M R Sanclean

Sept '90.

IN GOOD COMPANY

IN GOOD COMPANY

*The First World War Letters
and Diaries of*
The Hon. William Fraser
Gordon Highlanders

'He went in good company that day . . .'

*Lieutenant the Hon. William Fraser, Gordon Highlanders
writing of his brother, Lieutenant the Hon. Simon Fraser,
Gordon Highlanders, Ypres, October* 1914

EDITED BY

DAVID FRASER

MICHAEL RUSSELL

© Fraser Publications 1990

First published in Great Britain 1990
by Michael Russell (Publishing) Ltd
The Chantry, Wilton, Salisbury, Wiltshire

Typeset in Sabon by The Spartan Press Ltd
Lymington, Hampshire
Printed and bound in Great Britain
by Biddles Ltd, Guildford and King's Lynn

Contents

Preface

My father's letters and diaries, from which extracts are given in the following pages, concern the First World War on the Western Front. He served there consistently throughout except when wounded or injured (and excepting some months commanding a Corps School in France), and he served both at regimental duty, including battalion command, and on the front line staff. The war dominated his youth – he was a subaltern of twenty-four when it began, a lieutenant-colonel of twenty-eight when it ended; perhaps dominated his life.

The views and experiences related here echo a great deal already written about that war – the devastating strictures on much of the High Command and staff, the anger with incompetence and amateurishness, the pain of bereavement, the misery of physical conditions – there is little startlingly new. My father's record of the times may, nevertheless, be of some interest beyond his family. History is not only concerned with accurate chronology and analysis. It also attempts – or should – to convey that often most difficult of impressions: what it was like to be there. In this, perhaps, these spontaneous and youthful writings of long ago contribute something.

It is a 'something' particularly poignant to one of my own generation, born immediately after that struggle of 1914–18 and with childhood much affected by talk of it; yet subsequently living through later wars and other dramas whose impact and myth were so different as to make The Great War – as we grew up calling it – far more remote in spirit than its comparatively short distance from us in time might imply. It was a war which ended an era; which was conducted largely free of what would later be called ideology; which in the case of the British Army (although not their enemy) made, on the whole, far heavier demands than subsequently on human endurance, for the four long years in which the Army faced the main weight of German power. It was a war which involved unprecedented loss and suffering, and yet there is something else too, which may be found curious and paradoxical by some, yet rings with a familiar note in my own ears. 'I often wonder', my father wrote in his diary on 14 August 1918, 'how many, even of those who have suffered most, could they put back the hand of time four years and arrange it that there should be no war, would do so? Not I, certainly – I think I have seen more real happiness here in France during the agony of these days than ever I saw before.' Such must be set against the grief, and the frequent yearnings for the war's end.

It was a war in which simple patriotism was, for most of the time, an unquestioned faith; and in which consciousness of the rightness of that patriotism inspired both sides to a remarkable degree and for remarkably long. It was a war from which the British Army – tiny and professional in the beginning, huge and representative in the end – emerged believing that it and almost it alone had won the day. It was a war, as Corelli Barnett observes in his preface to *The Swordbearers*, 'as near as one's father's youth and yet as remote as the Crusades; lances of the *Garde Ulanen* scratching the summer sky of 1914; guns of Jellicoe's thirty-four capital ships firing the valedictory salute to British sea-power into the mists of Jutland; horizon blue and field grey; the Motherland, the Fatherland, *La Patrie*.'

My father kept a diary at the beginning and in 1915 – although the latter has not survived. He kept one again, continuously, from January 1917 until after the Armistice. He never took his diary into the trenches but wrote it up after a spell in the line; and he was, whether in or out of the trenches, a regular letter-writer, so that much appears in both letters and diaries which has required editing to reduce repetition. Here and there, particularly in the 1914 Diary, I have needed to insert some dates by guesswork and research in order to help the sequence, since these were often omitted. Place names, also omitted at the time in the interests of somewhat patchy security, were generally inserted by him later.

My father was a dedicated and thoughtful professional soldier and the overall picture contains much criticism – particularly of lack of forethought and competence in higher staffs – and much lamentation over lack of system in training. My father believed, with passion, that reinforcements were sent to France and

Flanders with inadequate initial training: that officers and NCOs never received the sort of systematic traning for their responsibilities which he thought should be essential prerequisites for promotion; and that battalions, in their turn, were given insufficient time and resources for training between battles or spells in the line. He took the view that tactical doctrine and knowledge of how to train men intelligently were deplorably ignored in the British Army. He was convinced that training, at every level, would have drastically reduced the casualty lists; for although he sadly recognised that the conditions of the Western Front meant that battles inevitably involved much loss he nevertheless attributed a great deal of that loss to inexperienced leadership and faulty basic training.

But of the underlying strategy my father had no doubts – any more than he had doubts of the fundamental justice of the cause. He was totally convinced that the war had to be fought and won on the Western Front; and that this involved attrition on a huge scale, and Allied offensives at the right time and place, under the right conditions – for he could not challenge the underlying political reality that the German Army was occupying much of northern France and most of Belgium and had to be dislodged. He quarrelled not with the strategy but with the tactics, or some of them – the dream of breakthrough, where he favoured the limited attack succeeded by others of the same sort elsewhere. His criticisms were, of course, those of a young man, often exaggerated and perhaps unfair like many such; but he saw a lot of the game, and although he was genuinely indifferent to honours, his Military Cross, his three awards of the Distinguished Service Order, as well as his three Mentions in Despatches (the fourth, referred to in the text, was in 1940) indicate that he knew that game pretty well.

In editing these papers I have excluded most which does not bear directly on the war. Most but not all; here and there I have felt that a touch of family news or occasional relaxation not only provides appropriate contrast to the rest but serves to remind that for the diarist these things were the background – remote though they seemed at the front – which made the mud, the boredom, the danger and the fatigue bearable. And although I have cut the more prosaic and routine diary passages to some extent I have not omitted them altogether. They convey atmosphere, and they emphasise that most of the First World War, like every other, consisted of tedium and monotony. Too strong a diet of battle would give a misleading impression of those years; but there is battle enough for a lifetime.

DAVID FRASER

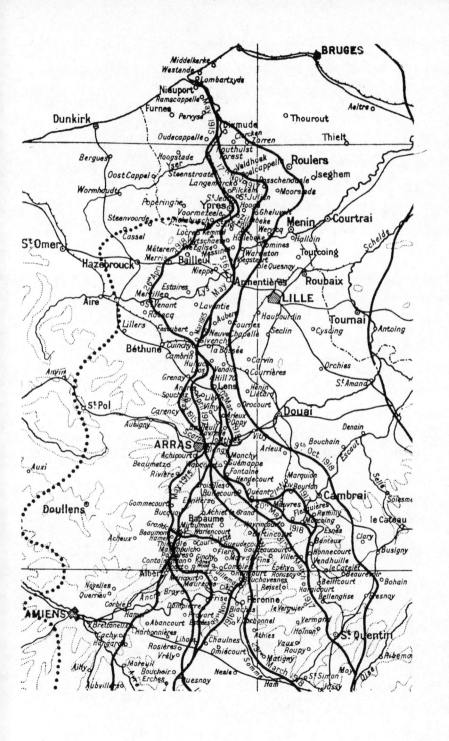

Introduction

William Fraser, invariably known as 'Willie', was born on 5 July 1890 at Philorth, near Fraserburgh in Aberdeenshire, the home of his father, the 18th Lord Saltoun. Willie's mother, Mary Grattan Bellew from Ireland, was a great-granddaughter of Henry Grattan, the Irish statesman.

Philorth had been built in the seventeenth century and much added to by Willie's grandfather in Victorian days. The house had replaced, as the Fraser home, an ancient castle in a more exposed position about a mile away which had been the original 'Philorth' and is now (1989) again the family's base. The lands of Philorth, constituting the Aberdeenshire parts of the historic earldom of Ross, had come to the Frasers through marriage to a co-heiress of the Earl of Ross in the fourteenth century.

Philorth lies in that north-east district of Aberdeenshire called Buchan – a district of hard weather and hardy people, of rolling farmlands, a bleak coast, a prevailing and powerful east wind, and few trees (although the carefully planted and encouraged woods of Philorth were excellent). Willie loved his home and everything about it.

He was the fourth of Lord Saltoun's four sons; said by his brothers to be the favourite (although he strongly denied it). He was adept at most games and all field sports, with an excellent eye, sense of rhythm and timing, and considerable manual dexterity. He was competent though not brilliant academically, a good Latinist and promising linguist, well-read and devoted to particular authors. He had, like most of his family, a sharp tongue and temper on occasions. And he was exceptionally graceful and good-looking.

Lord Saltoun had been, like his own father, a soldier, a Grenadier. With considerable regret he had resigned his commission in 1886 on succeeding to title and estates; but – largely through the extravagance of the previous generation – the family fortunes had been much depleted and he reckoned that even in those comparatively leisured days he could not combine management of business in Aberdeenshire with a military career. He was undoubtedly sad at this, and throughout life took keen interest in the Army; returning to it indeed, with command of a brigade, in the war of 1914 which broke out when he was already sixty-three. He was, therefore, unsurprised when he asked Willie (a schoolboy at Charterhouse) what he wanted to do in life and was told 'try for the Army'.

Lord Saltoun asked if Willie had any ideas as to regiment.

'I'd like to be a Grenadier.'

'Why?'

'Well, it was your regiment, and others of us' (an earlier Lord Saltoun had served with distinction in the First Guards, later Grenadier Guards, in the Peninsula and at Waterloo).

'The Brigade', said Lord Saltoun with finality, 'is for elder sons!' This was perfectly untrue, but like many Scottish patriarchs he had strong views on primogeniture. Younger sons, after a decent education and a good home, must make their own way. If they wanted to go into so unlucrative a profession as the Army they should not expect to join a regiment then supposed to require ample private means to supplement the meagre pay.

So Willie applied to join the Gordon Highlanders, the local regiment of Aberdeenshire and the North East (in which his father was Colonel of one of the Militia battalions); a regiment in which two of his brothers served as Reserve Officers; a regiment whose men included those same robust North-Easterners among whom he had grown up. No choice could have been happier. After a session at a well-known Norfolk 'crammer' and another spell in Germany learning the language, he passed with distinction into the Royal Military College, Sandhurst, and with even more distinction out of it. He then joined the 2nd Battalion, Gordon Highlanders,* in India.

Willie joined in time for a great march of the battalion across the sub-continent on a change of station from Calcutta to Cawnpore, a march lasting many weeks. He always remembered this with affection – the marching down the Grand Trunk road in the cool of morning, the pitching of tents and the explorations of

*He in fact, in very different circumstances, exchanged into the Grenadiers in 1927.

the local scene each evening, the sound of the pipes on the march and at Retreat in camp at dusk, the sights and smells of a still untransformed India, the India of Kipling's *Kim*. From Cawnpore, Willie moved with the battalion to Delhi, for the historic Durbar of King George V and Queen Mary, with ten thousand upon ten thousand of troops on parade, horse, foot, and guns, British regiments, Indian regiments, full dress, colour, display never to be repeated.

The Gordons had, as was the system in those days, been many years in India. Indeed the regimental families had remained there at their base while the men of the Battalion had been away fighting in the South African War between 1899 and 1902. Willie greatly enjoyed India, but every soldier likes variety and he was not sorry when, in December 1912, the Gordons embarked at Bombay and sailed to Egypt for a tour of duty at Kasr-el Nil Barracks, Cairo. Willie, on leave at home, missed the voyage and sailed to Egypt from England to join the regiment in their new station, a station which was to be their home until September 1914.

I
First Ypres
1914

*Willie Fraser's 1914 diaries begin at Philorth. 'Fine, cold day,'
runs the entry for 1 January in the dark green 'T. and J. Smith's
1914 Pocket Diary and Almanack'. 'Walked down by Mains of
Philorth with Abdy Gordon, he with gun, I with Bruce.* 4 duck
in reeds, got 1. Went on by bents, saw 5 teal and some snipe, got
1 teal. Flighted pigeon after lunch. A.G., Knockespoch† and self –
36 pigeon and 1 sparrowhawk. Lovely sunset – walked home.'*

*And so on. Britain was at peace. Willie, a subaltern, was home
from Cairo – home, and on a month's leave before attending a
machine gun course at Hythe. In due course he became battalion
machine gun officer: each battalion had two machine guns, with
horse-drawn limbers.*

*He had first started his diary just before leaving England for
Egypt in December 1912, had kept it in only desultory fashion in
1913, and resumed, with 'Good Resolution No 1. Really must
keep diary and good accounts this year' in January 1914. But the
resolution lapsed between 2 February and October, and when the
diary began again it was pencilled in a small, hard-backed Army
notebook ('Army Book 136'). Inside the cover was written: 'If
found, please send to Lord Saltoun, Philorth, Fraserburgh, Scotland.' The world was upside down. War had been declared on 4
August. The first pages were written on 9 October 1914 and bring
the reader briefly from Alexandria with 2nd Gordons, by way of
Southampton and the New Forest to Zeebrugge and Flanders.*

*The opening battles of the British Expeditionary Force, the
advance to and retreat from Mons, the turning point of the Battle
of the Marne, the follow-up of the withdrawing German Army to
the Aisne – these were over. What became known (somewhat
misleadingly) as the 'Race to the Sea' was on. Each of the
contestants – the Franco-British-Belgian forces and the Imperial*

---

*His dog.
†Gordon of Knockespoch, an estate in Strathbogie, Aberdeenshire.

German Army – attempted to turn the opponent's northern flank. Each moved a mass of troops – from other parts of the front, or from reserves where they existed or could be formed – to what became for both the new point of main effort on the Western Front: Flanders. What historians were to describe as the First Battle of Ypres was about to begin.

At Alexandria we embarked on the P & O 'Assaye', in which we had a very comfortable journey to Southampton – where we landed, somewhere about September 22nd 1914 – whence we marched to Lyndhurst in the New Forest, and encamped next to the Scots Gds, being brigaded with that regiment, the Grenadier Guards, and the Border Regt, the brigade being commanded by General Ruggles-Brise, who was Commandant of the School of Musketry at Hythe when I was there. At Lyndhurst Camp we remained until Oct. 4th, while the VIIth Division, in which we are, was being collected and equipped.

On the afternoon of Oct. 4th we received orders to be ready to move at once. The camp was immediately struck, but this was no sooner done than we received orders to pitch it again – which we did. Many ladies who were in the camp to see the last of their husband, brothers, etc., remained and had dinner with us. They were somewhat melancholy company, so at 9.30, the night being a fine one and we having received no orders as to the time we should move, a piper was produced and we all danced reels, and finished up with a game of rugby football with a pillow. Eventually we marched off at 11.00 p.m. and walked into Southampton in two parties, the first under the Commanding Officers, the second under Crawford – I was with the 1st party. Reached Southampton about 2.30 a.m. on the 5th, and embarked at 6.00 a.m., 1st party in the Lake Michigan, 2nd party in the Mineapolis. The second party had a very comfortable journey and arrived at Zeebrugge on Tuesday morning, when they trained to Bruges. We, on the cattle-boat Lake Michigan, were somewhat less comfortable. At about 12.30 a.m. on Tuesday we arrived at Dover, a surprise to all of us, and here we spent the rest of that night and all Tuesday, sailing again at 7.30 on Tuesday evening. The ship was very dirty, and there was about 20 sq ft of deck space for 70 officers, and very limited means of cooking food. The men were no better off. However we were all very cheery. Half battalion Scots Guards, The Staffords and ½ bn R.S.F.* were on board with us. Rony† among S.G. Officers. On Wed. about 4.00 a.m. we arrived at Zeebrugge having been escorted by a fleet of destroyers, and disembarked at 6.00 a.m. The bn. entrained and went to Bruges, where they found the other ½ bn and went into billets. I rode with the transport, which went by road (10 miles) as I wished to look after the Machine Guns and have a look at the country. Various delays occurred, but we got started about 3.30 and got in at 6.30. Good going with a long line of transport.

The battalion then marched to entrench a position south of Ostend: and thence moved by train to Ghent and entrenched another position east of the town. The Germans did not attack.

12TH OCTOBER On Sunday night we left our position E of Ghent very quietly, in fact so quietly that M.G. section and 1 platoon of B. Coy were very nearly left behind. We were in work some 600 yds from the nearest of our troops and had been told to be ready to move at once on receipt of orders. But it got later and later and no orders came. The cavalry who were near us moved away and we began to think something was wrong. I moved the limbers as near to the trench as possible, and about half-an-hour later a note arrived for Macbean, comdg the platoon, from McLean asking him to take his men up to a point behind the trenches occupied by the rest of the coy and await him there.

On this I decided to move and limbered up and sent the guns to join the main road through Ghent, and to await me at a point we knew. Then cantered off to HQ to try and get some orders. Found everything shut up and bn. gone. Rode down road to Ghent and caught up the limbers and we rejoined the bn a bit down the road. Reported that Macbean was probably still waiting behind our position and he was sent for and rejoined later.

*Royal Scots Fusiliers.
†Ronald Stewart-Menzies of Culdares, a cousin.

We marched all night from 11 o'clock, a hard march as the pace was very variable, and the men were tired with digging hard all day. Also the cobble stones, of which all the roads are made, are very bad for marching – we reached Somerghen at 5.30 am., and billeted there. Paraded again at 12 noon, but did not march until nearly 2 o'clock. Marched to Thielt and arrived about 8 o'clock, but did not get into billets until near 11.00. The men were waiting on the road in the cold after hard marching for 2½ hours – to one not 'in the know' this looks like bad staff work. However had a good night and I personally was awoken at 7am by a roll of musketry, which brought us all out of bed in a hurry, but turned out to be our own troops firing at an aeroplane. It was hit and came down about 8 miles from here. Rumour now says it was an English one. We move off about 10 o'clock, the bde m. guns brigaded, but where to I don't know.

13TH OCTOBER Yesterday we marched off about 10 o'clock, and marched a few miles. A column of the enemy was reported to be following us up, and we halted for some time, about 3 hours, when we resumed our march, and got to Roulers about 7.30. Found the bn was on picquet 2 miles out so marched out and joined them. A coy and ½ B were on outpost in trenches, the remainder were billeted at Rumbeke, M.G. Section among them. A very comfortable billet we H.Q. fellows had, with the chief padre, and I slept in a bed for the 3rd time running. The men were very tired last night and those on picquet had a very hard time indeed, more especially as they were all soaking wet, having marched the whole day in the rain. There was a muddle of some kind in getting us here, as the Borders came to our position first and had to march back. Today we march to Ypres and the battalion forms the rear-guard. Thank God its a fine morning.

14TH OCTOBER The morning did not long remain fine, and when we marched off it was drizzling, and for a long time we marched in heavy rain. No rations were issued for this day. However the M.G. section had a fair reserve of Maconnochie and biscuits and I managed to buy 3 chickens on the way, so they did pretty well. Reached our destination about 14 miles away in good time, and had just got into billets, when the alarm went, and we all had to turn out. A German column was reported marching down the road. However it turned out to be a cav. field ambulance of our own, so we turned in again. We heard guns during our whole march, and occasional rifle fire, and at last we appear to be approaching the long enduring battle of the Aisne. It was quite an easy march and there were none of the usual checks and delays.

Ypres, where we billeted, is quite a pretty little town surrounded by a wall and a moat. On the march we passed several chateau, and one in particular I shall always remember between — and —, a small red brick chateau, evidently very old, with a ripping old gateway and a coat of arms about it, and surrounded by a moat.

After the section was fixed up and everything seen to, went and had a shave and a shampoo, and purchased a few things I needed, including a saddle-bag and map-case. Turned in after an excellent early dinner, washed down by wine provided by the owners of our billet.

On that day Willie pencilled a short letter home.

Oct. 14th '14

Dear Mother,

Both Simon* and I are very fit, not that we see much of each other, as I am often away. We have had no fighting so far but any amount of marching, over these horrible cobble-stone roads, which knock one's feet to pieces. Of course I've got a horse but I always walk when we are on the march, and so far my feet are very good. We have been in billets sometimes, and sometimes in the trenches, and sometimes in neither the one nor the other, when we walk all night. As a whole the regiment have had a hardish time so far, been on outposts most nights, and some of the men are a bit done up. Also marching in a large force is a tiring job, with incessant checks.

*Simon Fraser, third of the brothers, was serving in the same battalion as Willie. They were very close.

I am keeping an account of things as they occur, more or less. No time to write much. Love to Father and Mary[*]

Your loving son
WILLIE

15TH OCTOBER Stood to arms at 4.45 this morning with orders to be ready to move at 6. Eventually moved about 7, and after marching out about 8 kilos, started to entrench a position. Have got quite a good gun position with quite a good line of retirement. It could be improved by some demolitions, but am not allowed to carry them out at present. The bn. has got quite a good position, with excellent field of fire for this country, but very extended. There are supposed to be German patrols about, and the Grenadiers who held this line last night killed three Uhlans, and the Border Regt on our left shot five, wounded two, and captured two, this morning. Our line here seems to be a section of a circle, surrounding the town of Ypres on the south, east and north, and held by a mixed force of French and English, but we none of us have any accurate knowledge of the general situation. Have been superintending the digging of my emplacements etc. all day and by degrees they are getting quite good, but there is a lot of work in them. Luckily the day has been fine.

16TH OCTOBER At 11 o'clock on that night orders came to be ready to move at 4 am next day and eventually at 5 am we marched off, only about 2½ miles. Then we halted for some hours and then moved up about two miles, where we billeted in a tiny village, Hooge. H.Q. in quite a good chateau. Got into billets about 6 p.m. but officers' food did not arrive until 8.30, which made us very late to bed. One of my numbers left most important part of the gun behind when we moved off from last position – went back to find it, and discovered it to have been collected by X Hussars who are now miles away. Very worrying indeed. The Germans appear to have taken up a position facing N.W. with their right thrown back facing west. In the small villages about they appear to have left the people quite destitute, and they are for the most part without blankets and without food, except for potatoes and vegetables. We are not far from them now, and with any luck should get at them soon. Yesterday we heard the account of our expedition to Ghent, from a German point of view. It described a brilliant German victory, and how a famous Highland Regt had lost 1000 men – which would have left us 19 strong. In reality of course, we never saw a German, they never attacked us at all, – they certainly shelled our position – 12 hours after we left it they may have carried the trenches at the point of the bayonet – as they say – we cannot deny it as we were not there to contradict them.

17TH OCTOBER This morning Wed 17 Oct. we stood to arms as usual at 4.45. There is, I believe, no more to be made today, except the necessary readjustment of troops – which means probably that we shall have to march 5 miles or so to rejoin our Bde with which we lost touch yesterday. Here we are close to Gheluvelt in the 21st Bde area.

3.30 p.m. This has been a day of rest, and has given us opportunity to get the horses with galls etc looked to. My little mare, which has been lame for 3 days – I have been riding the doctor's horse – is much better, and if we do not have much marching will soon be all right again I hope. Her cough, and she had a bad one, is going away. We are to remain tonight in this chateau as far as we know. I think we may expect an early start tomorrow and perhaps a scrap. Two hundred Germans were captured near here this morning. Two men came in this morning, who said they were French soldiers. They said that their battalion had marched into the German lines at Lille, and had been with a few exceptions captured. – Four days ago that was, and they had walked up here. They seemed to be all right, but of course they may be daring fellows trying to get information for the Germans. Anyway they have been sent to divisional H.Q.

20TH OCTOBER On Saturday night at 5 p.m. we got orders to march to rejoin the Bde, which we did and billeted in the small village of Zandvoort. H.Q. was at a small farmhouse, where they provided us with excellent coffee, and with eggs and chickens brought from our last billet we did very well. Next morning early we pushed on to a point S.E. of it, driving the Germans out, and prepared to entrench a position. Some German snipers annoyed us rather until they were cleared out by our covering party. We then went on with the entrenchments. M.G. position was with 'B' Coy. We had not done very much when they began to shell us with shrapnel and common shell. All the R.E. horses bolted, as did all my limber horses, burying the limber in a ditch. Went down to the limber and sent them off to catch horses, then went and got men from trenches and dug out the limber. The men worked well, because shrapnel and shell were bursting not too far away, and the road between limbers and trenches was swept once or twice. The horses were caught and we got them into a deep ditch, one wounded unfortunately. Then there was a lull and we got well on with the trenches and by the time they let us have it again we had the trenches pretty deep. A house about 20 yards behind us got it pretty badly, but they were bursting beyond the trenches. By dusk the trenches were nearly done, when they started on us again, but soon knocked off. I fancy they did not want our guns to pick them up from the flashes. They were about 1500^x away. We had four men wounded as far as I know. It's most unpleasant – that shell fire – spent the night in the trenches, all was quiet.

21ST OCTOBER The next morning two companies were ordered to advance and clear the woods in front of our trenches and the village of America about ½ mile to our front. They were soon ordered to retire, and about 2.30, we ourselves were ordered to retire. About this time we were being shelled pretty heavily, but the guns and all the section had been back with the limbers some time, so as soon as orders came I made my way back and brought the horses out of the ditch where we had put them, harnessed up and sent them at a gallop up the road and the section to follow them 100^x clear of the road. A shell landed within 5 yds of me on my way from the trenches to the limbers, a most unpleasant experience. We got clear without casualty, and rejoined the battalion at Reutel – inside an hour. Here we remained some time together with the Scots Guards, and about dusk were ordered to rejoin the Bde at Zandvoort. Moved off in rear of S.G. They took a wrong turn in the dark, but fortunately we did not follow them, as they did not get in till 4 in the morning whereas we were in by

7.30 in the evening. Spent a fairly comfortable night in same farmhouse as we had occupied 2 nights before.

22ND OCTOBER The next morning, ie this morning, we were ordered to make a reconnaisance in force towards Gheluvelt together with the Scots Guards. Halted for some time behind a hill after pushing forward for about ¾ mile while our artillery in front of us took on the enemy's artillery in the direction of Wervicq and Menin. The plateau in front of us was swept by shell-fire for some hours. However the reconnaisance went on and no damage was done, as their shrapnel was bursting too high or in many cases not bursting at all. Eventually our guns seemed to silence one of their batteries. Meanwhile we pushed across the plateau for a little over a mile, and were then recalled. This evening we took up a position on the right of the Border Regt – the S.G.* on our right again. The whole afternoon there has been very heavy rifle and artillery firing on the plateau, but we have not been engaged, although the Regt on our right have got through a lot of ammunition. There is no suitable position for M. guns to be mounted tonight but tomorrow morning at daybreak will find them in quite a good position on the right of our line. Hope we get something to fire at.

It is impossible to say with certainty on what day the diary was resumed. Probably 23 or 24 October.

Yesterday morning we dug ourselves in at the edge of a small wood, firing over our own trenches. In the morning there was heavy firing from the trenches below us, but I was unable to see what they were firing at – probably a few well-concealed German snipers – as a lot of bullets came over our heads. The limbers are concealed by a haystack close to us, and by the grace of God they have not yet been shelled, as the village close to them, and a farm

*Scots Guards. Willie used mercifully few abbreviations, although these will here and there be found:- GH (Gordons) SH (Seaforth Highlanders) A and SH (Argyll and Sutherland Highlanders) and BW (Black Watch).

200^x behind them, were heavily shelled all day. Nearly put them near the farm, but some good angel said 'don't'. They are covered with straw and should escape observation from aeroplanes. We are holding the rim of a vast amphitheatre and nearly the whole inside has been shelled. The only target we got yesterday was a cavalry patrol at 1275^x, but could not see what damage we did. The front held by the bn. was not heavily attacked, but the Borders on our left and the S.G. on our right were hard put to it. The enemy seem to be working round to our right, and we are holding too large a front in expectation of reinforcements which should have been here yesterday morning, but were not here yesterday evening.

They pushed up a gun within 1500^x of the village on our right yesterday and were shelling it all day. We had a quiet night on our front, but early this morning the Borders and S.G. were both hard at it. The only excitement so far this morning has been a battery of Krupps silent guns which have been shelling the road 150^x from my limber with the percussion shells. Big guns they are and the shell has a most awe-inspiring scream. However no damage so far, though some splinters fell round my guns 300^x from the burst. We have orders to hold on at all costs. Should like to get a target of some kind. Wonder what the name of this battle will be?[*] There are guns going all the time, but not much musketry fire at the moment. Forget when I last had my boots off for a few minutes, but managed a shave three days ago. We have no news of the outside world or of the rest of the war. I suppose this is only an affair of outposts in a war this size. Tobacco and matches are running rather short, the men are smoking the half-dried leaf. There is a lot of tobacco grown about here. My flint and steel are very useful. The heavy Krupp battery knocked off for a bit, but has started again now harder than ever – the shells sound exactly like an express train going through the air – and there is quite a perceptible tremor in the ground when they land. Wonder if our guns will pick it up soon.

A gun started shelling the windmill about 50 yds to the right of the limbers this afternoon, but our guns started on him at once and silenced him. However he got the windmill twice well, and set it on fire. Beyond this there has been no excitement in this direction, and it is thinking of getting dark. It's not very exciting sitting watching

[*] 'First Ypres'.

one's front and seeing nothing. Also it keeps on trying to rain and is grey and dull. Fear its going to be a windy wet night, the wrong sort to sleep out in.

They set fire to the windmill last night and it made a good blaze and the farm beside it caught fire from it. Suddenly Corpl. Andrews remembered that the steading was full of animals so we went up and let them out. It was a fine night after all and we got occasional sleep between very heavy bursts of firing from the trenches to our front. We could see nothing, so did not fire.

The diary consists of only two more pages:

The next morning sent down to the trenches and discovered that the firing had been at some transport they had heard to their front. It was a ripping October morning and an old cock-pheasant came out of our little wood and stalked about, not caring a rap for the firing which started again with the daylight. He should have, on an October morning!

They started shelling us in our wood early and gave it to the wood pretty hot, but never quite picked up the guns at the front edge of it and we were in action all day. A machine gun was putting a lot of bullets round the haystack behind which the limbers were, and Corpl Andrews was wounded in the leg and one horse wounded too. The horse is quite fit, but Corpl. Andrews will be laid up for 3 weeks. We got orders to retire that evening, and next morning had one gun mounted in 'C' Coy trench on right of our line. Did not like position but they wanted gun there. Found position bad when daylight came, owing to two houses in front in which the enemy had got machine guns and from which my position was commanded.

Was ordered to retire about 10 o'clock, did so without casualty.

The day before this had been an unhappy one for the regiment. A m.g. and shrapnel fire got on to two companies who had advanced to support the Border Regt., who were reported to have given way. When they got up they found the Borders snug in their trenches, with no room for them. It was in the ensuing retirement that the casualties occurred. Fred Sworder wounded, also Campbell Thistle. C.S.M. Kerr killed by shell which wounded Fred.

Reported the houses in front of trench and was sent to interview Bn H.Q. Got a gunner officer and we went and examined position of houses. Arranged to have 2 guns up before daylight next day to knock down houses.

We had a disturbed night owing to an attack on our front. Next morning, i.e. this morning, guns arrived and we selected positions by guesswork in a dense fog. Fog cleared about 9 o'clock and by 11 o'clock both houses were in a bad way. I am writing this in 'C' Coy trench from where the gunner officer is observing and they are still pegging away at the houses. It is another lovely day. Heard from Father yesterday, also wrote to him. We are all well. This morning they buried some of the poor fellows who were killed the day before yesterday. The pipe-major played the lament.

This last entry is likely to have been entered on some day on or before 27 October. On that day Willie wrote again to his mother.

Dear Mother,

Excuse the paper. The Bde has been in a very tight corner. We have got out all right with a good many casualties, but only 2 officers wounded. Your present, I firmly believe, saved me. Had a very lucky escape, and am sorry to say lost a gun. Fear the other Regts suffered more. Rony Menzies is killed or captured, the evidence so far as I can find points to the latter – so if his Mother writes to you, would you tell her I think he is captured.[*] I'm very fond of Rony. Would you send me out a new map-case, with or without a celluloid front, but if it has one, will you have a khaki or leather cover over it – also a Field Service message book, a good big one. The map-case should be able to hold this as well as maps. I've lost mine. Also some tobacco and matches and chocolate. Thank you very much for your last parcel. The torch is most useful. Could you send out some more batteries for it.

[*]He was.

[18]

Simon as fit as anything and doing jolly well. Am rather depressed at losing the gun. Perhaps I could have helped it, only had no men to carry it in.

Love to Father, and Mary and thank her for the socks. I am wearing them now. The nights are very cold. Could you send me a new pair of spurs and if Tantz would make a new pair of breeches and send them out. Am really very fit.

Your affectionate son
WILLIE

PS This letter seems to be all asking for things. The warm coat and woolly waistcoat are the comforts of my life. Fear all our kits are lost, so a vest and a pair of drawers would be most useful. They were chucked out to make room for wounded. A large box of tobacco just come. Thank you awfully. Will you send me two or three pipes.

In May 1915 an envelope reached Lord Saltoun at Philorth with a covering letter from Sergeant C. Holmes, 2nd Royal Warwickshire Regiment:

Sir,

I, Sergt. C. Holmes, have had this (Diary) in my possession ever since the 27th of October 1914. How I became in possession of it I will relate to you. On the morning of the 27th of October 1914 I was ordered to go and reconnoitre the country. After going about ¾ of a mile I came to a farm house which was occupied by civilians. I questioned him to see if he knew any troops had been locating anywhere around his village. He took me around the back and their I found rifles and packs belonging to the Gordon Highlanders. I made a report of this and then advanced a little further. I had with me 6 men at the time, all of a sudden a report from a machine gun rang out from our front. I at once sent 3 men to each flank. I crept on my hands and knees. The machine gun opened fire on to the left flank. During the time they was firing my right flank I crawled up and surprised them. I myself got up and rushed forward. There were 4 Germans with the gun. We took everything from them. By the time I had searched them my right flank had got up so they was well surrounded. This was where I found a wallet containing this Diary and have saved it all the time, carrying it with me in all engagements I have been in. Well Sir, it was on the 16th of May 1915 I got wounded and still I clung to this diary. I am getting along nicely. I am at a convelescent Home as you see is my address. Hoping you get it safely. I could not send it from France as it was not allowed. So I have stuck to it through thick and thin. Hoping Sir your son is still alive. I could not say for his whereabouts myself. Hoping you have had news of him. So Sir, I think I have explained all to you how I became in possession of this valuable Diary.

    I am sir,

Your Obedient Servant,
Sergt. C. HOLMES

Sergeant Holmes's letter suggests that Willie had been wounded and (temporarily) captured on or by 27 October. Dates are easy to confuse, and this cannot be, for on 28 or 29 October something else occurred which made that day one of especial tragedy for Willie. It was also during the following days, as his accounts make clear, that he was hit. On those two days a massive German frontal and flank attack fell on 20th Brigade. 1st Battalion Grenadier Guards were in position facing south, south of the road from Ypres to Menin and took the brunt of the attack, suffering appalling casualties. 2nd Gordons, on their left, were involved, albeit less heavily, in the same attack. A counter-attack from the north did something to force a pause and the line held.

    Letter to Lord Saltoun from Lieutenant-Colonel H.P. Uniacke, 3 November 1914:

My Dear Saltoun,

    It is with the deepest regret that I write to tell you that poor Simon was killed on the 28th Oct. when fighting a difficult rear-guard action. Willie buried him on the morning of the 29th in the grounds of an old chateau. The army has lost an officer of rare quality and we a brother officer who in a very short space of time gained not only our affection but won from us our greatest admiration by his solder-like qualities. Both your boys have done the most gallant and splendid work which has made them an example to all. Under the most severe conditions they have been always cheery and helped to keep up the spirits of the men. Twice only have I seen Willie anything but the soul of fearless content, once when he lost one of his guns and then when we lost Simon. Our grief at losing Simon is very great, so you both have all the sympathy of the whole Battalion. I only trust that the record of their splendid work may help in some way to alleviate your grief. Forgive this very hurried letter, but you will understand that I have much sad news to write, and have only just arrived in England rather weak after losing a good deal of blood from a shell, though very slightly wounded. At 3 p.m. on the afternoon of the first November I left Willie with his guns safe, I only pray that the God of Battles will spare to the end such a splendid officer as he is.

The fighting has been the severest of the war, and their artillery work is marvellous. There is no doubt that their very best troops and finest artillery has been concentrated against our immediate front. Our losses have been very heavy, and I regret to say amongst them Otho Brooke.[*] The last two days, 31st Oct. and 1st Nov., were the severest of them all. I shall be going out very soon but 94 Piccadilly will find me until then, when I leave this place.

We are all with you both in your grief over the loss of your son, whose death means so much to us and also to the Army.

H.P. UNIACKE

Lord Saltoun, a week later, received another letter:

Dear Lord Saltoun,

You will already have had information about what happened on the 29th of last month, but I think you will like to hear what I know.

[*]Captain J.A.O. Brooke received a posthumous VC. He was son of another well-known Gordon Highlander, Sir Harry Brooke – one of the Brookes of Colebrooke in Ulster.

In the morning, your son Simon and I were with our platoons in a trench on the left of the Gordons' position. The Germans came up on our left and drove back the troops there, and we had to take up new positions as we were enfiladed by a machine gun. In doing this I got a bullet through the flesh of my left arm.

When we had time Simon put on a field dressing for me and also attended to two of his own men who were hit.

We had to fall back to the village of Zanvoorde, when we helped to organize the men. About noon Simon very gallantly carried a box of ammunition to a machine gun over an open field under fire.

I rejoined him later and we took cover in a ditch during some very heavy shelling about 2 p.m. He had just offered me a drink of water and had changed his position to further down the ditch when a shell burst near him and though I ran to him at once there was nothing I could do. I am sure he did not suffer. I had to go to the hospital but Captain Huggins told me his body was brought in that night.

Although I knew him so short a time I regarded him as my best friend in the Battalion. We were the only two reserve officers and were in the same Company. I shall always think of his cheerfulness and fortitude whatever had to be done. He had an extraordinary aptitude for the work, and his men all liked him. The first questions of two wounded at Ypres hospital were for him.

I was very sorry to hear of Willie's ill treatment, and trust he is making good progress. My slight wound is nearly healed, and I hope to return to duty by the end of the month.

I remain,

Yours very truly,
(signed) PETER DUGUID
2nd Lt., 2nd Gor. Hrs.

'Willie's ill treatment' referred to his temporary capture on the evening probably of 1 or 2 November after his shoulder was smashed by a shell splinter.

At first he heard a yelled German order to shoot him, after capture. He was still in the German front line, the situation was confused, the atmosphere feverish and vengeful. Willie managed to attract the attention of a German officer. The latter snapped a question to his NCOs who had threatened Willie and Willie recognised the accent – he spoke good German, having spent a happy time in Frankfurt before going to Sandhurst in 1909. He managed to force a question on the German officer.

'Do you come from Frankfurt?'

There was surprise.

'Yes. Was –?'

'Don't you wish you were there now?' Willie said. 'On a Saturday night?'

He was in a lot of pain but said he managed, somehow, to exchange a grin with his captor. It worked. The German, clearly (remembered Willie afterwards) a Reserve officer and no very military figure, said firmly to his soldiers, 'You shan't shoot him! He's a British officer, he speaks German, he knows Frankfurt!' And shortly afterwards in the general melee the Germans withdrew and Willie managed to get lost and drop into a ditch where he lay in some agony, covered with mud and unrecognisable, until he saw British troops return and advance against the same Germans, moving through a wood.

Then an English and a Scottish soldier came running along either side of Willie's ditch. Willie tried to lever himself up and the English soldier yelled, 'There's one of the bastards,' and aimed a ferocious kick at Willie's mud-covered figure. The boot landed on the wounded shoulder and Willie – a man who rarely swore – let out a stream – or scream – of the strongest language he ever remembered using. The Scottish soldier stopped, his ear attentive. 'That's no a Jerry bastard,' he said, 'it's one of our officers.'

And so to casualty clearing station, field hospital and England. There followed sick leave – Philorth first, and then London, before a Medical Board and return to the front.

[London]
Dec. 29th 1914

Dear Mother,

How are you feeling today I wonder? I telephoned the result of the board yesterday. They looked at my arm and said they would give me two months leave if I liked. However I asked them if they did not think I should be quite fit in a month, and they said they did, so I said 'Make it a month'. Then the Colonel, whom I met in Aberdeen, said he wanted a reserve machine gun officer trained, and the end of it was that I said I would go in to King Street and help the staff there. But I took care to point out that I was still on leave and that if I wanted a day off I should take it, and that Saturdays and Sundays were holidays. I felt I ought to go and lend a hand, as I really am quite fit for that. I may stay till Friday here, as I find I've a lot to do. Things one ought to do, and had forgotten, always keep cropping up. And you will be at Newe* and Father at Edinburgh. Anyway I shall be back on Saturday morning barring accidents, such as Zeppelins. The train was over two hours late this morning. I could not get a sleeper at Aberdeen, so got out at Perth and got into the front train and found a sleeper there. So I scored off the Colonel and Mrs Uniacke, who were coming down too in the back train, as they must have been much later than me. It isn't near as cold here as it is at home. I saw lots of fellows in Aberdeen, including long Lewis Gordon, Ingleby, and Cunyinghame. I walked down Union Street with those three – all a long way over 6 ft – and felt positively ashamed of myself. Lewis is very worried, he is getting so thin, only weighs 17 stone 12 pounds now.

Your loving son
WILLIE

But while at Philorth he took the opportunity to send two long letters to his brother George.† George Fraser was a lieutenant, Royal Navy, and serving with the Grand Fleet. The second letter, writing an account from memory (although Sergeant Holmes, unbeknown to Willie, had his diary safe) covered some of the same ground: action – and grief – recollected in greater tranquillity, but without benefit of notes made at the time to assist chronology. The letter, however, is more explicit about the doings of some of the earlier days.

---

*Home of Sir Charles Forbes of Newe, in Strathdon, Aberdeenshire.
†George was the second of the brothers.

Dec. 7th 1914

My dear George,

I wrote you a letter the other day which you do not appear to have got yet. You appear to be very short of news of all sorts, so I will try and write you an account of our doings in Belgium. I did keep an account of the doings of the regiment, though of course I had to leave out anything that might be of value to the wily German. It was just as well I did too, because one night I had rather a ticklish job to do, so I gave this diary to another fellow to look after for me till I got back, and he promptly lost it for me. Well here goes.

There followed an account, remarkably close to the diary's missing account, of the days between 4 October and 26 October. Willie described the ground covered by the British trenches in front of Ypres as 'a sort of huge amphitheatre,' and sketched it in his letter:

The sketch is very inaccurate and nothing like to scale but it shows you very roughly what the position was like. The ground outside this amphitheatre was very wooded and enclosed, inside it was comparatively open fields. Which of course gave them an enormous advantage, especially in the use of their guns and machine guns. That amphitheatre was a real old shell trap, and was in addition swept by bullets coming over the ridges all round. Our trenches, i.e. those occupied by the regiment, were thrown back on the right – see sketch – and were not on the ridge and so were far less exposed than the remainder. Also we were never so heavily attacked so we suffered far less than the rest of the brigade. For the first two days I had a position in the small wood in rear of the right end of our trenches. We had rather fun there and I believe the guns did a certain amount of execution, though we never got a really good target in the wooded country to our front. Anyway they amused themselves for two days trying to shell us out of that little wood, but they never really got at us.

The limbers were behind the two haystacks marked in the sketch, and they did their best to get the stacks on fire but never succeeded. My corporal was wounded here by a stray bullet. It was about this time that Simon did a jolly good bit of work. Some of our men had been sent to a forward trench to help the troops who were in it but when they got there they found that the trench was being held all right, but there was no room in it for them. So there they were under the devil of a fire. The officer was knocked out and Simon was sent to reform them and get them back. This he most gallantly did and got the whole lot back.

Two days after I got my section out of the wood they got the range of it to rights and fairly plastered it with shrapnel, so that we were rather glad we weren't still in it. I can't give you much detail for the rest of the time we were in that position as it is very hard to remember what happened on which day. Part of the time the section was in the trenches and part of the time in reserve, but one way and another we were pretty busy all the time, and the same applies to Simon. There were infantry attacks by the enemy every night and usually two. They always attacked at the same time, with such regularity in fact that soon we began to set our watches by them. Their use of the machine guns was extraordinarily good, and of course the enclosed country through which they had to advance, favoured them a lot. Their snipers too were very clever, on one occasion one of them managed to crawl to a place about six hundred yards inside our trenches, and from there he began to have pot shots at our headquarters, which was at a farm in the large amphitheatre which I mentioned before. For a long time we could not spot him and he became a most infernal nuisance, as one could not put ones nose out without him having a shot at it. Eventually as it was getting dark two of our scouts were sent out to stalk him, and before long they returned with his scalp, and jolly glad we were to see it. One morning we were told that they had broken through the regiment on our left and I was sent up with one gun to try and help them. We got a very bad time and I had some of my best men killed, and we were unable to get into action on account of the hail of shrapnel. The trenches we had gone to help were empty, and there was nothing we could do. Don't know how we weren't all hit, I was hit by a shrapnel, which knocked me over but did no other damage as it hit part of my equipment and glanced off downwards, and beyond making a hole in my coat did no harm. I thought I had got a bullet in the back and could not make out why it did not hurt, and it wasn't till I had time to have it looked at that I found out what had happened.

Meanwhile in the few days before this, the other three regiments in the brigade had suffered so severely, that it was decided that we couldn't hold on where we were any longer, and it was agreed to retire that night and take up a position a bit further back, of less extent. We retired in the dark without being spotted, but for some reason which I never gathered did not take up the position further back, but marched a long way back to a place called Hooge on the main Ypres-Menin road, while other troops were sent up to the position which we were to have occupied. I suppose that they thought that we had had enough for the moment. Anyway we got to this place Hooge at about 2.30 am and the next day was a day of rest for the brigade, though I was sent off with the machine guns to be attached to the 21st bde for the day. We were in reserve all day so had nothing to do. In the morning before I started I saw Sim, he had just got a parcel from home and we had a talk about the various things that had happened. He was smiling and cheery as usual, and had just had a wash and got into clean things, which had arrived in his parcel, and he gave me a clean vest, which I went and put on. That, George, was the last time I saw Sim alive.

That evening the brigade went to take over an advanced line of trenches a mile or two to the left of where we had been before, and I did not rejoin the battalion until late that night. We were told to expect an attack by a whole German army corps early next morning, so we spent the night digging for all we were worth. The next morning was very foggy, one could not see more than 100 yards at first, though it got clearer as the sun got up. We could hear the Germans advancing – they come on quite slowly, line after line, saying 'houra, houra' all the time – and soon fire opened all down the line. We could not see what was happening on either flank on account of the mist, and the attack was not pushed home at our part of the line, but, after some time, we heard that they had broken through the Grenadiers on our left. I went off with one gun to see if I could be of any use. When I arrived I found that they had broken through, and were in possession of a small wood in rear of our trenches, and this the Grenadiers were making desperate efforts to retake, aided by one company of my regiment.

For a long time we had a real good scrap in the open. The Germans were in great force and we had no reinforcements up to make an effective counter-attack. We got back into the wood five times but were driven out again as often. They had managed to get up four machine guns and they were the cause of a good percentage of our casualties. I believe I accounted for a few of *them* with mine! That wood cost us some of the best lives in the regiment, among them Otho Brooke who was at John's with you and one of the finest fellows that ever drew breath. The Grenadiers started that day with only about 300 men left out of nearly 1100 and there they lost nearly all the remainder of their officers and a good many of the men.

We had to retire but managed to form a good firing line and prevented them doing much in the way of advancing. My ammunition was used up after a time and I sent the gun back and for the rest of the day was attached to the colonel as sort of temporary assistant adjutant. Towards evening we were relieved and were able to reform the regiment some distance in the rear, near the chateau which I mentioned before. At first there were only a little over 200 men and four officers but they kept coming in.

One of the platoons had managed to enfilade the Germans as they advanced in their thick lines to the attack, and were there about an hour and a half, before they had to retire, during which time they accounted for about 500.

It was about seven o'clock and quite dark when they brought in Simon's body, and I knew he was killed. I told you how he was killed in my last letter, so I won't go over it again. Poor old Sim. He went in good company that day, George. Well, I buried him next morning,* the attack had started so there was no one there but me. Some of my gun team dug the grave, and I read the burial service, or part of it, and the Pipe-Major played the lament. We had no cross with his name on to put up, and no time to put it up if we had had it. But I know the place.

---

* 29 or 30 October.

That day I was with the Brigadier, and the regiment made an attack towards Zandvoorde but had to retire again, as there were no troops to support them. I rejoined them in the evening and found they had had no food and water all day. Luckily I had sent back for both and our transport officer, Graham, who was a first class fellow, got them both up that night, so we were all right as far as that went. That evening another Fraser who was in the regiment was killed; I buried him too, in an old shell hole, he was a good chap too. The next day we were in the trenches and heavily shelled all day and in the evening I was wounded, and the Germans got hold of me but I managed to get away afterwards luckily. I was one of the last to be hit, and soon after that we were withdrawn from the firing line, as there was only one officer left.[*] I was sent to Boulogne where I was two days, I think, and then to Sister Agnes's[†] and a little later up here. My medical board is on the 24th of this month, and I ought to be pretty fit again by then.

I expect yours is the most difficult job though, watching out all the time for those damned submarines. Well I only hope their fleet comes out soon and when it does God be with you and you give 'em hell. Good luck, old chap.

Your affectionate brother,
WILLIE

[*] Out of 26, and that evening the Battalion strength was 205; it had been 812 a week earlier.

[†] King Edward VII Hospital for Officers, run by the redoubtable Sister Agnes Keyser.

II
The Ypres Salient
1915

First Ypres witnessed the virtual destruction of the British Regular Army. Liddell Hart long afterwards wrote of that Army:

The little British Army had a cognate sense that was unique. To this its very smallness, as well as its conditions of service and traditions, contributed. First Ypres, on the British side, was not merely a 'soldiers' battle' but a 'family battle' – against outsiders. The family spirit was its keynote, and the key to the apparent miracle by which, when formations were broken up and regiments reduced to remnants those remnants still held together. They attained their end – in both senses. Ypres saw the supreme vindication and the final sacrifice of the old Regular Army. After the battle was over, little survived save the memory of its spirit.

The casualties among the 'first seven divisions', the original Expeditionary Force, had been appalling. Henceforth the Army was gradually and enormously increased in size by the absorption of the New Armies, raised from volunteers on the outbreak of war. The old Regular battalions continued, their character inevitably changed.

The Germans, too, had suffered huge casualties in their attempt to break the Allied left in Flanders, reach the Channel Ports and roll up the Allied line from north to south. The attempt had failed. No operational decision had been achieved. The exhausted contestants manned the positions they had attained in the autumn fighting, manned them, improved them, here and there adjusted them by small local fights. So large were the opposed armies, despite their losses, that their lines were continuous. Across Western Europe the fighting front now extended, without gap or interval, from neutral Switzerland to the sea. In this long, livid scar upon the map of Europe the British positions east of Ypres made a deep indent in the German line – the Ypres Salient. It was a tract of desolate, waterlogged land which Willie was to know all too well in the next four years.

In the event Willie was not fit for service until March 1915. He *spent time helping out at the training depot at Castle Hill Barracks, Aberdeen, and getting to Philorth as often as he could. But on 11 March he was able to write:*

Dear Mother,

I have been passed fit at last and may go out any day now after Monday next. What are your plans, will you be up at Philorth by the end of the week by any chance? I could probably get away for the weekend. If you would send me a wire saying where you will be I will know more or less what to do.

The weather here has changed for the better, result we can get on much faster with the recruits' training. Another draft went last night, 100 men to the 1st and 50 men to the 2nd battalion. I went down to see them off, and they all looked as happy as they could be.

Had quite a good weekend at Newe last week, and Mary seems to be having quite a good time, and on Monday night I went out to Fairley and saw the Brooke family.[*]

Yesterday we had a big recruiting march, a turn-out of about 5000 troops and they looked quite well going past.

Otherwise there is no news.

Your loving son
WILLIE

And a week later:

Royal Hotel, Invergordon
March 17th 1915

Dear Mother,

I expect my wire this morning surprised you a bit, but I was surprised to have to send it – I will recount you my adventures.

I was sleeping the sleep of the just at 12.30 a.m. this morning when I was woken up by Ross. A wire had just come in from the War Office to say that I was to proceed forthwith to Cromarty to

[*] Of Otho Brooke VC.

[34]

take out a draft of 200 Seaforths. We decided unanimously that the 3 a.m. train, which was the first I could catch, was out of the question. So I left Aberdeen at 9.45. I had no time to do anything at all, not even to get my hair cut, and the result is that I owe four bills which I had not paid, one to Garden the gunmaker, one to the Mess for my mess-bill, and one to the Northern Club for some dinner I had there, and one to an iron-monger but I forget his name. Anyway its a very small bill and he is sure to send it after me, so that does not matter. I am enclosing a cheque for £10., which I am sure will cover everything easily. Would it be an awful lot of trouble to pay them for me? You see the War Office did play it rather low down on me, only giving me 8 hours and those in the middle of the night.

The other thing is, I wrote to the Army & Navy Stores ordering a set of Officers' web equipment, which is much better than what they dish out to us. It had not come, so I wired them to send it to meet me at Southampton and to send the bill to Father, which I thought would give them confidence. It won't be much, and I will pay Father back, but he might be surprised if he knew nothing about it.

Well, I left Aberdeen at 9.45, just caught the train, and got to Inverness at 2.20. Left again at 2.35, which just gave me time to get a bite of lunch. Arrived here at 5.10, we managed to drop an hour on the way as we were due in at 4.9, and found a wire waiting for me telling me not to cross to Cromarty, but to await the draft here. So went and telephoned my arrival to the headquarters, got some tea, and am now writing to you in the station-master's office, waiting for the draft. We leave at 7 o'clock this evening, its now 6.30 about, and shall probably get to Southampton tomorrow night.

Don't know when I shall post this. The draft has just arrived so I must stop hurriedly. The Colonel* has been killed, its awful. I can't realise it.

Goodbye, and best of love to you and Father. I wish I could have seen you again.

Your loving son
WILLIE

*Colonel Uniacke.

Dolphin Hotel, Southampton
March 19th 1915

Dear Mother,

I hope you got my letter all right. I had to give it to the stationmaster at Invergordon to post, but I expect he did it all right. We left Invergordon at 7 p.m. on Wednesday, and should have embarked yesterday, and crossed last night, but we were delayed by the snowstorm and did not get in until 8 p.m. yesterday. So we billetted here last night, the men in a large school and us, ie 3 officers including me, at this hotel. The draft were more than half drunk when we entrained at Invergordon, and with one exception there was not an NCO among them worth a damn. However I've had to do with intoxicated drafts before, so I had all the carriage doors locked at Invergordon, and allowed no one out of the carriages all the way down. So we got here without any trouble.

We did not sail today, I don't know why, but we got no orders, so it was impossible to let the men out of their billets, as we might have been ordered to embark at any moment. They got a bit restless towards 4 p.m. and I managed to ascertain that we would not embark today, and was able to let them out. I'm afraid there will be a lot of them drunk tonight, but it can't be helped. We shall sail tomorrow night almost for certain. I have got the web equipment I told you about in my letter, but I forgot to enclose the cheque, so send it with this. I don't know if you are still at Glasgow, but send this there as I expect you are. I was rather glad we did not start off right away as it gave me a chance to get a few things that I needed. I see there has been no mention of the Colonel's death in the papers, but I'm afraid it must be true, as our information came from Banchory, a wire to Mrs Uniacke. However, I am still hoping.

How is Father? I wonder if he is out of bed yet?[*] The two officers who came with the draft are quite nice fellows, one a fellow called Ranken, who was up at Oxford with Master.[†] I should have thought he was quite capable of taking the draft down himself, instead of lugging me all the way to Cromarty to

---

[*] Lord Saltoun suffered painfully from gout.
[†] Willie's elder brother, Alistair, Master of Saltoun; always called 'Master' in the family.

do it. However such is the way of the War Office. With love to Father.

Your loving son
WILLIE

Grand Hotel Moderne, Le Havre
21 March 1915

Dear Mother,

We embarked at Southampton last night, and got off about 7.30 p.m. Got here at about 1 a.m. this morning, but did not disembark until about 8 o'clock. It was quite a small boat, the Empress Queen, and the men had not much room, and the officers were herded like sheep into one large cabin. However by good luck I managed to secure about the best and also about the only cabin on board, which I shared with Ranken, the senior officer of the Seaforths with the draft, and so we were quite comfortable.

About 8.15 we marched off from the quay, through the town and out to No 14 Rest Camp, about 5½ miles. It was a perfect day, but the roads were very dusty, and even in that short distance some of the men got their feet sore. A great many of them are Stornoway lads and not much used to walking far probably. The docks were very quiet, there seemed to be nothing doing at all except in connection with unloading transports, and the town seemed very deserted as we went through it. The people have got used to the kilt, so we excited no surprised exclamations of admiration! or the reverse. We had one short halt on the way to the rest camp, and got there about 10 o'clock. The men were all medically inspected when we arrived, and 5 of them were passed unfit, two for being too old. It seems folly on the part of the doctors at home to pass men like that, and allow them to be trained and sent out; Waste of time and money. Then we had a kit inspection, and they had lost extraordinarily little on the way. I must say they all behaved very well, we had no trouble at all. One hundred and fifty of them left for the front this afternoon, under the two officers who were with them, and up to date I have received no orders. But I don't suppose it will be very long before I get off. The Rest Camp isn't a very exciting spot, and the food so

[37]

far as I have sampled (1 meal), compares very badly indeed with McConnachie and bully beef. So this afternoon I wandered down here. The place seems to have woken up since the morning, and there are any amount of people about. One sees a good many men minus a limb, and an extraordinary number of widows. We – one of our 3rd bn whom I found in the rest camp and I – chose a sunny spot in a cafe and drank beer most of the afternoon (only 1 glass each though) and then retired inside the cafe and had *café au lait*, and after that – here I am writing this. I am hoping to get orders to go up tomorrow. I send this to Philorth. How is Father's gout, daresay he is out of bed by now? With love to him and Mary.

Your loving son
WILLIE

Grand Hotel Moderne, Le Havre
22nd March 1915

Dear Father,

I wrote to Mother yesterday and gave her all the news. This morning I got my orders and leave for the front tonight, but to the 1st battalion. It really is most annoying to be changed over like that when one has got a lot of things out with the other battalion and especially my horse, quite apart from the fact that one has always been with it, and I know they want me to go back. However nothing can be done this side, all these things are worked from the War Office. Do you think you could manage to get me transferred to the second again? I believe General Macready would be the best fellow to write to. Anyway in the meanwhile my address is 1st battalion.

Isn't it awful about the colonel, and Crawford and Stansfeld both wounded again. Baird I believe has got some staff job, so I don't know who is in command of either battalion. There is really no more to tell you. The train leaves sometime after ten o'clock tonight, and may take anything up to 36 hours to get to the front. I will write again as soon as I get a chance. With love to Mother.

Your affectionate son
WILLIE

March 24th 1915

Dear Mother,

Here I am at last, not quite in the trenches yet, but going up this evening. Pelham Burn is staff captain of the brigade and I found him when I got here and the general is going to give me lunch, so as far as I've gone I have been very comfortable.

Came down from Havre in a meat train which took about 20 hours, we crawled all the way and stopped frequently. Got to the railhead at 10.30 last night and slept in the train. This morning I was sent up here in a motor car quite comfortably, and arrived a few minutes ago. The trenches are about 5 miles on from here now and Baird is still in command of this battalion. I go up with the transport after dark. Will you try and find out about Guy Westmacott for me, his firm Abrahams, Jonas, might know? I saw in the paper that he is wounded. I wonder how badly, am rather anxious about him. I was very annoyed at being sent to this battalion. It seems bad luck in a way. Especially when the 92nd has been having such a bad time. The weather is damp and seems inclined to rain. Hope it doesn't, the trenches are just beginning to dry up again. I wonder if Stansfeld is bad this time. I would rather like to know that too if you hear. This is the 8th Bde, 3rd Division – With love to Father and Mary.

Your loving son
WILLIE

Willie's annoyance at being posted to a different battalion was typical of any officer's reactions in any war. The battalion is a home, and a different battalion, even of the same regiment and wearing the same uniform, is alien – anyway at first. Furthermore the two battalions of the Gordon Highlanders, as was customary in British Regiments of the Line at that time, had been widely separated for years. Willie's 2nd Battalion had been in India and then Egypt (interspersed with the years of war in South Africa). The 1st Battalion, although it had also served in South Africa, had been sent thither from England to which it had returned; and had formed part of the original Expeditionary Force to France.

[39]

Disaster had then struck the 1st Battalion during the August retreat from Mons towards Paris and before the 2nd Battalion's arrival in Flanders. Forming part of Sir Horace Smith-Dorrien's II Corps the battalion had stood and fought at Le Cateau. Then, during the night of 27 August, there was a general withdrawal; and in an uncertain situation, amid confused orders and a dark night, the main body of 1st Gordons marched into a German force with a gun trained down the road. Due to a number of circumstances, some of them still obscure and having nothing to do with Willie's story, over 500 were taken prisoner. Among them was the eldest Fraser brother, the Master of Saltoun.

Willie refers to the 2nd Battalion Gordons as 'The 92nd'. The regiment was formed from the old 75th and 92nd Highlanders in that linking of Line battalions into two battalion regiments which had taken place during Cardwell's regime at the War Office thirty-four years before. The 92nd was the original regiment raised in 1794 from the Duke of Gordon's lands, while the 75th had been raised in 1787 by Colonel Abercromby of Tullibody and embodied at Stirling. The two regiments brought together as '1st and 2nd Battalions Gordon Highlanders' had, therefore, not totally dissimilar origins and traditions, although the 75th had not been a kilted regiment since 1809. Nevertheless in much of the Infantry the habit of referring to battalions by the old numbers rather than the new names persisted and was preferred, well after 1881 when the change took place; and Willie generally called the 2nd Battalion 'the 92nd'.

Willie's absence on sick leave meant that he had missed the battle of Neuve Chapelle, the first major British engagement of 1915 on the Western Front, in early March. His old 20th Brigade had been heavily involved, the 2nd Gordons losing 255 men, killed, wounded and missing – including the Commanding Officer, Colonel Uniacke, as Willie's letter of 17 March conveyed. Neuve Chapelle – like other attacks – was initially successful, but then foundered: the movement forward of artillery, reserves and supplies was too slow for the rapid exploitation the situation demanded, and the enemy's reactions and moves soon sealed the gaps and made British efforts to press the offensive further – which were made – both costly and futile. The battle affected the overall operational stituation not at all.

Willie now found himself a company commander in 1st Gordons, in 8th Brigade, 3rd Division, in the Ypres sector.

March 27th 1915

Dear Father,

Here I am, quite settled down really. I have been in this farm for three days now. It has been knocked to bits by the Germans and looks uninhabitable from the front, which fact we take advantage of. But it means that one cannot stir out by day at all, as it is quite in view of their trenches, and really one is more comfortable in the trenches. We all live together in an old pig-sty, i.e. 5 officers and servants and the headquarters of the company, and the men are close by in a sort of barn. The only means of communication by day is a communication trench not very deep and a foot deep in water, and we can't deepen it because the water would get deeper. I allow no one to use it but myself, as if we were spotted we would be shelled at once and possibly suffer heavily. So our life is entirely nocturnal, and we spend the night digging trenches. I was very disappointed at not going to the 92nd but I don't think they will alter it now, and here I am commanding a company and they have applied for me to be made a captain. I am keeping a diary which I will send you each week, about. Will you send me a copy of the Apocrypha? It's very interesting and lots of reading in it, but I didn't think of bringing out a copy. The regiment has been in the trenches now 8 days without relief, and there is no news of our being relieved at present. There are a few casualties from time to time but not many. About 2 per coy. on an average time they go into the trenches. We are 2 days in the trenches and two in support, but the supports are far less comfortable than the firing line I think. Love to Mother. Soup squares would be very welcome.

Your affectionate son
WILLIE

By the time Willie's letter of 27th had been written a frightful blow had struck. Lady Saltoun was the only member of the family at home at Philorth on the night of 24 March when an electrical failure caused a fire, a fire which took hold and largely destroyed the entire building. There was no loss of life and many of the contents were saved but it proved impossible to put out the fire sufficiently to keep any part of the house in a condition to be made habitable again. Philorth was never rebuilt, and apart from their London house No 1 Bryanston Square, Willie's parents were homeless and the place of his own dearest memories was no more.

March 29 [1915]

Dear Mother,

I saw the Daily Mail of the 26th early this morning and it contained a statement that Philorth had been totally destroyed by fire. I can't believe it. It seems so impossible. How could it have happened? It did not say that any lives were lost but that many pictures were saved. It means if true that the inanimate things, as well as the house, which help to make up your life are gone. It's too awful. I am afraid you and Father will be awfully upset, and poor old Master! But as I say I can't realise it or believe it till I hear from you. I don't know where to write to you.

I am sitting in a dug-out in the trenches, this is the 10th day the regiment has been in without relief, and although my coy is relieved in the firing-line tonight, I am afraid it is only to go into support. The weather is lovely but rather cold. Love to Father and Mary.

Your loving son
WILLIE

March 30th 1915

Dear Father,

We are in reserve today, came out of the fire trenches last night and all being well go back into them tomorrow night, and two days later go back to La Clytte – which is where B H.Q. and two of our companies went last night – for 6 days, which we are all looking forward to like anything. I can't believe this news about Philorth being burnt. I saw a small paragraph in the Daily Mail. Is it true and how did it happen? It's really too awful. So far we

[42]

haven't had much luck as a family the last few months, perhaps it will change soon. I am hoping that only a small bit of the house was burnt, the paper said totally destroyed, but I can't conceive that that is true. Was Mother or Mary there at the time? How did it happen?

I feel that to tell you what we are doing out here is silly under the circumstances, but I may as well. I was sitting in a dug-out in the trenches taking a bit of rest about 2 a.m. and reading the paper and that's how I found out about it. Things are really very quiet out here just now, we are engaged in strengthening our position here as much as possible, but it is pretty slow work. One great difficulty is the amount of water about in the ground still; as soon as one digs a trench it fills with water. The job we are busy at now is making communication trenches between the fire trenches and then running out saps and T-heads and building up more fire trenches in the gaps, thus –

Fire Trench   T-head   Fire Trench   T-head   Fire Trench

Communication Trench

In this way you get on much quicker as you can have men working from the ends of the fire trench and from either end of the T-head, and if you have enough men you can have two T-heads and so on.

I am sending you my diary* with this, which will tell you what we have been doing. With love to Mother.

Your affectionate son
WILLIE

In the Field
April 3rd 1915

Dear Mother,

I had heard for certain that Philorth was burnt just before I got your letter. It is awful news, and I can't tell you what I feel about it,

---

*But it has not survived.

to think that it is gone. But I know quite well that you and Father are the worst sufferers, it does mean to a large extent that all the inanimate things which helped to make up your life are gone. To have to get accustomed to something new, its comparatively easy for us who are young, however fond we were of it. But for you its awful. I am glad Father has got that brigade,* it keeps him busy, and while he is busy he will gradually get accustomed to Philorth not being there. Will you let me know when the business part is settled and what you are going to do? I won't worry you with a long list of the things I had got there, the most expensive item to replace will be my uniform which was all there with the exception of my feather bonnet. All my clothes were there, and it will be simplest for me to get some new ones when I need them. At present I need nothing. I had a fur coat there which I might replace if the Insurance Company does it, but it doesn't matter otherwise. The only things I'm sorry to lose are a few odds and ends of jewellery I had. It suddenly occurs to me that you may need an estimate of the value of the things I had there for purposes of the insurance business, if so I will try and make one out as far as I can. But I don't suppose the insurance covers my things in that way. I should think though that my uniform would cost me over £200. to replace, and that I had other clothes and things to the value of about £150. But lots of them were things I can get along perfectly well without, and unless the Insurance Company does it its not worth while to replace them. I am sorry about the dark-room,† it was the first thing I thought about when I saw the house had been burnt. I am sure that McKechnie‡ did splendidly and I will write to him. I got your letter written Monday yesterday, 4 days to come really, 3 days from London. Sometimes letters come quicker.

So you are stopping at Witch Hill,§ I am sure that Mr Brown is heart broken about the whole thing, and that half your energies have to be expended cheering him up. As for Davidson who saved all your things, he ought to have a D.C.M! Poor Master, I am sorry for him, he will be awfully cut up. He will realise everything

---

*A reserve brigade, forming and training in Scotland.
†Willie's mother was a distinguished and enterprising amateur photographer.
‡Head gamekeeper and a very great and loyal man.
§The house of the devoted factor of Philorth, Mr Alec Brown.

together when he comes back. We have had 18 days in the trenches without rest – I've been in ever since I came out – and 24 days with 1 day in billets, so the 4 days in and 4 days out scheme is not working at present. However tomorrow we go back to rest and shall be back 6 days with luck. All our casualties now are caused by snipers, and all through the head. Men will not take sufficient care not to show their heads. With love to Father and Mary.

Your loving son
WILLIE

In the Field
7.4.15

Dear Father,

Thank you very much for your letter. It's an awfully good note-book you sent me, but my idea was to write a diary and send it home to you at intervals and if I write it in there and cut out the leaves it will spoil the book. You see I don't much like keeping it on me all the time, though there is nothing in it that would matter.

The wrist watch has arrived a few minutes ago, and I am now wearing it. It's too awful about Philorth, I can't realise it at all, but its you and Mother who are bound to feel it most. We can so much more easily adapt ourselves to new conditions. But poor old Master will come home to find things very changed.

All you said in your letter about the G.S.* work at the N.C.† show was true, and far more also. When a true history of this war comes to be written you will be surprised. Very many have been sacrificed – I could tell you very many things that I cannot write. It's quite true that the way to get on is to get on the staff, and I think that if I was offered a job I should take it, especially as more regular officers are coming to the Regiment and one can be better spared. Also one has done one's bit of regimental work, and can see very clearly the ways in which junior staff officers make things difficult for regimental officers, and one might be able to do one's small bit to make that better. Pelham Burn has done an enormous amount in that way in this Brigade since he has been staff-captain,

*General Staff.
†Neuve Chapelle.

[45]

but of course he is a very wonderful chap in many ways. I try to absorb the lessons I learnt from him when I was in his company. There was an inspection by the general[*] this morning and I think he was quite pleased with the company. The weather has been beastly since we came out of the trenches, hope it will improve before we go back.

The Dardanelles show doesn't seem to be progressing much, seems they started in too big a hurry and without sufficient preparation. The watch you sent me went all the way out to the 92nd and back to Holt & Co and out here again via Philorth.

All is quiet, so there is no news. A new draft came yesterday and being on the spot I managed to do rather well for the Company.

Your affectionate son
WILLIE

In the Field
Easter Sunday

Dear Mother,

I wrote yesterday but one never knows for certain how long letters take. You should get it tomorrow or next day. We go in to billets tonight for a 6 days rest, all being well. The weather here has changed again, it's not nearly so cold, but damp and drizzly.

All the things from Fortnum & Mason have probably gone to the 2nd Bn but they will forward them on here eventually all right. Father was right (as usual) he tried to persuade me to get a pair of Cording riding boots, they are waterproof and you can get them, I know, at the A & N Stores. They are the very things for this work now. At present I am wearing rubber boots, but they are unhealthy things as one's feet are wet in them all the time, though never very wet. But the other boots are much better, and they can be taken off and pulled on in a moment. If you have time would you order me a pair, I hate worrying you with such rotten details just now, they should be very big, say 14½ inch calf and very roomy in the foot and across the instep, so that I can get on several pairs of socks if necessary. Anything in the way of biscuits and sweets and even a box of cigars are most acceptable just now,

---

[*] 'The General' generally referred to the brigadier-general – the brigade commander.

or cakes, you see we are sedentary just now and there is no difficulty about moving things.

I expect you will be very busy in London for a little bit and that Father will have to come down. I will write to him as soon as we get into billets. If the A & N Stores send me the bill for the boots, I will send them a cheque by return, or whoever it is you get them from.

This is Easter Sunday, it seems a funny way to spend it – further down the line the Germans have been trying to fraternise with our men, much as they did at Xmas time, probably with a view to trying to pick up information, but advances have been sternly repressed.

I shall have a lot to tell you when I come home that I can't write on account of the censor. Have you any news of George and Master?

Your loving son
WILLIE

Near La Clytte
April 12th 1915

Dear Father,

Herewith my diary up to date. I don't think I can add anything to it in the way of news. As you will see from it things are very quiet just at present. I have just had a letter from Mother, who seems to be very busy up at Philorth, and they seem to have found quite a certain number of things which were not burnt.

She said that you do not go to Stirling on May 1st after all, but the Army Authorities never make up their minds until the very last minute, and even then they generally find that what they have done is exactly what they did not mean to do, so they will just as likely send you as not, I should think.

I heard the other day that I have been made a temporary captain. Would you send me out a length of braid and two more stars to put on my sleeve? I shan't be able to get them here. I wonder what will happen about temporary ranks at the end of the war. It will be rather a jar to descend to subaltern again!

The weather has bucked up a lot, which is very fortunate as we go into the actual fire trenches tomorrow night, and it is misery if it is wet. At present we are battalion reserve.

I wonder when this old war is going to finish. One sort of half hopes it won't until one has really got at the Germans oneself. Also in the back of my mind I sort of half feel I should like to get something out of it. So many fellows have! No one has offered me a staff job or I might take it, if I was allowed to.

Percy Brown has come out here and has taken over command from Baird, which is really very unfair, as Baird has had command 5 months, and has pulled the battalion together damned well. And of course it is very awkward for Brown too, who is a very good fellow and an excellent soldier. However its a way they have in the Army. Baird is as sick as mud, very naturally too.

The 4th Bn. is in a way linked to us, half of them and half of us in the trenches together, while the other halves rest. They don't quite like to trust them to hold the line by themselves. They are extraordinarily good and full of go, but there it is – as Ogilvie, their CO, says, however good they are, they aren't soldiers and never will be. He (Ogilvie) is an excellent fellow, and gingers them up like anything.

We are in quite pretty country here, and all the birds are singing like anything in the mornings, and children are playing round some of the cottages and men are working in the fields, and as an accompaniment to it all, a continual rattle of musketry and the dull booming of big guns. And at intervals there is a complete lull, and one would never dream that the war was a reality and close beside one, were it not for ruined houses, great holes torn in their roofs, many without roofs at all. And holes in the fields, some 80 yards round, where a big howitzer has dropped a shell.

I suppose we shall be at peace again some day. How strange it will be to go for a walk in a place where there are no shells or bullets.

With love to Mother if she is there.

Your affectionate son
WILLIE

The 4th (Territorial) Battalion Gordon Highlanders had in February arrived at the Front from England and was in 8th Brigade with Willie's battalion. 6th (Territorial) Battalion had joined 2nd Battalion in 20th Brigade, and had fought with distinction at Neuve Chapelle.

In a dug-out
April 14th 1915

Dear Mother,

Imagine me sitting in a dug-out in a trench about 80–100 yards from the Germans about 4.30 o'clock in the afternoon. A certain amount of sniping and shelling going on the while – because that is what I am doing. We took over this trench last night, and could not make out why bullets were coming over from our left rear, while two men were killed right inside the trench yesterday, belonging to the company which I relieved. Anyway I spent last night heightening the traverses and parados and doing my best to make the trench a bit safer. And jolly glad I was when it got light this morning, because I found that about 1000^x away on our left flank, the German line swings right round behind us and can fire into us behind. I call it a bad arrangement, and have spent part of the afternoon making a sketch of the position to illustrate it, and writing a report. It beats me why someone has not pointed it out long ago and also done more to make the place safe, because we have been here for months, and apart from casualties, it upsets men's nerves a bit to think that they may get it from behind as well as in front.

This seems a very dull letter full of shop, but a dug-out is not an inspiring place. Luckily it's a fine day, though it was a bit drizzly this morning. Our trench runs along a hedge and I believe the small birds are beginning to nest all along it just as cheerfully as if the war wasn't. They were singing away like anything this morning.

There is a horrid black cloud appearing and the snores of sleeping men all round. I hope it's not going to be a wet night. It looks like it. I expect you will be in London by the time you get this. With love to Mary.

Your loving son
WILLIE

Willie's wound was periodically troublesome still and he was sent again to a field hospital for a short spell in the second half of April. On the 22nd of that month there was a new development on the Western Front. A German attack was launched supported by a large-scale discharge of chlorine gas. Throughout the early summer the Germans ceaselessly pounded the British trenches and attempted probing attacks all round the Ypres Salient. The British front held, at a cost of some 60,000 casualties. This was 'Second Ypres', a struggle which continued until mid-May. Like 'First Ypres' it claimed Willie as a casualty before its end. Meanwhile,

May 1st 1915

Dear Father,

Herewith my diary – I'm afraid it's a very uninteresting production, but then things are not very exciting just at present on our front, and if they were I should probably have no time to write a diary.

They have just been shelling a German aeroplane not far away, but I don't think they have got it as I hear them still at it. We don't see very many over here and when they do come they fly very high. I believe we bagged two near Ypres the day before yesterday. Ypres is only about 4 miles away. I am out of hospital again and quite fit, came out last night, and got bad news at once. Blair-Cunynghame, whom you met once in Aberdeen, was hit through the head the day before yesterday at one o'clock. He is still alive, and is doing as well as could be expected, but his chances aren't very great I'm afraid. He is a splendid chap. It will be awful if he dies, and a great loss to the Regiment.

The weather is still fine but it's very windy today, and dusty as a result. There has been far less shelling north of Ypres lately, i.e. the last three days, so presumably the fighting has slackened a bit. It was simply hellish up there for about ten days.

We have no news, except that I believe the Germans are all back across the Yser, in spite of what they say in their official account (which incidentally is nearly always the most accurate by a long way). No one seems to know much about this gas they have been using. I don't think it is deadly at the time and that good troops could stick it out all right, though its after effects are in some cases rather bad in the shape of a bronchial catarrh. Thinking about it, I should say the best way to meet it would be to fire continuously until it reaches you in order to keep the Germans in their trenches, and then to lie low as close to the parapet as possible until it is past. They couldn't attack until it had cleared, and it would take them some time to negotiate our wire entanglements. My company comes out of the trenches tonight.

Poor old Master. I wrote to Mother as soon as I saw he had been taken as one of the 39, but have heard nothing. I wish we had Winston Churchill[*] out here! But I don't think they can treat Master much worse than they have done all along. Poor little Rony Menzies! He isn't at all a strong chap. The worst of it is I feel we are in the wrong over that affair.

You know they have sent Brown away to the 6th Battalion now. Pelham-Burn has been made Bde. Major here.

I hear you go to Stirling soon after all; I thought they would send you all right. W.O. never has been known to make up its mind without changing it about 6 times in the process, and I suppose, people like Scottish Command H.Q. catch the infection.

Your affectionate son
WILLIE

Reference to 'the 39' was to a selection of prisoners announced by the Germans as for harsh treatment in reprisal for alleged breach of parole by others.

May 3rd 1915

Dear Father,

Here I am up at the H.Q. of our two first-line companies, and temporarily in command. I came up last night to take command of 'A' Coy, and as a preliminary had a bite of food with Lewis Gordon who was doing second in command, and was therefore commanding up here. After which we walked down to look at a

---

[*]Allusion obscure.

new trench which is being dug. We had not been standing there a minute, when there was a tremendous plop against Lewis' kilt, and I knew he had got one. He began to hop about like anything, so I realised it wasn't serious. We got him down into the trench and tied him up. The bullet had gone right through his hindquarters, quite a clean wound. We carried him up and he was tied up by the doctor and an ambulance presently arrived and carted him off. He was awfully sick at being hit just there, considered it most undignified, although I pointed out to him it was a jolly safe place to be hit, and that it was jolly lucky it hit him and not me, as it would have hit me much higher up! So here I am in command up here. They landed a shell into one of our trenches this morning and wounded two men, one rather badly I am afraid. This gas is jolly stuff isn't it! Apparently it either does you in at once or within 7 days, or if you live through it your lungs are pretty well done for, and if you don't get consumption you get chronic bronchitis. Such is war these days – It only remains for them to poison the water, which they will certainly do if they have to retire. They were using the gas again yesterday and it could be easily smelt here, which is miles away from the area where they were using it.

I see it is solitary confinement for those thirty-nine. I expected it. They are dirty devils. I suppose we shall get at them in the end. But we must just play their own dirty game as far as the gas goes. One thing anyway I'm certain of – if they expect to humble Master in any way they will have a signal failure.

We have no news from beyond Ypres. Blair-Cunynghame is doing as well as possible. At first they thought he had no chance, but now they think he will live. I have felt he would all along – I do hope so.

With love to Mother and Mary.

Your affectionate son
WILLIE

May 10th 1915

Dear Mother,

We've had so much moving about the last few days that I've had little time to write at all. First of all we were sent back to the trench area after two days rest instead of 6, expecting to be up nine days. After two days we were withdrawn back to La Clyte, and at present we form part of a sort of flying column, which may have to rush off anywhere at any minute, which gives one a most unsettled feeling altogether. It's very windy today, still blowing from the north, but too strong for gas at present.

Isn't it awful about the Lusitania,[*] a corporal in the regiment had his wife on board her, and of course he has heard nothing.

The Germans are still pushing very hard north of Ypres, and absence of news makes us think that our attack in the south[†] is not progressing so well as it began.

[Continued 11 May] This letter was interrupted yesterday by orders to be ready to march as soon as possible, so for a few minutes all was bustle and rush, but eventually it turned out to be a practice turn out, and we did not have to move off after all. Everyone seems to think that Italy is coming in at last, so I hope (but don't believe) that by the time this reaches you, she will have done it. And the Lusitania, nothing can excuse that! Result will be a lot of talk by America, but no action. They are still pushing north of Ypres and using gas very freely. But respirators seem fairly effective and in the last attack covered by gas the Germans, advancing in the expectation of finding a trench empty except for dead and dying, paid a pretty heavy toll. Also their attacks seem to be less disciplined than they were. But they are still pushing very hard.

The weather is glorious, but it still gets very cold in the evening, and I often think I would like my British Warm coat. But we have had to reduce our kits and I can't carry it. We are always ready to move, which ties one down a lot, one can't get away for evening rides and loses one's exercise.

An aeroplane duel took place over our trenches the other day. I just missed seeing it, rotten luck, but our fellow downed the German all right.

There isn't any news to tell you, I'm glad you've found a really nice house in Stirling for Father!

Your loving son
WILLIE

[*]The liner had been torpedoed on 7 May by the Germans with the loss of 100 lives, including some Americans.
[†]At Aubers Ridge.

PS Since writing this orders have come for us to move tomorrow, and by dark we may be hard at it. But I don't quite know, it may just mean a new line of trenches, but I may not be able to write for a few days.

On 12 May Willie's 8th Brigade took over trenches from another division in the area of 'Hill 60'* a division which had been attacked, accompanied by gas, in the previous week. The Regimental Historian described the scene which met the 1st Gordons: 'In the trenches still lay the bodies of many men killed by gas a week before. The Gordons buried them and returned hundreds of rifles, precious at a moment when there were hardly enough at home to equip drafts for the front . . .' and on that day Willie was again hit.

May 14th 1915

Dear Mother,

I expect you will see in the papers that I am wounded. It's not really so at all. I was going down to some new trenches we took over at Hill 60 with my company, when a stray bullet at its last gasp went through the flesh of the inside of my thigh. I couldn't feel any exit wound and thought it had just gone in and stuck there. So after we'd finished the relief I went back and got the doctor to tie it up. We found it had just gone through and I found the bullet inside my breeches, so I'm sending it home for you to look at. But the silly ass of a doctor insisted on sending me back and at the dressing station they gave me anti-tetanus injection which made me really ill, after which they gave me morphia and packed me off to the base (Boulogne) and now I am at the Canadian Hospital, Le Touquet, feeling an awful fraud. It's rather rot, because we can't afford to lose officers like that. However I hope to start back tomorrow if I can manage it. It was the night before last I was hit. The worst of it is we (the Regiment) have just taken over rather a nasty bit of line, so you can imagine

*Near Ypres.

what sort of rotter I feel, being away at such a time. However things may remain quiet there, I pray they will. If we have a scrap and I'm not in it, I don't know what I'll do.

The Germans are still pushing very hard indeed east of Ypres, and have got it all their own way as regards artillery. Suppose all ours has gone down south. Anyway they are able to pound our trenches flat, without any opposition from our guns. Hope we manage to keep them out, but it will be hard work I expect.

It's a beastly day, cold and cloudy and very different from the weather we've been having. I only got here a few minutes ago.

Please write to the battalion as usual, because I shall be back there by Monday at the latest and I hope before. It's a mistake sending me down here at all, and if I had had the sense to refuse to be injected against tetanus I should never have come. Only they told me that I shouldn't feel it, so I let them do it. With love to Father and Mary.

Your loving son
WILLIE

No 2 Stationary Hospital,
First Canadian Expeditionary Force,
Le Touquet
14th May 1915

Dear Father,

To look at the address you might think I was wounded, but as a matter of fact I am just doing a skrimshank. Walking down to the trenches the night before last I got a spent bullet through the fleshy part of my thigh. I thought it had stopped in, so as soon as I had time I went to have it tied up, and we found it had just gone in and out again. However the doctor would send me back and they sent me as far as the base. Goodness knows what for, because as soon as I got here today I saw the doctor and am off back again tomorrow. They gave me an anti-tetanus injection, which was probably a good thing, as it made me feel iller than I've felt for a long time! However it passed off in 24 hours, and I am quite hungry again. The wound is nothing, I shan't be able to ride for a day or two, and it makes my leg the least thing stiff, but one does not want to ride much or walk much in the trenches.

There is no news. The German official report in todays Times is terse, but pretty accurate. They have not got through east of Ypres but are pressing very hard, and they acknowledge a French success north of Arras, which is rather more extensive than the report would have one believe.

This is the Golf Hotel at Le Touquet, where Sim stopped when he came over to play golf last year. How times are changed since then and its under somewhat different circumstances I am stopping here now.

They have just moved us up into a nasty bit of the line, and it was on the way down to the trenches with my company that I was hit, so you can imagine what sort of rotter I felt when the doctor said I had got to go back. But Baird said I must go, so I went. However I shall only have been away for about 3½ days when I get back. I wish to goodness I knew if we have been attacked in the meanwhile. I'm afraid it's quite likely. The trenches my company are in are not too nice as the Germans are in the left end of both of them, with only their barricade and ours in between. I think we should try and bomb them out but had not time to look at the place properly. Don't fancy Baird will like them to stop there long.

Your affectionate son
WILLIE

Willie was confident that he would soon be back at duty. No letters survive between 14 May and 7 July, so the pattern of his life for some weeks is unclear. But a letter to Lord Saltoun from the temporary commanding officer of 1st Gordons – Major Baird – reveals that Willie's wound was thoroughly unpleasant and took long to mend, involving another spell of sick leave.

June 10 1915

Dear Lord Saltoun,

Your letter of Sept 7 (I hope you mean June 7) reached me today. It is a great blow to hear that Willie is so bad. He never wanted to go sick at all but the doctor said it was wiser and I insisted so I fear I am to blame to some extent for his misfortunes. In any case I am obviously paying the penalty for it.

We have just been relieved after doing 13 continuous days in a particularly poisonous part of the line in front of a town of which you will doubtless guess the name as it begins with 'Y'. We were very heavily shelled and had a good number of casualties. My adjutant has just been taken away for the staff and I am stranded once more with 1 officer (Turnball) of 4 years service and 25 officers with service ranging from 9 months to 3! The situation is not a pleasant one and after doing 7 months as stop gap CO without the slightest chance of ever being confirmed in the post, I am beginning to feel a bit disgusted.[*]

Please give Willie my best love. No one has yet been appointed Bn M.G. Officer.

Yours sincerely,

W. BAIRD

Willie's absence from 1st Gordons after this second wound was fortunate in one respect. The battalion's trenches were very heavily shelled at the beginning of June, when bombardment finally destroyed the old city of Ypres. The battalion lost sixty-eight. Willie escaped this as well as the fighting in the second half of June – a series of savage German attacks and bombardments which left the enemy much where he had started but still holding commanding ground around the rim of the Salient.

Willie's letter of 7 July shows him about to return to duty. It also appears that he had been given a certain training responsibility within 8th Brigade as a whole, and that, while not formally a member of the brigade staff, he was attached to it.

Near Poperinge

7th July 1915

Dear Mother,

I got here yesterday at about 3 p.m. in a very hungry and unwashed condition. Got into the train at Boulogne but we did not get off until about 2 a.m. by which time we were seven in the carriage, which made sleep difficult, but I managed it and slept until 6 a.m. at which hour we got to Hazebruck. There they sent me of to Steenwerk which they said was our new railhead, but when I got there I found it wasn't our railhead at all, and had to go all the way back to Hazebruck and then on to Poperinge which is our railhead, and near which the Battalion now is. We are back resting and have been for three weeks now, and its done everyone a lot of good too. We go back to the trenches on Sunday night and shall probably be in about 12 days, as a Brigade that is.

I am going today to St. Omer for a day or possibly 2 days to see the Commandant of the machine gun school to see if he has got any new schemes worth adopting. I have also got the bombing and sniping to supervise. We are organising the bombers and snipers into a separate unit in each battalion. I will write to Father about training bombers and snipers, because there is no doubt that fellows coming out without experience in bombing are at a very great disadvantage, and there should be an officer who knows something about explosives in charge of the bomb-throwers in each battalion. But I expect Father will have some difficulties in getting a supply of proper bombs, there are lots of kinds, and of course men can't be taught about them if they can't see them and use them. It's an awfully important thing though.

It's quite warm here, though not frightfully hot. It will be by the end of this month though, I expect. I have to start for St. Omer in a few minutes so must go and get a bite of lunch. Love to Father and Mary.

Your loving son
WILLIE

On 19 July it may be that Willie's training of specialists bore fruit. The machine gunners, bombers and snipers of 1st Gordons were used in a small-scale but successful attack to eliminate a German salient at Hooge, and Willie was especially commended.

Dear Father,

I am glad the bombing letter was some use, and enclose the copy of a lecture I gave our bombing officers the other day. It's put very briefly, but is I think fairly intelligible if read in connection with the story I sent you. It's got no information in it which would help the Germans, so I send it through the ordinary post. The other thing I believe I could be of use in would be machine guns. I wonder if it would be possible for you to have your Machine Gun Officer – the Brigade one I mean – sent out here for a week. He would learn more than in a year at home. You see I have a course going on all the time in the Brigade, and he could see the trenches and emplacements and every sort of thing. He could start and be back with you in 10 days I think, and we will look after him out here. Lots of fellows do come out like that and I should think you could work it through the C-in-C. Our general would be very pleased to do all he could for him, I know.

We are hoping against hope to be left where we are for the winter. There is a certain amount of shelling but its a paradise to some places we've been in lately. However a rumour is abroad that we may very soon be back in a certain rather unpleasant place we lately left. This bit we are in now would be a good spot to come to for instruction.[*] Another most important thing to teach the men is to build really strong dugouts. You can go all over our lines out here and scarcely find a single dugout worth a damn. The great thing is to dig deep, drain it well, put on a very strong roof – about five or six rows of sandbags, a layer of broken brick in or out of sandbags plus 2ft of eath on top of that. Beams 10 to 12ft by 9" by 3" or 4" make a very good support, but not more than 2ft apart, with layers of corrugated iron on top to support the sandbags etc. I will start the next page with a diagram of one. It is most important to have that sort of thing for bombers and bomb-stores, and behind every m.g. emplacement, so that the men can sit and do their job as safely as possible during a bombardment. And of course, the bomb-

[*]Near Givenchy.

stores must be very strong and should be fitted inside with wooden cupboards for the bombs.

The beautiful drawing [see opposite] above is a sectional view of the ideal dugout. Where the ground is well-drained it can be made, and of course a drain can be run out of it, and steps taken to prevent water running in. Also the floor can be boarded if one can get material. I think the actual bomb stores should be smaller, and a large bomb store should be composed of several small dugouts. You have to cut a sloping path down to your dugout to get in by, and the entrance should face away from the enemy. I will try and draw a picture to show this.

This is the same dugout, but this picture [see opposite, below] isn't to scale. It shows the steps down to the entrance cut in the ground. Anyway one ought always to make dugouts as strong as possible, and in order to do this without a huge erection which sits up and asks to be shelled, one must get down into the ground.

I am afraid Warsaw is gone. The Germans hoisted a large placard with '*Warsaw gefallen*' written on it about 3 days ago, so we knew long before it was in the papers. But it didn't depress us in the least as we are all too busy here to worry with Warsaw. Also the Russian army is intact as an army and they will return all right. However I expect we shall have the best part of a million Deutchers over here before long with nearly all the guns in the world.

We have a cheery time to come before the winter, there is no doubt about that. There is a bit of a show just coming off, and we are doing a bit of gunning our way to try and draw off some of the Dutchman's fire. So I daresay he will return it with interest later on and our cubby hole may become too lively.

8th Brigade
Aug. 15th 1915

Dear Father,

We have been here 3 weeks and have done a lot of hard work and are just beginning to know the place thoroughly. And today we hear we are going back to Hooge. I don't know what battalions will say when they are told. It will take all the heart out

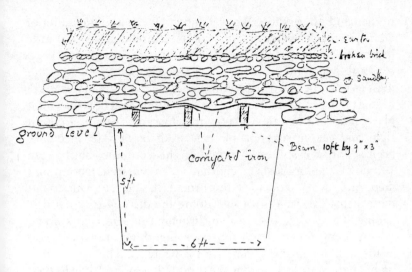

earth

broken brick

& sandbag

ground level

Beam 10ft by 9"x3"

corrugated iron

5ft

6ft

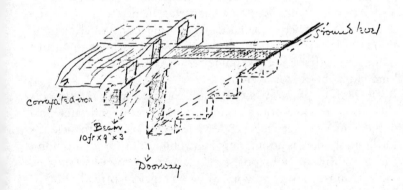

Ground level

corrugated iron

Beam
10ft × 9"×3"

Doorway

of men and officers too. We were up at Hooge and took a bit of German trench, which the division which relieved us promptly lost and a good bit more besides. Another division was sent to retake it, which they did, very well too. The place is in an awful mess as it has been shelled continuously for weeks, and it was the nastiest place in the salient before, and Ypres Salient is the worst place in the line by far. And now this division is sent up to put it right, and clear up other people's mess! All the work the men have been at for weeks goes for nothing. This continued shifting up and down the line costs us enormously in material, labour, and men. And since October last this Brigade has been moving round the salient – never out of it – doing the dirty work for other people. The people responsible sit behind in arm chairs doing their juggling, and getting KCBs and other things thrown at their heads, and not caring a damn for the wretched fellows sweating blood in the trenches, getting one thing half done and then hunted off to begin another, and never seeing any result. It makes one feel absolutely murderous.

The Germans are angels compared to some of our Corps Commanders etc. The worst of it is they are never within miles of a shell or bullet and there is no chance of them getting killed and making way for better men. I'd rather be dead in a ditch than on the staff of some of these fellows. The only one who was worth a damn, Smith-D.[*] had to go home because they were all jealous of him. Hope the censor opens this.

The Staff Capt. is on leave so I am doing his work for him. It's very good practice doing all these fellows jobs, and later on I might manage to get a job as Bde Major somewhere with luck. It's the best job there is about, only I am a bit junior for it. Shouldn't care for Staff Capt. job, too much Quartermaster work to suit me. But one must know the work to be an efficient Brigade Major. The post is just going. Love to Mother and Mary.

Your affectionate son
WILLIE

---

[*] Sir Horace Smith-Dorrien. He had been dismissed by the Commander-in-Chief, Sir John French, in May for reasons most thought petty and personal.

[62]

Dear Father,

Many thanks for your letter. I expect London was a bit dull just now, probably worse than Dumfermline in some ways. I am quite fit again, as I got away to the seaside for a couple of days and had a good breath of ozone well away from the smell of chloride of lime and cresote which permeates all areas occupied by our troops. This is a most bloody country, there is no other word for it. The weather has broken and it has rained steadily for 24 hours, and the whole country is a morass, just as it is all the winter. It's awful to think that the dry weather has finished and that these awful winter months are beginning again. The worst of it is that the authorities have taken no steps to provide huts or tents for the men – we are supposed to be resting now – and this rain has caught them unprepared, and the poor devils of men are all in open fields with no shelters but wretched bivouacs made of waterproof sheets and blankets.

I daresay it won't be very long before your brigade come out now, but I hope sincerely for their sakes that it won't be before next Spring all the same. It really is beyond description, the absolute misery of existence for the men in this part of the line in winter.

I am very glad to hear they have taken Master into the country up in the mountains. I can imagine it must be a tremendous relief to get away from a town like Halle to a place where there is more than a few ugly houses to look at. He has been more than a year in Germany, now, and with every prospect of being there another year I am afraid.[*]

I rather fancy the Dardanelles show is about as bad as it can be, and the Russians seem to be taking knock after knock. But the worst part of the whole show is these strikes at home. I think a great many fellows out here are beginning to ask themselves whether the damned country is worth fighting for, and I'm rather inclined to agree. If those strikers were out here they would be lynched.[†] I would like to see 20% of them shot straight away, and it would give me the greatest pleasure to be one of the firing party.

[*]And was there until 1918.
[†]The home front was subjected to industrial strikes in both World Wars. The reaction of the soldiers tended to be that of Willie.

One's blood simply boils at the thought of them. And one thinks of all these thousands of fine fellows dead, and the hundreds of thousands out here now who all hold their lives at a moments purchase, fighting for a damned country which breeds such a lot of cursed traitors that it can't even remain united when it's fighting for its life. The Germans may have their faults but at least they are patriots and do remain united. If we had been in Germany's shoes the war wouldn't have lasted 10 days.

Your affectionate son
WILLIE

Sept 17th 1915

Dear Father,

I'm afraid I have had extraordinarily little time to write lately because I've been very busy for reasons you appear to have an inkling of. I'm afraid my letters aren't very interesting at present, but you see one can't put down on paper anything in the nature of future operations.

This is as always a warm corner, and we have quite good bombardoes with heavy and light stuff everyday, just to keep the Deutchman on his toes a bit and knock his various works about and try to kill a few of him. It's very good medicine for him, bad for his nerves and gives him plenty of work to do. He usually retaliates, but just here I think we give him as good as he gets. I do think that we have got about as much stuff for guns as he has here, though I wouldn't tell the munition workers that for anything, and anyway it's not nearly good enough to have as much. We want 5 times as much and then there will begin to be a chance of finishing the war.

We are still fearfully short of material for making dugouts and m.g. emplacements and trenches, which hangs up work a lot. It's extraordinary how difficult it is to know where one is in a maze of trenches, and in a place like this where the Germans have been in and out several times, and lots of trenches have been blown in and aren't used any more and new ones have been dug, it's ten times more difficult. George seems to be all right at the Dardanelles, good work knocking out a Turkish battery.

I should think it's ripping up there now. This country would be very pretty if it wasn't battered out of all recognition. You've no idea how a country can be knocked about by shells. Of course in this bit, shells go each way in hundreds every day and often enough in thousands. Love to Mother and Mary.

Your affectionate son
WILLIE

Congratulations to George on the Turkish Battery.

On 25 September a new British offensive was launched by nine divisions in the mining areas of Loos.[*] The operation had been forced on a reluctant French and a much more reluctant Haig by the obstinacy of Joffre supported by the counsel of Kitchener (Secretary of State for War) who thought British participation in a general offensive essential, both to sustain Anglo-French unity and to help the Russians who had taken some hard knocks: 'Warsaw gefallen.'

The British attack followed a sustained bombardment, including a large-scale gas attack. 3rd Division were not directly involved in the main attack, so Willie's brigade did not engage: but his former battalion, his beloved 92nd, lost seventeen officers and nearly 500 men.

Loos was a disaster. The battle depended on prompt and efficient handling of reserve divisions. As so often the initial assault had a fair measure of success; the failure was in its exploitation. One consequence of the battle was the replacement as Commander-in-Chief of Sir John French by Sir Douglas Haig.

But meanwhile, on the same day as Loos, a subsidiary attack was launched by 3rd Division eastward astride the Ypres-Menin road. German trenches were taken; and in the ensuing counter-attack the same trenches were lost again. The two Gordon Highlander Battalions in Willie's 8th Brigade, 1st and 4th, lost in sum 32 officers and 645 men, of whom 68 were killed. On the concept of this operation Willie was caustic; on the performance of the men enthusiastic. While on what he learned of the main operation at Loos he was bitter.

[*] A village just north of Lens.

Sept 28th 1915

Dear Father,

The salient as usual has been a lively spot with Hooge as the centre of attraction. As the show is now finished it can't do any harm if I give you an account of it. But first I must mention a most extraordinary paragraph I saw in the paper today, which was put down as the official report of the C-in-C and dated from G.H.Q. the day after the fight, so that they must have been aware of the true state of affairs when it was written. It stated that we had attacked on a considerable front north and south of the Ypres-Menin road and had taken trenches on both sides, but had been forced to evacuate the trenches north of the road, but (and this the odd part) had retained the trenches for 600 yards south of the road and were consolidating the ground won – Which is a damned lie. You can't usually believe a word of our official reports, but barefaced lies of this description make one ill. We were driven out of the whole line the same day as we attacked, entirely due to the Boche's much heavier and more effective artillery. You see we attacked right at the point of a narrow salient where we were subjected to artillery fire from 3 sides, and where it is impossible for us to use the number of guns, or get them so close up, as one can in a straight bit of line. Why we were made to do this I can't tell, probably the Corps. Commander could tell you. There are lots of places where we could have attacked with a fair chance of success, and against positions which it would have helped us far more to capture, and it would equally have made a diversion to help the fellows down south.

The real reason was because this wretched division was up here. As it was, the 1st G.H. found the wire on their front intact and never got in at all on the north of the road, but managed to get in on the south with 1 coy, which was eventually cut off. The 4th G.H. did splendidly. They had a very strong bit to take, found the wire uncut, crawled under it and took the place. But the Germans were very clever, they shelled them terribly in the position, and then put a barrage of fire behind them and cut them off by bombing down the trench from both ends. The Royal Scots stopped in their position longest, but were eventually bombed out too. You see the Germans were able to isolate all the points in turn with artillery, and used it extraordinarily well – never made a mistake all day. But ours was a damned good show, the men were splendid, and I certainly think we killed more of them than they did of us, although we got no ground. We exploded a mine which probably did in a good many, and we got 160 prisoners. They were Prussians and good clean-looking fellows. As you might expect their trenches were wonderfully well constructed, far better than ours, which is natural, because their organisation is far better, and they don't keep changing troops from one bit of the line to another as we do and they have everywhere got the highest and dryest ground, and they can get as much material such as sleepers and concrete as they want. Whereas we have great difficulty in getting anything we want.

In the bombardment they blew in all the communication trenches leading up to one point, and the next day a doctor had to bring down some wounded on stretchers over the open. They sniped at him whenever he showed himself, but never fired a shot at any of the stretchers.

They asked the other day if the general could recommend anyone as Bde Major to a Bde in another division and he sent in my name. I daresay I shan't get that either, as I should have heard by now I think. But I really don't mind very much. One just takes the job that comes along and tries to do it. I'm rather fed up with seeing fellows blown to bits and don't mind when the war ends. It's heart-breaking all the good fellows of the 1st and 4th G.H. killed. Splendid men, but they never had a chance. No men could do more than they did. With love to Mother and Mary.

Your affectionate son

WILLIE

Oct 14th 1915

Dear Father,

I suppose all the papers are busy acclaiming great victories in the south. I can't read the stuff they write now, it makes one ill when one has an inkling of the real facts. It's the same old tale, staff work in the higher commands simply appalling. It has been the same in every push we have made during the war, and as the staff officers are not the fellows who get killed by their own mistakes, they remain to make more. And they are usually too pig-headed to learn. The men of some of these new divisions were simply sent forward like sheep to the slaughter; part of the show was simply criminal.[*] A German officer captured summed up the situation by saying 'Your men are magnificent, but your staff work and generalship awful'! Just about right he was! You know, one really does begin to have doubts about the outcome of the war, the way we sacrifice men for nothing is so terrible. Our show here the other day was simply another instance of the same thing. As soon as I can I will send you an account of our fighting here.

I haven't heard any more about that job I told you about – don't think I shall get it now, but it's possible I may get another.

Our general has gone to the Corps now – he is a great loss to the Brigade, but he may instil some of the rudiments of the art of war into the Corps Commander and staff. Though I fancy they are too pig-headed to learn much.

I'm afraid this is a depressing letter, but I'm not very cheerful just now. Don't think that the outlook has ever been so bad since the war began.

I began this letter 3 days ago but had not time to finish it, as we had a sort of scrap in the middle. Of course here we aren't in the big push at all, but we are always scrapping in a niggly sort of way, and the Germans and ourselves keep blowing up mines and generally try and make the other fellow keep his reserves and not send them off to the south.

I am sorry to hear you say Master isn't getting enough to eat, I thought he was happier up at Clausthal. I am sorry to hear you've been laid up too, that is rotten luck. Love to Mother and Mary.

Your affectionate son
WILLIE

On 19 October a new brigade, 76th Brigade, was transferred to the 3rd Division; 1st and 4th Battalions Gordon Highlanders were moved to this incoming brigade, and Willie was sent to the Brigade Staff. He was told he was to have the coveted appointment of Brigade Major, but this was later changed and he found

---

[*] Loos.

himself kept at brigade headquarters without a proper job and irritatingly superfluous, although not for long. He took this hard: meanwhile he went on a week's leave, confident that he had a good and interesting new appointment, but disappointed of it on return, when a black and uncertain period temporarily set in. Willie had his share of proper ambition.

22.10.15

Dear Father,

Many thanks for your letter. I had one from Mother too. It is a bit of luck getting a B.M. job. It's a G.S.O.2 job you see. The routine work is all right – the great thing out here is to have as little paper as possible and to cut down what you send on to battalions to a minimum. Also to be able to write orders shortly and clearly. One has a lot of tactical work too of course, but I have done that part of the job for a long time in the 8th Brigade. I found this Brigade* had brought out reams of useless paper, which I had to go through and tear up, which I did ruthlessly. But the Staff Captain doesn't know how much and has the lawyer type of mind, which is a disadvantage. Also the clerk is new and doesn't know his job. I was offered a job as G.S.O.3 to the 2nd Army, but didn't take it. It's a soft job, and one they would never have given to any but a Staff College fellow before the war, but not as good as the one I have got. It's a safe job though and sometimes when one is done up, one thinks that worth having, but not really, you know! They have pulled the division out to rest, and I am jolly glad. We needed it.

I may manage to get home for a few days soon, when I have got things fixed up here. 'Here' is a nice little French village, and no shells and bullets flying about, which is a rest in itself. I have been in the trenches nearly all the time since I came out last at the end of June.

We got in last night and the Brigade is billeted all around. Our old 8th Bde Staff is scattered now – the general gone, Pelham-Burn gone, me gone, and Macready the Staff Captain going soon. Wish he was here as Staff Captain. The weather has been kind to

---

*76 Brigade.

us lately but I don't know how long it will last. It's getting pretty late in the year now.

I quite agree with your 'Oh for a strong man'. That's what we need, I wonder what Sir E. Carson's retirement means? I think he is, or rather was, the strongest man in the government. But these fellows will go on shilly-shallying and telling the country we are winning. We're not – no, not by any means. If we had had a national spirit to compare with Germany's this war would have ended long ago.

Your affectionate son
WILLIE

After his week's leave, the blow fell.

76th Bde
5–11–15

Dear Father,

Here I am back here, and at present I haven't got a job. It really is rot: If there's nothing for me to do here I might as well be at home. It's very annoying though, not having a job to get down to. And anyway I expect I shall get left in the end.

There is no news much, but everywhere there seems to be a feeling in the air that the Germans are hard put to it. However it's probably all imagination. Nothing much is happening out here at present, and all the interest seems to be in the Balkans. The French papers say the Russians are sending 600,000 men to Bulgaria, but you probably know more about that than I do.

I had quite a good journey over here, without any exciting adventures, and managed to get a car at Boulogne to bring me on from there. I brought the partridges out with me and we had some for lunch today and they were very good indeed.

I think that this is the best address to write to for the moment anyway, but I will let you know as soon as anything turns up. Seems to me I should be better doing some job at the Scottish Command than doing nothing here! Anyway I shall go and see the division tomorrow probably and find out if anything has turned up.

It was ripping being at home for a bit, but it makes one hate being out here worse than ever. I wish I really thought the war would end in the Spring as they all say. That's what the Americans think, and they always say the looker-on sees most of the game. Love to Mother and Mary.

Your affectionate son

WILLIE

76th Bde

7–11–15

Dear Father,

I am here doing nothing at all, and I have just heard unofficially – but I know it's quite true – that I am going to be sent to command one of the new machine gun companies they are forming. Well I won't go, that's all about it! I'd far rather go back to the Regiment than go and command a crowd of scallawags like that. Here I am seconded from my Regiment, and without a job! They make me a Bde Major and take it away again, then I am promised another job of the same sort, which they then say I can't have, as I am to go and command this d-d m.g. company. Which isn't even formed yet. And meanwhile I am doing nothing! One is pushed about from pillar to post, because the authorities are too muddle-headed to know what they are doing. So if Ewen F can give me a job and can work it so that I am allowed to take it – I will take it like a shot.

At present I am absolutely fed up. I think it's perfectly damnable the way they treat one. Anyway, one thing's clear. Go and command a scallawag crowd called a machine gun company I will not! I've seen too much of that sort of thing out here already for that. And anyway it leads nowhere.

I'm afraid this letter is a bit of a grouse, but I feel very strongly about it, and I have been treated most damnably. There is no news. We heard a good deal of gunning today. I am sending a lot of documents on grenade work which I hope will fetch up all right and be useful. They are all things I have made out from time to time for the 8th and 76th Bdes.

Your affectionate son

WILLIE

Dear Father,

It's quite true – there's nothing to do but lump it cheerfully. Of course I couldn't really ask for a job at home! So I've lumped it, and I trust fairly cheerfully, outwardly anyway. But all the same this machine gun business is an absolute dead-end. I am writing this at the machine gun school where I have come for a 3 days course, as I hadn't much to do. All I have found out confirms me in what I thought, that so far from being a means of getting on, it is an absolute bar from getting anywhere, and from that point of view one is far better with one's battalion. So if I can I shall go back. Though it's doubtful if I shall be able to, and anyway it's a bit of a come-down to go and command a company in a battalion in the Brigade of which one has been Bde Major. And apt to knock the keenness out of one, for a few minutes anyway. However, such is life.

Thank you very much for your letter and you would probably hear if you asked that these machine gun companies were very good billets, because they are trying to boost them up, but, as I say, for anyone who wishes to get on, it's an absolute dead end.

It's very cold here and has been snowing and freezing and doing all sorts of things. The trenches are getting awfully wet and falling in all over the place, and in a very few places will they be any better than they were last winter, and I'm afraid that we shan't strike one of those places. So it's not a very cheerful outlook from our point of view. Nor for the Germans opposite, though I can't think their trenches can be very bad because they almost invariably have the higher ground, and have always had unlimited material. I wonder what things are like in Serbia? I often think it might be more amusing out there in many ways. I hope the Americans are right and that the war will end in March.

Love to Mother and Mary.

Your affectionate son
WILLIE

Dear Father,

I send you herewith some papers I promised some time ago. The Brigade is back in the trenches and its quite funny to hear guns and bullets and things after being away from them for a month. I am with Bde H.Q. – a sort of paying guest. No definite job to do, and taking up room in a headquarters which is none too big in any case. A d-d nuisance in fact. It really is extraordinary to leave one here doing nothing, when we are supposed to be short of officers. However it's on a par with the conduct of our authorities in the large things of the war.

We have got the only bit of line in this part of the world which is anything approaching good. In parts our trenches are quite fairly dry and also we are on a crest line, so that the ground behind the trenches is hidden from view. There is a lot of mining going on though, and as we had been very neglectful in that form of warfare in this bit up to a month or so ago – the Boche up to date has had the best of it. But we are getting down to him now I believe, although he is still probably in the best position. But I do think that when we get going we can usually do him in underground.

I was down at the M.G. school as I told you, the other day and met a lot of fellows from the 1st Army. Their tales of the awful mismanagement of that Loos show fairly opened ones eyes. We ought to have been right through them if we had had our reinforcements up at the proper time. However that's past and it's no good looking back and regretting.

Things look black indeed in the Near East – in fact as far as I can see they look bad everywhere, and one's reason tells one-as far as known facts go – that if the war ends in less than a year or eighteen months the advantage is bound to lie with Germany. And yet the Americans still say that Germany can't last beyond the end of the winter. I wonder!

Your affectionate son
WILLIE

Soon, however, disappointment was overtaken by a proper appointment, as Staff Captain 27th Brigade in the 9th (Scottish)

Division. And thus Willie ended 1915 – still in the Ypres Salient.
His first Mention in Despatches (of four) was in November 1915.

Dear Father,

I wonder if you ever got some documents about bombs and grenades work I sent you home some time ago? I hope they arrived all right. The posts have been very upset lately and one never knows if its coming or not. The wet weather has begun in earnest, and the trenches in many places are in a dreadful state, its all one can do to keep them together at all. So we hope the Germans are in a bad way too. We know they are in many places. The latest trench rumour is that peace is all arranged and will be signed on the 14th of this month, also that Hindenburg, or Hinderbody as the men call him, has been captured by the Russians.

Did you read in the paper about some lunatic Americans, headed by Ford of car fame, and mostly composed of newspaper reporters, and cinema photographers, – who have chartered a liner and intend to make a tour of all the governments of Europe in order to arrange peace? Did you ever hear of such a mad scheme? They seem to imagine we are scrapping for the fun of the thing!

I expect it is pretty cold up there just now, and your warriors won't care about drilling as much as they did in the summer. It's not very long before it will be 1916, and this rotten old war going as strong as ever. There is a lot of gunning going on in this part of the world every day. The other day the Canadians had a bombardo, and fired 11000 shells at the Germans. They made sure it was an attack and retired, and began to shell their own front line, which was quite satisfactory. They fight well the Canadians, but are an undisciplined crowd, and I forget how many thousand pounds a week the division spends on drink, but its something colossal. Have you any news from Serbia? I don't like that business.

Love to Mother and Mary.

Your loving son
WILLIE

III

France and England
1916–1917

At the end of 1915 the German Chief of the General Staff, Von Falkenhayn, concluded in a written appreciation that while England was the principal support for the Western Entente, Germany's method of defeating her should be by destroying, through attrition, the French Army. England would then have no effective instrument on land. To force on France a great battle of attrition there must be an offensive against some point which would force the French to commit every Frenchman to its defence. Falkenhayn chose Verdun. On 21 February 1916 the great battle began.

Falkenhayn's object was not breakthrough but destruction of French division after French division, by forcing upon them the necessity of counter-attack and exposure to massive German artillery fire. To achieve this the Germans planned and executed – ultimately at huge cost – a series of limited advances: limited in range but enormous in terms of the mass of men and material employed. The battle made of 1916 a year of crisis for France. The crisis dominated the first six months of the year.

One consequence of Verdun was that the brunt of any Allied offensive operations in 1916 had to be borne by the British Army. A joint Franco-British offensive to take place in July had already been agreed in February, before the German attacks at Verdun started. Thereafter the French part in this offensive was inevitably and progessively reduced as Verdun made its own terrible demands. It had been agreed between the Allies (with Haig reluctant over both place and date) that the area for the summer offensive should be in Picardy: the Somme.

To his joy Willie's brigade was moved out of the Ypres sector.

Dear Father,

I must say I have been very bad about writing lately, but I have had a most colossal amount to do. However things are settling down a bit more, and the Bde Major is back from leave, so I have more time. We haven't had a very good day to usher in the new year, as it is blowing and raining together. I wonder what will have happened by this time next year – this time last year we never thought we should be where we are now. I forgot if I told you but Harry Pelham-Burn* is now commanding a Battalion in this Brigade. I went and saw the new year in with him last night, and we had a very good dinner and managed to get through a fair amount of champagne and old brandy. At present leave is coming fairly regularly, and I daresay I shall manage to get back for a week in about a months time – granted nothing untoward happens. We have moved out of that beastily salient now, thank heaven. The first time I have been out of it, and when we go back into the line again, it will be elsewhere, as things are at present, that is.

I am still at this Staff Captain job, and I don't like it much, but it's all experience. We are not very much in touch with the outside world just at present, because the posts are all upset by weather and mines and submarines etc. and we don't get the papers every day. However we seem to be going to send some troops to Egypt – I shouldn't mind going there at all, to a nice warm climate where there is no mud! That's our worst enemy out here, the mud, but it's not so bad in this part of the world as round about Ypres.

Your affectionate son

WILLIE

An unusual new Commanding Officer for the 6th Royal Scots Fusiliers arrived in the 27th Brigade that winter.

---

*He had been Willie's company commander in the 92nd and was ultimately to be his brigade commander. At the time of this letter he was commanding a battalion of another regiment, although shortly to be given command of an amalgamation, the 8th/10th Gordon Highlanders.

Dear Father,

I got your letter this morning written on New Year's Eve. It took a long time, but it's just luck how long a letter takes these days, because the mail is very irregular. I'm having rather a slack time just now, just enough work to keep me occupied all day, which is about right. It's an odd thing, but the other day they sent Winston[*] to command a battalion in this Brigade, and I believe he is going to do all right! But of course one feels that he is only using the bn. as a stepping stone to a Brigade, and I suppose the whole thing is a political advertisement. I went down to see how things were going today and stopped to lunch and he seemed to grasp the situation and was quite intelligent generally. I don't know how much longer we shall be out of the line, but not very much I shouldn't think. Though the longer the better from our point of view.

We've been having all sorts of amusements, boxing and concerts and football matches, just to keep things going. But we put in a good deal of work too, drilling and training and bombing etc. The men are all fairly comfortable in barns, where they do get dry straw to be on, and they get exercise, so when we go back to the trenches they ought to be fit again. The worst of the trenches is, that living in them one gets no exercise. I hope the end of the war will be in sight next Hogmanay, it will be a bad business if it isn't. However we've all got so accustomed to trenches and bullets, that life without them seems unnatural, and a time when there is no war seems a wild extravagant dream.

Your affectionate son
WILLIE

23.1.16

Dear Father,

I am sending herewith 2 receipts I should be most awfully obliged if you would keep them for me – as I am sure to lose them out here, and being a Staff Capt is making me most horribly methodical.

[*] Churchill.

We are bound for the trenches in a very few days now, and once we get the move over and are properly settled in our new quarters I hope to get leave for a few days, probably about the end of the first week of next month. We had a most glorious day today, and I took an afternoon off and rode over to Eecke where I was billeted once with the 3rd Division and saw my old friend the curé there. He is an awfully good old chap, exactly like the pictures of the jolly old priests of the middle ages, with a comfortable corporation and a cherry red face framed in a halo of snow white hair. It does one good to look at him. He appeared quite pleased to see me, and we sat and bucked in fluent French for about an hour, and drank one another's healths in a bottle of white wine.

Our new trenches are good, I believe, though I haven't seen them yet myself, but of course the country behind is pretty muddy and the road very much cut up. But the mud contains a larger proportion of water than it did in the salient, and is therefore not so hard to get about in. I suppose you have no news of when you are going to move?

I went to a regtl. concert of the 6th R.S.F. the other night – C.O. Winston – and he had Seely[*] – who commands a Canadian Bde – there too. The show ended by Seely and Winston getting on the stage and making flattering speeches about each other in their best platform manner, amidst the applause of the audience. Each then called for three cheers for the other, which were heartily given by the soldiers, most of them with their tongues in their cheeks – I suspect! I regret to say that I was laughing so much that I clean forgot to rise and give any cheers for either of them, which incident was all the more lamentable as I was sitting in the front row just below the stage. It was very funny but a bit unusual at a regtl. concert! I think they both look on soldiering as a vote-catching campaign to bear fruit after the war.

Your affectionate son
WILLIE

And after a short leave at home –

[*]Colonel Rt. Hon. Jack Seely, later Lord Mottistone. Secretary of State for War in 1914 at the time of the so-called Curragh Mutiny and a Cabinet colleague of Churchill's in Asquith's Government.

Dear Father,

How are you getting along?

The French have been having the devil of a battle at Verdun, and have lost about 78 guns, they say, and 17000 prisoners and a good many casualties I suppose. But they are quite pleased with themselves. They say that thirteen German divisions lost about 60%, and that the casualties in many others were heavy, and that they have not required to touch their reserves to meet the attack. Some people think that the attack is worn out, but I don't think so. I think the German plan is an advance with a limited objective, and what we have seen is the first bound. In about a week they will make the second, or try to. Of course they may attack elsewhere, but they seem to have used a lot of men to make a diversion, which is what the Verdun show would become in that case. And if so the diversion has failed. But I don't think they have failed yet by any means, though I think they will.

There was quite a good show on this front, ie. the re-capture of the ground lost while I was on leave!* My old Bde was sent up to do it, and they did it and got a bit of original German trench as well. That was the 1st Bn of my Regiment. All this took place yesterday in the early morning. A German counter-attack was repulsed; I don't think it was a very vigorous one. Very likely they will have a more energetic attempt before long. We've been fairly quiet down here so far.

Love to Mother and Mary.

Your affectionate son
WILLIE

Dear Father,

I was very pleased to get your letter. It is rotten luck about the Brigade, but I suppose there's nothing to be done, and anyway it's a great thing to know that you've turned out a thundering good article, even if you are not going to be able to use it yourself.†

---

*On the Ypres-Comines canal.

†Inevitably, because of his age and health, Lord Saltoun, having trained his brigade, had – much to his disappointment – handed over the command

[81]

We've been having very cold weather with a lot of snow and frost, but today it is like summer, brilliant sun, and as warm as anything. We have been moving into a new H.Q. and it has been rather a job one way and another. However we are more or less settled at last. My present general is rather a footling, brainless little man, and rather like a spoilt child in many ways. Also he has no more idea of commanding a brigade than of walking on his head. However, he's got some good points. But sometimes things are a bit difficult. Luckily the Bde Major is an excellent fellow, and between us we carry on all right.

We have got some Russian officers going round the line today, having a look at things. I haven't seen them myself. I did mean to go along with them, but couldn't get out in the end. The place is a mass of aeroplanes today, which is a damned nuisance as it means that one has constantly to be getting the men under cover. Also this is a place which is pretty certain to be spotted and shelled before long, and there is no place to put the men in decent safety when that happens.

I think this big push at Verdun is a good thing myself – if the French can down them that is – because the attacker is bound to have most losses at this game, and if they could afford it they would wait to be attacked, and not attack themselves.

Your affectionate son
WILLIE

March 22 – 16

Dear Father,

Many thanks for your letter. This goes to Bryanston Square as you will probably be there when it arrives. The weather has turned to rain, which makes work in the trenches very hard indeed. One does as much in one fine week as in two months of wet or snowy weather. Work in the trenches is never ending, and here it is very hard, because although this line has not altered for 16 months, no proper system of work has ever been laid down, and the whole place was in a lamentable state under the circumstances. The higher commands ought to lay down the whole trench system, and then a continuous and sensible policy might obtain – but they don't.

[82]

The best and latest reason for the German attack at Verdun that I have heard is – 'that the Kaiser died on Jan 15th, and the Crown Prince wished to make the announcement of his succession popular by a big success on this front'. This comes from the Corps Commander who heard it from someone who heard it from the King of the Belgians. So it must be true! We've got a new Brigadier, G.F. Trotter – one-armed fellow – he was a Grenadier. Perhaps you know him?

I don't think there is any news, the wireless reports all quiet at Verdun, but the wireless is always in the papers the same day. It's a month now since I left. The time has really gone pretty quick. If all goes well I ought to get home again about the 10th of May.

Your affectionate son,
WILLIE

On 13 April Willie received the welcome news that he was to be appointed brigade major of 151 Brigade in the 50th Division. Brigade major, the right hand man and chief staff officer to a brigade commander, was a key appointment and Willie (rightly) thought it was best filled by someone like himself who had seen plenty of fighting as a regimental officer. The supply of trained staff officers, of course, was wholly inadequate to the demands of a hugely expanded and expanding army; and officers like Willie, who had regimental but no formal staff training, were increasingly used for key appointments with the front line staff, expected to learn the job on the job. Willie was not yet twenty-six.

14.4.16

Dear Father,

I have just got your letter of the 12th and am awfully bucked to hear what Col. Gordon says about Master. I should greatly like to hear the whole story of that time.

You are right about the leave question, it is all stopped now, and so I shan't get home as soon as I thought after all. I heard last night that I have been appointed Bde Major of the 151st Bde, 50th Div., and expect to have to go tomorrow. I'm just a wee bit nervous about it, because its a strange division and I know no one there I don't think. I wish it had been my old 3rd Div.

It's not in a particularly pleasant place I don't believe, but that doesn't matter as one is out here to scrap. The great thing is to be able to put the job through well, because after all the majority of Bde Majors out here are fellows with 15 to 20 years service. I hope my new Brigadier is a good fellow.

Your affectionate son
WILLIE

H.Q. 151 Bde
4.5.16

Dear Father,

I am very happy in my new Brigade, my new general is a very good fellow indeed, also I am beginning to discover the secret of happiness. Which is to do one's job and trust in God.

About this Irish outbreak,[*] of course it is disgraceful and out here we regard it as entirely the fault of the Government which did not take proper steps at the proper time. As for Kut[†] – we knew it was coming some time ago. Only about 3000 British troops were there which doesn't make much odds in this war, and the Indian troops made no odds at all, really. I think myself it was the greatest mistake to send a relieving force – because after all it's no use killing Turks. It's these beasts opposite us we want to kill! As for the responsibility – I believe it is true that Gen. Townshend's orders were to go and guard the oil-fields. But he is a gambler in military matters, and finding his star as he thought 'in the ascendant', he made a dash for Baghdad and got scuppered. That is what is said, and what all those whom I have met who know the man believe to be true. But it's been an unfortunate week all the same, so something good is bound to happen to counter-balance it.

Out here I tell you we have all got our tails right up. We think the Boche has lost all ginger in the offensive, and that Verdun had been the heaviest blow he has yet received. As soon as he finds himself unable to arrange and carry out big offensives on either

[*]The Easter Rebellion in Dublin.
[†]A British disaster at Kut-el-Amara in Mesopotamia.

[84]

front alternately, he loses the greater part of the advantage of his interior lines. When his troops are pinned down at all points, as is nearly the case now I believe – he is done. All we must do is to wait until we have sufficient men and munitions for a terrific offensive simultaneously on every front, and the end will come. It will cost much blood, but it's a sure thing. Absolutely certain. We are fools and we make many mistakes, but we are a 'chosen people' and we shall not lose. That is my view anyway.

I hope to get home about the 27th of this month, all being well. I could get away a week or two earlier probably, but a very great friend of mine is getting married on June the first, and I have promised to be his best man. He is a splendid chap, and has collected a Military Cross, a D.S.O., a Legion of Honour, and has been recommended for the Victoria Cross, and every one has been thoroughly deserved. And is probably the youngest Bde Major out here, being a year younger than I am. We have been through one or two scraps in company which teaches men to know each other well. So I am very keen to see him through the greatest adventure of all. I should like you to meet him – he's a fellow after your own heart, and Mother would fall in love with him at once.

You will have read all about this gas attack which failed utterly. They used a lot of gas, but we knew all about it beforehand, the guns did 'em before they got off the mark I think, and the few who got off had a rotten time too. We are out of the line for a bit resting, and have got glorious weather and a glorious bit of country to rest in. I seem to get through a fair amount of work all the same, but try to cut the paper down as much as possible. Far too much writing goes on in this sedentary war – far more than in peace time. The thing is that G.H.Q., Army and Corps staffs, whose real job is to be planning big operations, have nothing to do, so they come interfering in the jobs of divisions, brigades and even battalions, just to feel they've done a bit of work. So we spend much time answering silly questions.

Your affectionate son
WILLIE

The friend whose best man Willie was to be was Billy Congreve of The Rifle Brigade. 'He has been recommended for the Victoria

Cross' Willie wrote (in addition to the DSO, MC and Legion of Honour) and Billy Congreve indeed won the VC – but later, on 20 July 1916; and posthumously. He was killed on the Somme. Willie was utterly devoted to him. Billy Congreve's widow, Pamela Maude, ultimately became Willie's wife.

15.5.16

My dear Mother,

It's been a real noisy day today and the Boche has been bombarding very heavily indeed without stopping at all. At present we don't quite know what he is up to, but I think myself it's demonstration. However it's not very pleasant, though we have had no shells just where we are. But of course it's always a bit awkward when one doesn't quite know what he is playing at. This is a very desolate country now and it will be a terrible business ploughing it up again after the war.

The weather has been very hot indeed which is a bit trying as one's steel helmet becomes almost red hot and heats up one's head a bit. I don't quite know how long letters take, but I think that in the normal course of events we ought to be out of the line again by the time you get this. I hope so anyway.

We are still pretty weak in numbers. It's very hard to give you any real news as one doesn't know what one can say.

Your loving son

WILLIE

Willie had been only two months with his new brigade, in 50th Division, when a mishap occurred which kept him from active service for some time. In June 1916 Lord Saltoun received three letters.

[18 June 1916]

My Lord,

I am writing to tell you that your son Willie (our Brigade Major) met with an accident this afternoon. He was returning from the trenches when his horse bolted, and when negotiating an awkward corner in a farm yard and amongst some old trenches it came over and threw him. We quickly got him down to the Dressing Station.

The Dr says he appears to have fractured a rib. He is also bruised and suffering from slight concussion. I told him I would write and let you know what had happened. He will be writing to you himself in a day or two.

We are all so sorry the accident happened as we had grown very fond of him. However we hope to have him back in a few weeks. Please don't worry at all because I have told you all. I know parents are apt to worry and always think accidents or wounds are worse than they are when a stranger writes home.

Yours sincerely,
W.B. LITTLE (CAPT)
Staff Capt 151 Inf Brigade

151st Infantry Brigade
B.E.F.
23 June 1916

Dear Lord Saltoun,

Your son, my Brigade Major, had a fall from his horse on Sunday last 18 June about 1 p.m. He had been up in the trenches with me and I had ridden on while he was talking to a colonel. When close to Brigade HQ I saw his horse loose following me. I turned back and found him at a farm being attended by some men and an officer so I went to the field ambulance and got a doctor and a motor ambulance and brought him back. He was sent to the Casualty Clearing Station at Bailleul the following day and evacuated, I believe to Boulogne, two days later. He had slight concussion, and had broken two ribs. I sent in daily to enquire after him and I understand he had recovered from the former but I fancy the ribs will take some time to heal. I don't think you have any cause to be alarmed as I understand his injuries are not dangerous, though serious.

It appears from what the groom who was accompanying him said that his horse was frightened at something and took charge, bolting up a narrow path to a farm – there was a sharp bend there with some men standing by 2 cisterns. The horse shied off them or your son pulled him off to avoid the men and the horse charged into a bank revetted with sandbags, putting your son off.

I understand that your son asked my Staff Captain, Little, to write to you and he has done so. Fortunately the accident only occurred a few hundred yards from the ambulance so I was able to get medical attendance at once.

We were all very sorry to lose him and shall be glad to hear how he is getting on. As you say, he is a gallant fellow and remarkably knowledgeable for such a young soldier. I am sure you have every reason to be proud of him. I only took the brigade over a few weeks ago and I have found him very helpful.

Wishing him and yourself the best of luck and for him a speedy recovery and return to duty.

Yours very truly,

T.T. WESTMORLAND

[23 June 1916]

My dear Lord,

With the mail today I received a letter from Willie together with yours, so I expect by now you will also have received one from him. He wrote from No 9 Stationary Hospital, Boulogne, but said he expected to be moved over to England in a day or so. He says he is much better and I am glad of this. I'm afraid it will take 5 or 6 weeks for his ribs to heal up. I believe the Drs were most afraid of his head as he had given it a nasty knock. However he says himself that it feels quite all right and he should know best. I am so grieved that the accident happened as it means someone else will be appointed in his place. We are so sorry to lose him. I hear from his servant who saw him off on the train from the C.C.S. that he was looking well and very upset at having to be sent down country.

Yours sincerely,

W.B. LITTLE

It is not clear exactly what happened thereafter. Willie was on sick leave in Scotland in August, implying that his injuries from the fall took time to mend. His August letters are concerned with trivia, with sporting and social activity, with family. In the following January he refers to having been before a Medical Board and 'passed fit at last'. Furthermore when he ultimately returned to France – in April 1917 – he referred in his diary to being back 'after 9 months at home', implying continuous disability and leave from at least the previous July, 1916.

Willie's division was not involved in the earlier phases of the Battle of the Somme which began on 1 July. In the first three days over half the strength of 2nd Gordons became casualties and two weeks later 1st Gordons suffered almost as badly in the operation round Longueval and Delville Wood. 50th Division were sent to the Somme area later, to take part in the September advances – limited, painful, and producing no operational result in terms of ground won. The Germans also suffered terribly in the Somme fighting, a circumstance often neglected: there is little doubt it contributed to their ultimate collapse. In the meantime it seemed to the British to have brought tragic loss for little gain.

From Willie's later diary – and the absence of letters – he appears to have entirely missed this savage episode. He later avowed – surprisingly – that the move of his division south to the Somme from Flanders was welcomed by all, in spite of the battle's grim reputation. 'The Ypres Salient', he said, 'was so unimaginably dreadful *in the conditions of life it imposed on the men that any place and any dangers were preferred!' It seems likely that this was culled from the experience of friends rather than his own – unless, as seems improbable, he was passed fit prematurely, returned to duty for a few weeks in September and then collapsed again. No letters survive to support this and it can be presumed that Willie, mercifully, escaped the Battle of the Somme.*

He took the losses of his friends there very hard, but particularly and shatteringly the loss of Billy Congreve, which for long dominated his feelings and to which his diary entries often painfully adverted. Billy's father, Sir Walter Congreve, himself a holder of the Victoria Cross, commanded a corps on the Western Front and did so, unlike some, amid universal respect and admiration. Willie knew and revered him, and as Billy's closest friend visited him whenever he could, and often spent time*

---

*Won at the Battle of Colenso, 1899.

on leave at the Congreve family home at Chartley in Stafford-shire. The end of 1916 found him staying at Chartley. Still medically downgraded he had been ordered to report, as an instructor, to the Senior Officers' School at Aldershot.

In January 1917 Willie again began to keep a diary, omitted throughout 1916. He also later stuck within its covers copies of certain reports he wrote on operations during the year. The early weeks were spent at the Senior Officers' School, and the diary entries are concerned with the minutiae of training, lectures, schemes, riding school and the personalities of his fellow instructors. There is plenty about his visits to London, and to the houses of friends in Hampshire; and about the eccentricities of his recently acquired motor car. He encountered the usual human difficulties.

[DIARY] 15 MARCH 1917 Fine day – somewhat colder. March discipline demonstration took up this morning. Spent the after-noon dealing with reports. This part of the course is very unpleasant – it's always an evil job to have to write reports on officers. They all have to see them. Most were quite happy about theirs', but one fellow was very worried about his. He also upset me a good deal by telling me I had not taken much interest in him or helped him, but had rather looked upon him as a fool. Which is very disturbing – one feels that one has been a failure as far as he is concerned; and the fact that it was all quite unconscious on my part does not help matters. He is very touchy I think – but the fact remains that he has not got as much value as he might have done from the course, and goes back in bad heart. I wish he had spoken to me sooner.

And the lesson is 'be very, very gentle with the lame dogs'.

There is little comment about the war. On 24 January he was able to record: 'attended a Medical Board and was passed fit at last'.

He was not, however, released from instructing at Aldershot until 25 April. Then, to his joy, he was told that he was getting command of a battalion at the front – which battalion was for the moment uncertain.

[DIARY] 26TH APRIL 1917 Fine day. Left Charing Cross at 7.45 and got to Boulogne at about 12.30. An uneventful journey. Met Brand and Umfreville on the boat. Brand and I had lunch together at Boulogne and he got a lift in a car to his destination. My train does not leave till tomorrow, so Umfreville and I put up at the Folkestone. Am rather glad to get a good night's rest.

The last time I was at the Folkestone was with Billy, when he was going home to be married. Happy days.

April 26th 1917

My dear Mother,

Here I am safe and sound so far, having passed the various dangers of the sea. I was rather sleepy when I left this morning, so I left a book that I wanted in my sitting room. It's a red book called 'Notes for Commanding Officers'. Will you please send it to me when you know my address. Which I can't tell you yet as I don't know it myself. It was most awfully sad having to go just as George arrived, but the world is inclined to be a bit contrary sometimes. And I believe the good days are coming soon. At least I hope so.

I found Brand on the boat coming out and another fellow who was with me at Aldershot.

I find my train doesn't go until 7 a.m. tomorrow, and I had no luck in finding a car going in my direction so I am stuck here for the night. And not a bad thing either, really, as I shall be able to make up some lost sleep. I don't suppose I shall get to my destination until this time tomorrow. It's delightfully warm and sunny – this sort of weather makes war seem more of a sin that ever.

It seems to me I have spent most of the time eating since I have been here – there doesn't seem to be any shortage of sugar etc. I will write again as soon as I get to my destination.

Love to Father and George,

Your loving son

WILLIE

[DIARY] 27TH APRIL 1917 Left Bolougne at 7.30 a.m. Changed at Etaples and got to St. Pol at 12.30 p.m. Lunched there and with some difficulty got on to the 51st Div. on the telephone, who promised to send a car for me. Waited about at St. Pol having found a companion in much the same circumstances – Watts in the Somerset Light Infantry. My car arrived about 6.30 and I went off to div. H.Q. about 6 miles away. There I found Dick Cunynghame as G.S.O.1 and Lawrence Carr G.S.O.2 I am to take over the 6th G.H. in Pelham's Brigade, which is splendid. Dined at Div. H.Q. and remained there for the night. It does seem odd to be back again after 9 months at home, all seems to be much as it was when I left.

At home the war seems to progress – here it seems to have remained just where it was. However one day it will end.

28TH APRIL 1917 A glorious day. Got up about 8.30 having fallen asleep to the sound of gunning in the distance and slept like a log.

Had breakfast and lunch at divisional H.Q. Spent the morning writing letters and talking to the general. There was an attack this morning on the whole corps front, but no great success was attained. Possibly the most satisfactory part was a Boche counter-attack on the whole front of the 37th div. which was beaten off with heavy loss.

After lunch Lawrence Carr drove me over to the 6th G.H. where I found Adams my 2nd in C and Newson my adjutant. Went on to Bde H.Q. where we had tea and found Pelham, looking not too well, I thought. He needs a month at home and should get married into the bargain. He and I walked down to my H.Q. together and I made the acquaintance of several more officers.

It is a difficult job, this taking over of a strange battalion – and my predecessor seems to have been a splendid fellow, which does not make it easier. The battalion look splendid though, and they must not be let down.

IV

Arras

1917

Willie was now a battalion commander – at twenty-six. 6th Battalion Gordon Highlanders was a Territorial battalion entirely raised in the North-East, in Aberdeenshire and the Moray Firth counties. It had mustered on the outbreak of war at Keith and been one of the first Territorial battalions to be sent to France, in November 1914. Thereafter the battalion had at first formed part of Willie's old 20th Brigade – although after his own departure, wounded. Soon after arrival the battalion was in the trenches.

It was in the sector occupied by 6th Gordons, among others, that one of the strangest incidents of the war had occurred, between Christmas 1914 and 3 January 1915. The historian of the battalion told the story.

Christmas Eve the Germans spent in singing carols, and, the night being calm, they informed our men that they did not intend to shoot on Christmas Day, asking at the same time that we also should refrain from violence. 'No shoot tonight, Jock! Sing tonight!' was one of the remarks they made on Christmas Eve. Little attention was given to this, but on Christmas morning, when our men were at breakfast, a cry was raised that the Germans had left their trenches. Springing to arms, they could scarcely believe their eyes when they looked over the parapet, and saw a number of the enemy standing in the open in front of their trenches, all unarmed. Some of the enemy shouted 'No shoot!' and after a little, a number of our men also got out of their trench.

Meantime Colonel McLean had come up on his daily tour of inspection, accompanied by the Padre, the Rev. J. Esslemont Adams, minister of the West United Free Church, Aberdeen. They had just completed a burial service over one of our men behind the line, when the Chaplain, looking up, observed the strange sight at the front trench, and drew the Commanding Officer's attention to it. Colonel McLean ran along the front line and ordered the men to come down, but they pointed out that more of our men further along were standing 'on the top,' and that a number of the enemy were out on their side and gazing peacefully across. The Chaplain, who had followed the Colonel, said to him, 'I'm off, sir, to speak to the Germans; maybe we could get a truce to bury the dead lying in No Man's Land.' Coming to a little ditch, which ran along the middle of the field between the lines, he held up his hands and called out, 'I want to speak to your Commanding Officer. Does anyone speak English?' Several German officers were standing together, and one of them said, 'Yes! Come over the ditch.' The Chaplain hurried forward, saluted the German Commander, and began to talk to him and his staff. Almost at the same moment a hare burst into view and raced along between the lines. Scots and Germans leapt from their trenches and joined in the eager chase. The hare was captured by the Germans, but more was secured than a hare. The truce of God had been called, and the rest of Christmas Day was filled with peace and goodwill.

Dotted all over the sixty yards separating the lines lay the bodies of the dead. Spades were brought out and soon each side set to work to dig graves for the fallen. The Chaplain had seized his opportunity and had urged both Commanding Officers to agree to a short religious service after the dead had been buried. This was arranged, and about four o'clock that quiet afternoon took place what must remain one of the most memorable Christmas services of all time. On one side of the dividing ditch were British officers, with soldiers in rank behind them; on the other, German officers with men of their regiments about them; between them stood the Chaplain, an interpreter, and a German divinity student serving with the Saxons. The Padre read the 23rd Psalm in English, the German student reading it after him in German. Then a short prayer, which the interpreter had translated, was read sentence by sentence by the student after the English form had been recited. At the close the Chaplain stepped forward and saluted the German Commander, who shook hands with him and bade him farewell. It was an impressive sight –

officers and men, bitter enemies as they were, uncovered, reverent, and for the moment united in offering to their dead the last offices of homage and honour.

The spirit of friendship and goodwill did not end with Christmas Day. Both sides were only too glad to snatch a brief respite from the discomfort and misery of the mud-filled trenches. A friendly understanding was come to, by which they warned each other of the approach of any of the Brigade or Divisional Staff. On their appearance the 'truce' seemed to vanish, and trench routine became normal. A few rounds were fired well into the air, lest by accident a frontline combatant might come by harm. As soon as the Staff left the line, the truce revived, and friend and foe again swarmed into No Man's Land. The informal character of the truce sometimes created embarrassing situations. During one such visit the Brigadier, passing along the front line, looked over the parapet and saw a German fully exposed. Turning to the nearest rifleman, he ordered him to shoot the German down. The man wishing to give the enemy a sporting warning, fired high. The German took no notice. The Brigadier became annoyed and ordered the private to shoot again. This time the soldier fired wide, but near enough to cause the German to look up in pained surprise. 'Shoot again' ordered the Brigadier. The soldier obeyed, and so near was the bullet that the incautious enemy dived headlong into his trench.

A number of the Germans were fluent speakers of English – one said he had been a waiter in the Hotel Cecil – and conversation was always possible. The greatest friendliness prevailed. All kinds of 'souvenirs' were exchanged – coins, buttons, and pipes; while quite a busy trade went on in barter. Bully beef and jam were in great demand, and were exchanged for sausage and chocolate; cigarettes and tobacco were the price of German cigars; and British rum purchased wine or cognac. In these beverages they pledged each other's health, and to all appearance the War was at an end. Strangest perhaps of all, and most abiding proof of truce, was when it was dicovered that there were barbers among the enemy; a number of our men were shaved by them in No Man's Land.

The truce lasted from Christmas, 1914, to the 3rd of January, 1915. Its end had more formality than its opening. On the afternoon of the 3rd of January a German officer approached our lines, accompanied by an orderly who acted as interpreter. They asked for an officer. Capt. Dawson, of 'D' Company, left the British trench and advanced over the open to meet them. The two officers gravely saluted, the German officer then informing Capt. Dawson that instructions had been received that the ordinary conditions of warfare must be resumed. After some discussion of the time, watches were compared and were found to differ by nearly two hours; it was then agreed that the truce would lapse after the expiry of an hour. That day only a few shots were fired, but on the following day, in obedience to orders, volleys were fired all along the line. A 'feu de joie' passed from the 2nd Gordons through the 6th to the Guards, rifles being in the proper position, muzzles well in the air. Immediately after, a message passed right along the front, 'Pass it along – the Kaiser's dead!' The truce was over.

[*From D. Mackenzie,* The Sixth Gordons in France and Flanders, *Aberdeen, 1921.*]

The battalion had fought at Neuve Chapelle, its first major battle, in which the Commanding Officer had been killed, as well as 15 other officers and 290 men; at Aubers Ridge in the summer of 1915; and at Loos – where the battalion again lost its Commanding Officer and from which it emerged with little more than shadow strength to await reinforcements.

Then in April 1916 6th Gordons had joined the 51st (Highland) Division, with which famous formation it was to serve for the remainder of the war. On 20 July the battalion had been sent to the Somme area, and on 1 August was committed to the holding of High Wood. In November 1916 the Battalion had taken part in the attack on Beaumont Hamel, a highly successful limited attack at comparatively low cost. Trench warfare and some skilfully conducted raids had alternated in the following months with periods of rest. On 9 April 1917, however, the battalion had taken part in the first phase – and on 23rd in the second phase – of what came to be called the Battle of Arras; immediately before Willie's arrival.

The British Army went into the Battle of Arras with high hopes. It was believed that only the lateness of the year had saved the Germans from ultimate disaster during the later stages of the

Somme fighting. During the preceding weeks the Germans had withdrawn in the Somme sector to a rearward line, well prepared and very strong, known to the Allies as the Hindenburg line. South of Arras the front line left a shallow German salient. The British offensive was conceived as a convergent attack against the shoulders of the salient.

Surprise, as so often, was subordinated to intensity and protraction of the preliminary artillery bombardment. The Germans were alerted and well-prepared and had paid particular attention to defence in great depth, realising that nothing could generally stop the initial success of a British attack but that the artillery preparation which preceded it usually nullified its effect by destroying the ground over which the exploiting troops, supplies and guns had to move; while the defender could redeploy and concentrate on comparatively clean ground.

A parallel French attack was a tragic and expensive disaster and Nivelle, the French commander, was dismissed. In the British sector, however, and tactically, Arras was conducted very successfully – accompanied by gas. 6th Gordons took part in the northern or left-hand part of the attack against the right shoulder of the German salient. The 'creeping barrage' – adopted since the Somme – was admirably effective. Then, in the second phase of the battle, on 23 April, the battalion had found itself isolated after a successful initial advance; had suffered heavily; and had lost its Commanding Officer. Willie was assuming command of a battalion which had seen plenty of fighting, and tragic loss; casualties in the Arras fighting which started on 9 April were already 500 by the time Willie arrived. The battalion was temporarily in a rest area, west of Arras.

[DIARY] 29TH APRIL 1917 Glorious weather. Church parade in the morning, and spent the remainder of the day getting acquainted with the officers, and the working of the battalion. Also found an excellent place for a rifle range. Had a meeting of company commanders in the evening and went through the programme of work for tomorrow. This is a delightful spot, and the men are very happy here after some stiff fighting but I'm afraid they won't be left to enjoy it very long.

Two company Commanders – Hutcheson and Fleming came to dinner.

30TH APRIL 1917 Perfect weather. Summer seems to have come with one bound, leaving that slow-coach spring to come along later. Inspected 2 companies in the morning and found them very weak indeed. We are badly in need of a new draft.

Had some difficulty about getting the field for my range – so rode up to the Bde office and saw Pelham, and it is all right. So we started digging this evening. Had two good demonstrations in the afternoon for officers and NCO's and afterwards inspected the transport, which was good, though the horses are poor – the result of a short ration and hard work. The divisional band played here this afternoon – Gony-en-Ternois is our village.

Had a meeting of coy officers at 6.30 to discuss work for the week and other details. In future this will be a daily affair. Walked down to see the range which is going on well.

Had two coy commanders, Leggatt and Fortune to dine.

May 1st 1917

Dear Father,

We are still behind the battle, and I believe it is just possible though not probable that we may be for some little while. It would be a very good thing if we were because the last draft have not been turned into soldiers yet and we are badly in need of another one. We are all together (the battalion that is) in quite a nice wee village and the weather is glorious, and the men lie about in the sun and enjoy themselves. I'm not working them too hard – about 3 hours in the morning – because they need rest quite as much as training. However I find plenty to do myself, getting the hang of things and trying to make things go as much like they did in the 92nd in peace time as possible. Orderly pipes to play the calls and all that sort of thing. It helps enormously.

I am very lucky – it is the best battalion·in the division. The men all come from Donside way – and they have got a very strong battalion spirit and also a great reverence for the 92nd. In fact they are splendid fellows and I think we shall be very happy. But as I say, I should like 3 weeks training before we go back to the battle.

I wonder how George is? I expect he is enjoying his leave, but I wish we'd been able to hit off the dates a bit better. I daresay your picture is finished now. I wonder if you would have it photographed and send me a copy? If George has his done I would like one too. Now I've got to rush off and inspect HQ. details – so I must stop. Love to Mother and George.

Your affectionate son
WILLIE

[DIARY] 1ST MAY 1917 Uncle Harper inspect the division's transport in the morning. I was not very satisfied with the way in which mine turned out – but it will be better very soon. Inspected two companies and the bombers in the morning. The specialist instruction is very good. The instructors have always been left out of the trenches and that system is proving itself to be the best one.

Today we got the range finished and tomorrow they start firing. The pipes played retreat in the evening and then we had a concert arranged by the padre which went off very well.

Dined with Pelham at Bde H.Q. There were five 92nd fellows there. Dick Cunynghame, Laurence Carr, Stumpie Maxwell, Pelham Burn and myself, and we sat bucking till midnight. The pipes of the Argylls played very well indeed. I'm not quite sure their piping isn't better than our pipers'.

Stumpie drove me home in his car and I got to bed about 12.30 a.m.

'Uncle' Harper was Major-General G.H. Harper, who had taken command of 51st Highland Division in September 1915. An officer originally of the Royal Engineers, he soon showed himself a divisional commander of great distinction. He was intelligent, reflective, and a first-class trainer of troops who learned meticulously the lessons of the fighting on the Western Front and ensured that they were applied throughout his division. Willie much admired him. Harper was as far removed as can be imagined from the stereotype of a First World War general (always something of *a caricature) – bluff, insensitive and remote from the fighting troops. Instead he understood every aspect of the division's work from top to bottom, and was universally trusted and revered.*

[DIARY] 5TH MAY 1917 Glorious day again and very hot, but the evening got quite cold and looked like rain. Had the attack practice with one company for the Divisional Commander in the morning. A fellow called Neil Munro, who is going to write a book or something, came to lunch. Went down to the range after lunch.

In the evening Pelham lectured to all the officers in the Brigade, and then we went and watched the football finals. After which we had a concert which was assisted by some men from the Divisional troupe and the men seemed quite happy.

But they aren't as fit as they look yet, they need more rest, and it would be folly to put them over the top again before they have had it. Some of these high commanders must realise that even Highland soldiers are human.

Got my first letters from home today and very welcome they were too. But it gave me a lot of writing to do this evening and it's not far off midnight now.

May 6th 1917

Dear Father,

Very many thanks for your letter. I would like all my letters sent here plase. I don't think there will be many bills among them. Yes – they have made me a Lieut. Col. It's only temporary of course. I keep the rank as long as I keep command.

I have been very busy one way and another – we are still resting but not for much longer I am afraid. We have been having glorious weather which has made it a real rest, very different from what we used to call rest in some places that I have been in. How is the war going? I very seldom see a paper and then it's usually two or three days old. Not that the papers are always quite accurate in their statements. I was very glad to get my budget of letters, ten days is quite a long time to go without hearing from anyone – though the time does slip away very quickly.

I rode over to the division today and saw old Uncle Harper our div. commander. He is a dear old boy and a very capable one into the bargain. I asked him to dinner on Wednesday so we shall have to give him a good dinner. I told Mother about my last dinner party which was quite a success.

I'm afraid a destroyer in the North Sea isn't a very safe job, but then there aren't so very many safe jobs about, at least not jobs it would interest one to have. I hear the French have had a bit of success.

Goodbye – and love to Mother.

Your affectionate son
WILLIE

[DIARY] 9TH MAY 1917 A glorious day. Took two companies in the attack practice in the morning, after which went down to the Range, where a Brigade Rifle Meeting was taking place. We did not do very well in that I'm afraid – but there it is. All our best NCO's are gone and so far we have not had time to make new ones. However that is a point which I am getting down to now.

10TH MAY 1917 Early rise and early breakfast at 5.30 as we had to move off at 6.20. I was a bit astounded when I got to the starting point to find the leading company was not even on parade. A very bad show and I let the Coy commanders have it straight on that point. Also the C.S.M.'s.

We got off at 6.30 and marched to Liping St Flochel where we entrained, and got to Arras about 11 a.m. Bad staff work there and the men were kept hanging about until 12.30 at the station, which is very often shelled. However, we got into billets eventually. They were pretty dirty and one was both dirty and very unsafe, so I refused to occupy it and got another far better billet in its place. I think they are housed fairly safely now. Find I can get a rifle range here – good work. Don't know how long we shall be here. Turned in early.

11TH MAY 1917 They shelled the town pretty well all last night with single shots. We had no casualties, but its not very pleasant. Personally I made sure they weren't falling near the men's billets, or this one luckily, and went to sleep.

[DIARY] 12TH MAY 1917 At 8.30 a.m. we moved out of Arras and marched to Blangy,* bivouacing near there. It was a very hot day and there was no shade. However the men soon made themselves comfortable in some old trenches. In the afternoon I saw G. Trotter, now commanding the 51st Bde. Last time I saw him was dining at the Carlton. Thought we should move up that night to position of reserve, but later got orders not to move until 2.15 a.m. So we spent a very pleasant night under the stars, it reminded one of days in the Egyptian desert, or rather of nights. Except that there the night is full of peace, here it is made hideous by the report of guns and the scream of shells over head.

13TH MAY 1917 At 2.15 a.m. we moved off. Had some difficulty in locating the trenches we were to occupy, the Fampoux-Oppy line. However eventually we got settled in very comfortably, and remained there all day. It was very hot. In the morning I went up to Bde H.Q. and had a good look at the country from an O.P.

Got back to lunch at my H.Q. and spent a day doing various small jobs in the bn.

14TH MAY 1917 Had intended going up to the line in the morning but put it off owing to rain. However the adjutant and I went up later. We went all round the front line with Scott, commanding 1/5th S.H. During the night both he and the bn on his left had pushed forward and constructed a line in advance of the original front line. There was intermittent shelling going on, but we were very lucky and missed the worst of it. The line seems by no means bad, but requires a good deal of work. Had lunch with the Bde on the way back. Found that A. Cator is commanding the Bde next to us, his H.Q. being beside ours. Went to see him after lunch and we went and watched a bombardment of the Boche lines. The old Boche was very quick

*Just east of Arras town, as was the French line.

with his retaliation. He put a few shells near the battalion's position, but did no damage.

15TH MAY 1917 A very hot day. The Boche started a very heavy artillery bombardment of the positions held by the battalions of this Brigade in the line at about 9 a.m. All our information is to the effect that he intends to retire on the Queant-Drocourt line and I was inclined to think that he was firing off the ammunition near his guns. In the morning I went back to the transport lines to inspect a class of N.C.O.'s working under the R.S.M. Returned to the bn. about 3 p.m. to find the bombardment continuing. It continued until about 9 p.m. At 11 p.m. we had just lain down, when a verbal message came from the Bde ordering the bn. to proceed at once to relieve 1/5th S.H. and part of 1/8th A & S.H. in the front line. After issuing necessary orders I went to Bde H.Q. (as ordered) to find out what was up. It was a very dark night and the operation was very difficult, as some of the officers had had no opportunity to reconnoitre the position they were to take over.

The bn. was just moving when they were assailed by a very heavy barrage of H.E. and lethal gas shells, which caused confusion and considerable delay. It was necessary to adjust gas masks and the ground was a mass of old trenches, battery positions and shell-holes.

Few experiences are more disagreeable than an enemy attack made during a relief in the front line of one battalion by another. In this case the German use of gas greatly added to the unpleasantness.

[DIARY] 16TH MAY 1917 The first companies arrived at bn. H.Q. of 1/5th S.H. at about 2.15 a.m. and moved off at once under guides. Soon after, the second company arrived and moved off. But owing to the mud (it had been raining and the ground was very marshy in places), the relief was a slow business. The two rear companies arrived and were put into positions of support. At about 3.30 a.m., long before the relief was complete, the enemy opened an intense barrage of heavy shell, and it was impossible to carry out the operation. I do not think I have ever seen heavier shelling and as battalion H.Q. would have crumpled up at once if hit, it was unpleasant even from the personal point of view. The Germans worked round both flanks and then delivered a frontal attack. However the line held and he was eventually driven back with very heavy loss. In fact I do not think that a great number got back, and his losses in killed from rifle and machine gun fire were very heavy. The situation was obscure for the greater part of the day, but by evening it was clear that the day might be reckoned as a success for us. The men fought very well indeed. That night we were relieved by the 154th Bde and the relief was carried out in absolute quiet.

Casualties for the day – killed 13 – wounded 67 – missing 32. Officers – killed 2, wounded 8. Map and full account of operations attached.

Willie's report on the operations of 15 and 16 May follow in his diary, given in detail company by company.

[undated: probably 16 May 1917]

Dear Father,

Many thanks for your letter. We are in the war pretty well now and it's not all joy. However, 4 out of the last 5 Boche shells were duds and didn't burst. Also they wouldn't have done us any damage anyway. It's nice sunny weather and at present I am sitting in a trench, not too uncomfortable. But it's a beastly noisy performance, guns going off everywhere and shells bursting in dirty black clouds. It's much noisier than it used to be and we make more of the noise. The bit of line I've taken over isn't altogether a 'peace line', just awkward you know, but not too bad on the whole. The flies aren't bad yet either which means one isn't so uncomfortable as one will be later on in the summer. Of course we go on pushing small shows, and it's not all our own way as the papers make out. The Boche has still got guns and knows how to use them and he has still got soldiers who know the game very well indeed. No, the war isn't a picnic even yet.

I'm very glad that Master is at Crefeld and happy; I suppose his longing to see a trench is natural enough, but you know a trench is a thing one soon has enough of. I daresay your picture is finished by now and if it is I daresay you won't be sorry – it's hard work sitting.

I'm sure George had a good time when he was home – dry land and a good time are the same thing for a sailor.

The dirty dog of a Boche has just put one rather closer than usual!

How is Mother? I'm very glad the Humberette sold at once. She must have fetched practically what we gave for her.

Goodbye and love to Mother.

Your affectionate son
WILLIE

[DIARY] 17TH MAY 1917 At about 3 a.m. the relief was complete, and Scott (comdg. 5th S.H.) and I were able to leave. Intermittent shelling had again begun, but we were lucky enough. We called at Bde. H.Q. and reported all well. Further along the railway embankment we found Campbell (2nd in C 5th S.H.). He had commandeered a dugout and prepared breakfast – bacon and eggs and tea, and I thoroughly enjoyed them.

After which I walked back to our bivouac at Blangy. There had been a good deal of rain and it was still falling – and the going was bad. Found most of the bn. already in – except the one company which was relieved last. Fixed up one or two things such as getting the 'cookers' for the men's breakfast, and then turned in. I slept wrapped in a tent, until my valise arrived, when I got between the blankets. But was too tired to sleep very well. About 12.30 I woke properly to find Gen. Congreve in the camp. He had ridden over to see me, which was awfully good of him. We had a bit of a crack and then he had to go off. In the evening we went into Arras, where we billetted in the same place as before. By the time I got to bed I was able to sleep like a log.

18TH MAY 1917 In billets in Arras. Was very worried because the general (Pelham) began to write nasty remarks about the time the bn. took to move off on the night of the 15th. I do not think he realises the difficulty of the circumstances, but I do know that I had not realised quite what a one man show this must be, and there is no doubt we should have moved off sooner. Though as events turned out it was fortunate we did not – we should have been too weak to hold so long a line against a heavy attack. But I feel I am to blame – through inexperience. One *must* see to *all* details oneself.

However it is all well in the end. Spent the day writing the report of the action and working off the paper which had accumulated. In the evening Pelham and I both went to dine with the XIII Corps. He was dining with Stewart (B.G.G.S.) and I with Gen. Congreve. We had a long talk about Billy's picture – there is something wrong with it. I stopped the night, and slept the sleep of exhaustion. That wee battle tired me a lot.

May 19th 1917

Dear Mother,

We are now back again. We had a bit of a battle, you probably saw in the paper that we regained all lost ground, which is true, not that much was really lost. But the main thing is that we killed an awful lot of Boche, the ground is thick with them and the authorities seem fairly happy. I lost a lot of officers though, I'm afraid. I have been awfully busy there is always a lot to do after a show, and reorganisation becomes more difficult each time. Last night I went and dined with Gen Congreve whose H.Q. are near here. We had some rain when we were up forward which made the ground deep in mud. I have never seen a more concentrated bombardment of heavy guns, than that with which the Germans preceded their attack, it really was tremendous and lasted a whole day without intermission. However the infantry attack was not up to their standard really, and rifles and machine guns did their work. At last we have got away from these damned bombs. We had no bombs in the last show at all. Forgive a very short letter, but I must be off. Love to father.

Your loving son
WILLIE

May 20th 1917

Dear Mother,

Thank you so much for taking all the trouble about my clothes and the bills. I think the best way will be to pay off Furley Lewis out of the proceeds from the sale of the car, and send the rest to Child's for me. Thank you very much. We have had rather a strenuous time lately – there is no doubt that this is a strenuous game. We undoubtedly killed an awful lot of Boche, but we lost some good officers and N.C.O.'s ourselves, and it's hard to fill their places. And more and more does one have to see to every detail oneself. If you say exactly what you want done and keep hammering at it – it gets done fairly well, but then one cannot expect more. They all try awfully hard, but it's rather a case of the blind leading the blind. They are good fighters though. If one could only get made up to strength and then go into what we call 'peace trenches' – ie a part of the line where no offensive is taking place – for a month and then get a month or 6 weeks right out for training purposes, then one could have a magnificent battalion indeed. But otherwise one must just rub along.

The men are splendid, but the subordinate commanders are not experienced or well-enough trained to be good leaders, except in the case of very exceptional fellows – so that one does not get full value out of the men's capacity.

It's been very warm but today we had some rain, which cooled the air a bit. I have been writing letters at odd times today and a lot last night. One gets very behind hand with one's correspondence when in the line, and it does make a difference out here – hearing how things are going at home.

Your loving son
WILLIE

[DIARY] 21ST MAY 1917 A fine morning – training. We have got all the companies together which helps a great deal in the matter of supervision. Afterwards went and inspected the N.C.O.'s class, but it came on to rain which was rather a bore. Managed to fall into a trench and gave myself rather a nasty bruise. In the afternoon inspected the transport; they are far better than they were, but can be better yet. After which we hunted the country for a place to have a bn. parade and found one, I think. Wrote letters, and in the evening went to dine with the Company officers. They are all living together, there are not many of them left I'm afraid. They gave me a very good dinner, which is a very good sign.

Wrote up my diary when I got home, had got rather behind hand with it, but at last I am up to date again. To bed about 10.30 p.m.

22ND MAY 1917 A wet day – continued training indoors.

During the morning got orders to send 400 men under Adams to bury cable. They are to live in huts near Blangy and work at nights. It taxed all the resources of the battalion to provide 360 without taking the 50 men in training as Lewis gunners and bombers. The remaining 40 we got from the T.M. batteries. The whole show is an awful nuisance – it disorganises training and makes the proper reorganisation of the bn. impossible for the moment. However there it is. Drove over to Duisans with H.P.B. to see Jim Burnett, but found the 1st bn had left and gone farther back. We saw Haldane on the way, who asked us both to dine tomorrow. In the evening I dined with the division. They had the massed drums and pipes of the division playing, 103 pipers, which is a lot. I thought they were very good considering they have had only one rehearsal. Got back about 11.15. They put one or two shells into Arras, but no so many as usual.

May 22 – 1917

Dear Father,

Apparently the authorities are all very bucked with the little show the Brigade put up the other day. I have just had the Corps Commander in to see me, smiling all over his face, so I took the opportunity to tell him a few home truths. It's just as well to let 'em have it when you get the chance. They aren't usually so amiable. Sir Charles Fergusson* it was – he asked to be remembered to you. And telegrams from every sort of commander have been falling over each other for the last few days.

I told all the men about it after church on Sunday, and they

*General Sir Charles Fergusson of Kilkerran, formerly Grenadier Guards.

laughed till they cried nearly! Because we hadn't been thinking so awfully much about it.

But now I've no battalion left, I've had to find a huge working party to bury cable and all the poor devils are out digging. It's bad luck on them – I told the Corps Commander that too. When there are these thousands of fellows loafing behind the lines! Labour bns. composed of crocks are apparently more valuable than good fighting men and can't be allowed to dig in the shell area.

I am hoping we shall get out for a proper rest soon – the battalion needs it badly – a chance to really train the men. The Corps Commander said we should. This division had never had it yet in two years. All the same they captured a Boche document the other day giving the British divisions in this army in the order of their fighting value from the Boche's point of view and this division headed the list.

It's most awfully good of you to have taken all that trouble about the whisky, but if there's a lot of trouble in managing it, please don't worry. It's been a real wet day today and the country is a sea of mud as a result. The lightest shower turns this chalk soil into greasy slime. I hear from Mother you are going to take a house in the country. Perhaps you have it by now.

Goodbye and love to Mother.

Your loving son,
WILLIE

[DIARY] 23RD MAY 1917 Weather fine. Spent the morning inspecting the specialist classes and the class under the R.S.M. These latter are getting on well, but require a bit more gingering up especially as regards 'turn-out'. Must also ginger up the bombing and Lewis gun instructors as regards drill and personal appearance.

In the afternoon the adjutant and I went for a walk to Blangy, where we had a good look at the old German line. It showed proof of an extraordinary capacity for work, and jolly good work too. The whole trench was lined with brick and cement, the fire-step of brick – all the shelters for snipers etc. were of brick and cement, and the dugouts (the place lies low and you cannot dig deep) had all two to three metres of concrete on them. There was one fortified house with a machine gun in it which would have kept out a 9.2. shell I believe.

Further up the line had been very heavily shelled, but even then most of the dugouts were intact. I wish one could have a camera – what a diary one could make. These villages are an awful sight – nothing left. Mangled remains of iron, chimneys and girders and masses of broken brick and barbed wire, mine craters and shell holes and sandbags – the whole in a state of chaos. This is war nowadays, though war comprises many worse things too.

24TH MAY 1917 In the morning the general and I went to see the NCOs' class. They are getting on fairly well. Then we went and saw the Lewis gun and bombing classes doing musketry. It is certainly very hot – the weather I mean, not the musketry.

In the afternoon the adjutant and I went for a walk and sat about in the country. It was very pleasant and I went to sleep and dreamed of days when there was no war. What a day for lying in a punt on the Thames, looking up at a gorgeous blue sky through the leaves of a shady tree, doing absolutely nothing!

In the evening McDonald (6th Seaforths) and Johnstone (his 2/in/C) came to dine and we had a very pleasant dinner and sat talking until midnight. How war changes things. There is McDonald, before the war a radical lawyer in Fraserburgh – now commanding a battalion of Seaforth Highlanders and doing it damned well. And he is a jolly good fellow too – but I fancy he has changed his views on many things, he has got the broader vision now. And of course there are thousands like that – so there is hope for our country yet, when these fellows come home again.

Don't think there were any shells in the night.

24th May 1917

Dear Father,

Many thanks for your letter of the 19th. We are now in divisional reserve and are fairly quiet in the day, but a few shells at night. My men are out digging – which I hate, because its very tiring and means they must sleep in the day – so it knocks all training and reorganising on the head. I daresay you guess fairly accurately where we are. The Vimy Ridge is a most extraordinary sight now, one can walk over it, a mass of mine craters and shell holes. Some of the German lines near the Scarpe are extraordinary – parts are not too much damaged – they were lined entirely with brick and concrete and dugouts with 2 or 3 metres of concrete on them. It's a place where you cannot dig very deep. But nothing one can make without going 30 or 40 feet underground will stand against a heavy shell with delay action fuse. It's true enough that the engineers strike is a most disgraceful show, and it has undoubtedly had a very great effect on the shell output, and I should not be surprised if it had not already been felt out here.

You know one often feels that the country is so rotten that it's hardly worth fighting for. Why should all these fine fellows risk their lives on behalf of creatures who go out on strike about three times a month? The serious thing is that all the best get killed – it's the degenerates and wasters that we preserve like so much gold – when it would really be sound to get as many of them killed as possible. I think myself that a very great number of the men fighting out here now will emigrate after the war.

I think really it's very doubtful if we can beat the Boche on the field of battle – but our stupid papers aren't allowed to tell the truth, they simply fill up with trash – which if it were true, would mean the German was beaten long ago. And the people at home believe it. Love to Mother.

Your affectionate son
WILLIE

[DIARY] 26TH MAY 1917 Very hot. Went round the various specialist classes in the morning, also selected some ground where we can dig trenches.

The detachment who have been digging came in this afternoon – very tired. Because this morning they were twice shelled in their bivouacs, which made rest difficult, even after digging all night. Went for a walk in the evening in the other part of the town, where there are nice gardens and shady trees. We sat and watched men bathing in the moat for an hour or more.

Played a game of bridge after dinner.

They started lobbing these big armour piercing shells into Arras about 11.30 p.m. and kept it up all night.

28th May 1917

Dear Mother,

Many thanks for your letter and for all the trouble you have taken about my bills. I'm not worried by the noise or the work so far – though no one can pretend to like being shelled. If things remain normal we shall be back in the rest area by the time you get this, and out of reach of shelling.

I'm sorry you have not heard from Master, I expect the letters are being hung up.

We got two escaped prisoners back the other day, further south – and from their accounts the prisoners (the men that is) are being treated very badly. The French prisoners and the Russians are being used to carry rations up to the front line and to work in the front line – and the food consists mainly of stewed turnips. I hope we shall do the same for the Boche prisoners – they are swine. I fear it's going to be a long while yet before we are able to make them pay for it, – Russia has let us down properly. But I think it would be a very good thing if the treatment our men got at the hands of the German was more widely realised at home. It makes one more furious than ever with these strikers. I shall be glad to hear you have got a house in the country. I'm sure it's awfully hot in London now. Love to Father. Goodbye.

Your loving son
WILLIE

May 29th 1917

Dear Mother,

I think we probably go back to rest tomorrow. I wonder if you would mind sending me out my small whole cane fishing rod and a reel and line? The rod is in the cloak room and the reel and line in the wooden box in my room. There ought to be some fine casts and a few flies there too, but if not would it be an awful lot of trouble one afternoon to get me a few casts, fine ones, and a few small flies? I should think a few dry May flies among them. I hope to get some fishing in the evenings where we are going. Of course I don't know for certain, but one may as well have a rod in case. The time slips away, doesn't it – almost in June now and very soon the summer will be over. It's odd how short the summer seems out here – though we shall see some good old scraps before it is over I think.

The Boche has got an awful lot of guns on this front just now, and an awful lot of men. I think he must have left the other front almost entirely to Turks and Austrians. The Italians seem to be doing fairly well – if he keeps on succeeding he may get his tail up and do a bit of fighting yet. But it's here we've got to fight the war out, and we shall need all the Americans before we win it, I'm afraid.

Love to Father.

Your loving son

WILLIE

PS: Could you send me some more writing paper. It's hard to get here.

[DIARY] 29TH MAY 1917 Continued digging. It was much cooler today. Uncle Harper came round and criticised.

This is our last day in Arras with any luck, and then back for a rest which the whole division needs.

30TH MAY 1917 The transport moved off very early and the men followed in buses about 1.30 p.m. and arrived at our first rest-area near St. Pol. at about 4 p.m.

I rode on in the morning to Ecoivres where I found Gen. Congreve. We went for a walk in the morning and among other people we saw Freddy Dhulip Singh, whom I met at Woodbastwick* long ago.

The general has got a large camp for worn out horses – very well run indeed and I'm sure it saves many lives. Poor old beggars, they looked very happy – though a bit thin and worn in places.

I also heard about the French fighting in Champagne and the Boche tunnels. These tunnels ran back as much as 300 yards from the 2nd line and had one or two M.G. emplacements at the end, and a garrison of perhaps 20 machine guns in the tunnel to replace casualties. They did not show on air-photos and had not been bombarded and they held up the whole French advance.

*Home of the Cator family in Norfolk; old friends.

The general ran me over to the bn in his car in the evening and I found them settled down in a topping wee village. Lilac and thorn trees red and white, rhododendrons all doing their share. A real resting place.

6th Gordons had at last moved to a place where they could rest and train and absorb reinforcements clear from the perpetual shellfire and interruptions which had made even periods in reserve restless and disjointed in the recent past. The battalion was in billets about five miles south-east of St Pol.

May 31 1917

Dear Father,

Here we are in a most delightful wee village – full of flowers and trees and hedges, and the war is miles away, so we have temporarily forgotten what sort of noise a shell makes. We got in here yesterday evening and shall remain for a few days, after which we move on again by route march. But I think we shall be out of the line for quite an appreciable time with any luck. It's extraordinarily quiet and peaceful and one can lie under a tree in a shady garden in one's spare time. And of course the men do the same and it does them all the good in the world. There are any number of thorn trees covered with masses of red-blossom. Coming from a country which is trampled brown and every-where cut up by shells one appreciates this sort of place. I'll tell what strikes one most in France at the present time – the fact that every square yard is under cultivation. All the men are away, but the old ones and the women and the children are all working. And there's no question of an eight hour day – they start with the dawn and they finish with the dark. If you talk to any of them about it, they say 'pour la patrie'. It's a somewhat different spirit to the one which prevails in the agricultural districts of parts of our country! But all the same France is having a pretty critical time just now. Strikes in Paris on account of meatless days and high prices – and one way and another things are a bit rocky.

I can't help thinking this may be the deciding year – though it certainly won't bring about a military defeat of Germany – with Russia in the state she is in. Love to Mother.

Your affectionate son
WILLIE

Congratulations on being made a general.

[DIARY] 31 MAY 1917 So we're finally out of the line again – good! I slept with a huge window open by my bed and the moonbeams and the smells of the may and lilac and the trees sent me pleasant dreams. It was a cool morning and the companies went route-marching. In the afternoon we got a draft of 8 officers plus 45 O.R. None of the officers have served out here as officers before. All have been promoted from the ranks and none of them were N.C.O.'s when sent for Commissions, so they sound not too good, but we hope for the best.

I walked over to Maisnit-St-Pol where the 6th S.H. are and had tea with McDonald and we had a talk about odd things. He has got a good H.Q. and a charming garden by it.

Walking back it struck one what a beautiful country this is. Rolling downs – all cultivated – unbroken by hedges, the reds and browns and greens all merging into one another – the farms are all grouped into small villages, each situated in its grove of bushy trees, elms, limes, poplars, chestnuts, all mixing their various shades of green, and above them the spire of the tiny church, pointing the straight path to the skies, – so easy to see, so hard to follow – and over all the soft evening light, and a gentle breeze whispering tales of happiness.

1ST JUNE 1917 These are lazy days. I don't mean that there isn't much to do, but that there is a temptation not to do it. The sun is so warm and the breeze so gentle. But we do it all the same, and one must not let go for a moment. There is a very great deal of ginger required here. I saw many things on parade today that make one's job seem very difficult. But then what a splendid thing to succeed, to succeed so well that one was satisfied oneself that one had succeeded.

I had a very straight talk to the N.C.O.'s this afternoon and I told them what I thought without mincing words. I hope it will do good. I think so, because they are mostly triers, I think.

3 JUNE 1917 Uneventful day. A draft of 25 (mostly conscripts) arrived in the middle of the night (Saturday night). Church parade in an orchard – then reorganisation of companies into 3 platoons. I know it is a bad system, but one is ordered to carry it out. I have elicited that it has been evolved without any regard to tactical requirements and it will break down on that issue alone.

A new draft of 72 arrived this evening, having marched from Tincques. Mostly conscripts and one can easily foretell the number that will fall out tomorrow.

4TH JUNE 1917 Commenced our march for the north. Left Foufflin-Ricametz at 6.30 and personally I was quite sorry. It's a very pretty wee place and it has been a very pleasant 4 days. Judged the time to Bde starting point just right, but of course we started far too late. I had urged the necessity of starting early – but in vain. I saw R. Campbell on the way through St. Pol.

It was a very hot and dusty march – we did not reach our destination until 12.30, and 30 men, nearly all the last two drafts, had fallen out. However they did not have a happy time, as they all were forced to finish on foot and then be medically inspected before dismissing. It's a good thing we march independently tomorrow and can start early.

With the adjutant I reconnoitred the first half of our march for tomorrow, in the evening and found we could make a very valuable short cut.

Had all feet inspected and washed and all socks washed. There was an excellent stream for the purpose running past our billets.

It's a wonderful country, up on the plateaus between the valleys, one can see for miles. This system of collective village farming certainly works '*a merveille*' in this country.

5TH JUNE 1917 Passed the starting point at 4 a.m. having given the men a cup of tea before starting. Marched for one hour, after which we halted one hour and ten minutes for breakfasts.

Continued the march and reached our destination DELETTE, at 9.20, i.e. between 13 and 14 miles in 4 hours and a quarter. Two more fell out, both last draft men. Which proves I think, the value of marching early with good arrangements. The billets in our new village are excellent and the Lys runs through the village. Remainder of the day spent in washing feet etc.

I went and tried to catch a trout with a live may-fly in the evening – with no success.

8TH JUNE 1917 Marched off at 5 a.m. in Brigade Column. Broke off from column after 2 miles and shortly after halted for breakfast. Finished the march into Arques* shortly after 9 a.m. Good billets, but more in a town and not so pleasant as the country villages of the last few days. Was billetted myself in a chateau with a delightful garden.

Nearly saw Ally Boyd, but just missed him. The Guards Division are all round here.

It rained a little in the afternoon.

We hear good news of the attack. Apparently they have got Wytschacte and Messines and about 6000 prisoners, and have killed a lot of Huns.

On 7 June General Plumer's Second Army had attacked at Messines in the Ypres sector. Supported by the detonation of a number of enormous mines under the enemy positions the attack was a huge and comparatively inexpensive success. The battle was conceived as a preliminary to a major offensive east of Ypres – intended to attract German resources and deny to them the possession of the commanding Messines ridge.

[DIARY] 9 JUNE 1917 Marched off as a battalion. Starting point at 4 a.m. Breakfast on route at 5 a.m. and got into billets at Maison Bleu Ganspette at 9 a.m. Good billets but very scattered, and not much training ground I fear. Rode round and found two quarries which will make good ranges, and managed to get one or

*Just east of St Omar.

two fields for parades. We shan't do so badly – but we get a lot of muck from the Division about training and organisation which is quite impracticable and rather worrying. However, no matter.

H.Q. are billetted in a delightful chateau belonging to the Comte d'Hespel, who lives here with his wife and some daughters. They are nice cheery girls and Madame la Comtesse is very kind. We played tennis this evening. I have never been billetted so well in France. Madame was showing me her photograph book this morning, and there I find Crawfurd and Billy. Billy was here just a year ago, shorly before he was killed. And they all loved him of course, and were awfully interested to hear I was a friend of his.

June 10th 1917

Dear Father,

In answer to your question 'East or West' I reply 'North'. The place where the battle is now I have often told you about on the map, and the position captured was probably the strongest one on our front.

I think they have done good work. I didn't hear the mines go up, but I believe the noise could be heard in London. They were terrific. So you may be coming to do some work behind the lines. Well I think if you are strong enough later on you would be happier there than anywhere.

The sun has gone today and it's much colder. The news from the interior of Germany is encouraging – but there is no doubt the French are in a fairly dicky position. The question is – will they stick it out? And it isn't every French man who gives you an affirmative answer. Goodbye.

Your affectionate son
WILLIE

June 10th 1917

Dear Mother,

Thank you so much for sending the rod.

I hope by the time you get this you will be settled down in the country again. I'm sure London has been trying lately. We are out of the line for three weeks anyway, I hope – and I am billetted with a French Comte and his family in a chateau and when I have a moment off spend it playing tennis with the family.

The men are well and clean – clean kilts and polished belts and buttons go a long way towards winning a battle!

We were on the march from the commencement of the month until yesterday – and by the end the battalion were beginning to know how to march. It's a priceless job this. I've not been so happy since the beginning of the war. In my work that is.

Goodbye.

Your loving son
WILLIE

[DIARY] 19 JUNE 1917 Another morning on the range. In the evening went to the Divisional Horse Show. It would have been a very good show, but was spoilt by very heavy rain which came on about 5 o'clock and never stopped. Our limber and light draught pair got a first prize. Saw Long – he has come to command the 7th G.H.

In the evening we had a dinner party and most of the family came – Monsieur, Madame, Mlle Marguerite and M. and Madame de Colnet. It was quite a success and I think they all enjoyed it.

21ST JUNE 1917 A quiet day. Went round all the companies in the morning and had orderly room in the afternoon. In the evening wrote a lot of letters. And said goodbye to our hosts, for tomorrow we leave this most pleasant billet, where one has been made most welcome and I for one have been as happy as anywhere in the last 11 months. It's quiet and peaceful and in the evening one has people who are not soldiers and who are of the same world – as we say – to talk to, which is a great relaxation indeed.

And they were most kind all the time. And I shall miss the view from my window.

22ND JUNE 1917 Breakfasted at 6.30. The head of the battalion passed the starting point at 7.25 – in pouring rain, very heavy indeed. We had a march of something about 7 miles and got in about 9.30, to our new area at Booneghem. The billets are not very commodious – it is in a flat, marshy, country, intersected with canals, and reminds one of the Norfolk Broads, or parts of the Fen country. Some of the men have to go to their billets in boats. So there is plenty of water even without the rain we had today, which continued very heavy until about five o'clock. But there seems to be no training area of any kind whatsoever, no fields available at all.

I walked to Clairmarais Forest in the afternoon and found a place where we could make a range if they will let us cut a few trees. But it is a walk of an hour and a half. However we can probably arrange to billet companies doing musketry at Clairmarais. Rode over to the Bde H.Q. in the evening. Conference of O.C. Coys at 7 p.m. Dinner and an early bed, quite tired.

23RD JUNE 1917 The last day of another week. It was a glorious day, sunny but not too hot. Went round the companies in the morning – they have all got fields where they can carry on their training.

I hear Gen. Congreve has lost his hand, an awful thing. I'm afraid he will be just as careless of himself when he gets back though. The men are happy here, paddling about in punts and lying on the grass.

24TH JUNE 1917 Church parade in a green field on a glorious morning. It always strikes one that this is a priceless opportunity for padres of all denominations, to make religion real to men, the most wonderful thing in their lives. But few seize it as it might be seized. I don't think even yet that they aim high enough. There's no doubt that in war, in the constant presence of death, men's thoughts tend to become less material and more spiritual. Gillingham said that all religions had failed out here, but that I don't believe. Perhaps the majority of the parsons have failed.

Went over to Clairmarais and reconnotired ground for training, and after lunch rode over to the Bde to find out about various things. Wrote letters when I got back.

A new draft of 60 men (Argylls) arrived today. I believe they are a good lot, but it's a pity they have to send us Argylls. It does not make for *esprit de Corps*. However, must have a talk to them and see what can be done to make them Gordon Highlanders.

Went fishing after dinner with a bit of cheese as bait, but no success.

26TH JUNE 1917 Rode round the training area which we have been allotted after lunch. It is covered with beautiful standing crops, and they will be partially destroyed. Of course it's all paid for, but what use is money to pay for the destruction of a man's work? It all seems very sad and hard on the people, but I suppose it's war. Anyway the men have got to be trained, that's quite certain. But the authorities should tell the people, and not leave it to us; I cannot compete with widow-women, who come and ask me what is to happen to their poor cows when their pasture is destroyed, and what themselves are to eat, when the crops they have worked hard at for months are trampled down. And they are all so good to one when one is billetted on them, they give up all they can, and they certainly realise the war as no one in England realises it.

29TH JUNE 1917 A hot damp day. Walked over to Clairmarais Wood in the morning with the Company Commanders to have a look at the course for wood-fighting tomorrow. In the afternoon went to a Conference at the Brigade about forthcoming operations. A difficult job we have to do.

Went on to a lecture by Gen. Bols on the Messines Show. Not very instructive as his division had a walk over, and his arrangements were never put to the test by the Boche.

The wood-fighting for tomorrow is counter-ordered.

A draft of 23, mostly old N.C.O.'s arrived today, which is a great help.

30TH JUNE 1917 Heavy rain from 10.30 a.m. till 3 p.m. Rode out to the training area (6 miles) to see a demonstration of drums of boiling oil to hurl at the Boche. All the Knuts were there, the only thing that was absent was the demonstration. So we waited an hour and a half in the rain and then came home.

The General was talking about Adams – I'm afraid the dirty work comes to me. He is too old to be 2nd in command to me and the general won't recommend him for command of a fighting bn., so he will have to go. But I hate telling him, more especially as he is a jolly good fellow and does his work with all his might.

But he is filling a place for which a younger man who can be trained to command a battalion would be better suited.

Rode into St. Omer and had a tooth stopped and had tea at the Bde on the way back.

1ST JULY 1917 Church Parade at 9.45 followed by Communion Service to which I went. Had never been to a Presbyterian one before.

Afterwards broke the news to Adams. He was very good about it, but very cut up I'm afraid.

Walked over the taped course of the trenches we are to capture in the afternoon, and later rode over to the Chateau d'Eperlecques to tea. Found the d'Hespel family in good form, and on excellent terms with their present guests, a Brigadier this time – Gen. Daly and his staff. He seemed a very good fellow.

Rode back by 7.30. Fleming and Fortune came to dinner. About 10.30 got a message that the G.O.C. was expecting to see some wood-fighting tomorrow – rather a shock in view of the fact that all the transport moves tomorrow. However managed to fix it up. It's a good exercise for the men and officers.

Bed about 11.30, rather late for me.

2ND JULY 1917 Fine day. We had the wood-fighting stunt.

As I was walking down to Clairmairais I saw a fellow with a long pole with a square-shaped scoop on the end, scooping great square blocks of peaty looking mud out of the bottom of one of the canals. It appears they take this and dry it and burn it like we do peat.

The stunt went off all right. Uncle was there and H.P.B. and they walked about and the former talked a lot. And the men got mixed up in the wood and I think the officers learnt something.

Had a lecture to all officers in the evening – I think they took it in.

The transport moved off at 2.30 – we shan't see them again till tomorrow night.

V
Third Ypres
1917

July 2nd 1917

Dear Father,

Many thanks for your letter. I wonder why they have broken up the camp at Crefeld so suddenly, and where they have sent Master? I hope he strikes a good place again. So you are going to leave London. I am very glad I must say and I'm sure you will like it better. Where is Rickmansworth?

Meanwhile our rest is over for the moment and we get on the move tomorrow and return to the war. I have been here now more than two months – it's gone very quick, but it seems a long time. One begins to date the time from one's last battle. The days of what we call peace trenches are over, and the semi-open warfare is the order of the day now, until we get to real open warfare.

I don't think the Boche like being in front of us any more – he didn't enjoy either of the last two shows and probably is not looking forward to the possibility of their repetition. We have had some very heavy rain the last few days, but today is sunny and cheerful once more. This is a country intersected by canals and if you want to go for a walk across country you have to go in a boat, because there are very few bridges. It's a very busy life, we have to make the most of any opportunity to train.

I still have my old grouse against the training at home. It's absolutely rotten. We have to train our men as we get them. I sent in a report the other day which may possibly get somebody the sack. If so he will deserve it. Of course they have got the wrong fellows looking after the training. Goodbye, and love to Mother. I suppose the photo of George's picture is not ready yet?

Your affectionate son

WILLIE

[DIARY] 3RD JULY 1917 Had a small outpost scheme with the officers in the morning. We moved off through the marshes after lunch, having said goodbye to our host, who was a good fellow. He had formed a great opinion of the men.

Got to St. Omer Station, where we were to entrain, at 3.30 – to find our train was not expected for an hour at least.

It turned up about 4.50 and the troops in it were clear by 5.15. We entrained by 5.30, and the train moved off about 6 p.m.

We got to Poperinghe at 8.30 to find our guides waiting for us and a three mile walk brought us into camp. Huts in the back area, shelled at intervals.

Back in Belgium again – well I don't like the country – but I always thought somehow that I should be here to put up a cross on old Simon's grave, and it looks as if it was to come true. After that I daresay my connection with Belgium will be severed.[*]

This bn. has never been in Belgium before, and signalised the fact by burning one of its huts down before turning in for the night. It made a beautiful bonfire.

4TH JULY 1917 First day in huts. The Boche is shelling the back areas to an extraordinary extent – so far we have been lucky.

Went down to see the transport in the afternoon and then on to see Brand, who is in a farm not far from here. Found him very cheery and longing for the end of the war.

A lot of shelling not too far from us after dinner.

5TH JULY 1917 Long came to breakfast and told me something about the line. A little training in the morning. In the afternoon Uncle appeared and we went to see the model of the Boche trenches. It's extraordinarily well made. While we were looking at it a Boche aeroplane appeared and attacked some of our sausage balloons and babel broke out. All the Archie's[†] and machine guns in the neighbourhood started on him. The observers in one balloon came down in their parachutes, just in time as he got the balloon immediately afterwards, which burst into

[*] In fact Willie served there as Military Attaché and lived in Brussels from 1931 until 1935.
[†] Anti-aircraft guns.

flames and completely burnt up before it came to earth. The Boche then retired behind a cloud and bided his time and we went on discussing the attack. And then suddenly he appeared again and the observers in another balloon took refuge in their parachutes. But he missed that balloon and the Archie's missed him and he got away. He was a stout fellow, although a Boche.

In the evening the officers played the sergeants at football – it was a good game and ended three all. Nearly all the battalion was looking on, but fortunately no shells were about.

(My birthday – 27)
July 5th 1917

Dear Mother,

The Russian show is good news isn't it – I certainly never thought they would come again at all. But I don't think they can make it a real big success, I doubt whether their organisation will stand much strain. But if they kill a few Boche that's something. How they managed at all, when the plan of attack has to be vetted by every private soldier before they start, I don't know!

Any news of Master yet? I suppose not, it's a bit early to have heard.

I heard from George the other day, but nothing about himself, all about the Russians. And Mr Wallop writes and tells me all the chatter of London Town. Our latest rumour here is that King Albert and his Queen have been arrested as spies.

Love to Father. I hope you are both happy in your new house. We are all full of cheer out here. Goodbye.

Your loving son
WILLIE

The first Russian Revolution had broken out in March. The Tsar had abdicated and a Provisional Government had been formed – ineffective, and succeeded by another in May. The latter Government, led by Alexander Kerensky, was superficially committed to the continuance of the war. Discipline and order, however, were progressively eroded throughout the Army and a system of Soldiers' Soviets established.

A few days before Willie's letter the Russians had, despite their disorder and loss of will for war, carried out an attack against the Austrians with a certain measure of success, and it is to this that Willie referred. The offensive was quickly checked and effectively counter-attacked by German forces – a counter-attack which drove the Russians back to the frontiers of Russia and out of Latvia and Lithuania.

[DIARY] 6TH JULY 1917 Very hot day. Went up to the line in the morning to look at the country from an OP. A long hot walk, but I think one got an idea of what it looks like.

Got back about one o'clock to find that we relieve tomorrow night and that I had to go back and reconnoitre the line. Snatched a somewhat hurried lunch and then to saddle once more. Found Campbell walking on the way up, so walked with him. Went all round the line – it was very quiet fortunately and one got a good look at things.

Got back about 7.30, quite tired. Had a bath and dinner and did some office work. And then inferno opened in the front line, and still continues. It sounds from here to be a bit south of our line – but it sounds like business on the part of the Boche. I only hope we get our night in bed and are not hoicked out in the middle to go and counter-attack or something, because I'm tired.

7TH JULY 1917 Usual sort of day one spends before going into the line. Wandering round to see all is in order, arranging for the men who will be left behind etc. etc. The battalion marched off by platoons at 8 p.m. and met our guides near the Canal.

The night was quiet fortunately and we had a good relief, but rather slow. This was owing to some of the guides getting mixed and to the great crush of men going up. Finished at 2 a.m. and McDonald comdg 6th S.H. went off and we turned in.

Willie was now back in the Ypres sector. It was new to 6th Gordons.

[DIARY] 8TH JULY 1917 Turned out at 5 a.m. and went round the line, also explored the sector on our right from which we have to attack. The trenches on that flank are very wet and some of the C.T.'s* blown to bits. It will be a hard job forming up. Got back about 8 a.m. and had breakfast and lay down for a bit. But I don't sleep much up here – the Boche is putting over a lot of shell (especially round my H.Q.) and there is the responsibility which does weigh on one a bit. So I read – Emerson is as good for freeing the mind as anyone.

Went round the line again later on, and found fault with one or two things. I always seem to be finding fault with something. I suppose that is my job, or part of it. However they all take it in good part.

9TH JULY 1917 Usual shelling through the day, but the morning from 5 o'clock till 8 is quiet as a rule. My H.Q. is usually shelled heavily at 3.30 a.m. Went round the line early and did some more reconnaisance in the right sector. Saw about boards being put in to mark gaps in the wire. There was a bit of a mix up about that. Went round again in the afternoon. After dinner thought I would go and see all the men were happy in the front line. Got back about 11.20, and at that moment the Boche started a most intense barrage along the line of my H.Q.

It lasted an hour during which time it was an unpleasant job even getting to the signal office to talk to the Bde. who were a bit excited. I thought my line was all right and that the Boche was raiding on my left. This proved later to be correct, but he failed to get in. However his fire knocked in some of my trenches and I had some casualties. He has been shelling the canal bank with 8″ and 11″ shells and a few casualties have been caused to reserve companies. An unpleasant 24 hours. By good luck he missed our H.Q. It's awful losing good men though.

10TH JULY 1917 The weather has cleared after two wet days and the sun is out again. We have got on to repairing the battered trenches, urgent because of the relief tonight. Went and saw the gaps in the wire cut by my lads last night. They seem all right. But it's a bad place to jump off from.

*Communication trenches.

[131]

Was round the line very early, and got back to breakfast after which I waited in, expecting the C.O. of the battalion which relieves us tonight to come up. However he didn't. Sent him down full instructions and made most careful arrangements for guides. Went out in the afternoon with O.C. tunnellers to show him where to make H.Q. for Scott and self for forthcoming operations. Found the trenches cleared for a 6″ shoot by us. However risked it and did the job in peace.

We were relieved in the evening, the relief being complete by 1 a.m. which was not bad under the circumstances. Luckily it was a very quiet night. Had one casualty going out.

But for three days in the line have had 10 killed and over 20 wounded, which is very heavy. It has been a sleepless time rather.

11TH JULY 1917 Got back to camp at 3.30 a.m. The men had tea and cocoa and turned in. Breakfasted myself about 9 a.m. and we marched off to Poperinghe to entrain at 9.30.

We were supposed to entrain at 11.15 but the train was not ready until 12.45. We got to St. Omer about 4.45, 4 hours for 20 miles. No wonder, as the engine has to be stopped every mile or so to have water poured on the brakes or something of the sort.

We had a long march after detraining and got to billets about 8 p.m. There was a mix up there owing to bad staff work. All this time the men had had no solid meal as the cookers had to go by road the day before. It's absolutely criminal to treat men so, after they come out of trenches and I shall write and say so.

July 12th 1917

Dear Mother,

I was very pleased to get your letter dated the 8th. I wrote on the 5th or 6th, so you will have got that by now. I am awfully glad you have at last moved out of London and have got a nice place. One is apt to be just a bit worried when you are in London and these raids are going on. I'm afraid they are rather serious.

We have been having a tour in the line but are back again for a few days. It was an unhealthy spot and one did not get much sleep, so am a bit tired, but another night's rest will put me right. The men want a sleep too. Here we are out of the range of shells, and have no worries in that way. And the sun is shining again which makes us happy. We aren't too hard to please. It's when its real wet in the trenches that circumstances are unpleasant. But after all it doesn't matter much. It's good news that Father is fitter and likes his small car. I expect when you get into the way of it she will be very easy to crank. I think you have to twiddle those small cars round once or twice.

I heard Master had been moved but did not know you had heard from him. I'm glad of that. I have been out nearly three months now and if I was in the Guards Division you might expect me home in a few days; they do more play and less work than the rest of us. As it is I think in about two or three months I might get a few days.

But I like my job, and the unpleasant times aren't always the unhappiest, though its awful sad when the men are killed. They are such children and I don't suppose they realise much. One feels a sort of personal responsibility for every one of them.

Goodbye and love to Father.

Your loving son
WILLIE

[DIARY] 13TH JULY 1917 Glorious day. Company inspections and baths for some of the men in the afternoon. Also a staff ride for officers and N.C.O.'s over the trainng area. It is all right as far as the black line, but after that the ground becomes quite unsuitable, and I have had to find some fresh.

They are now busy trying to take away my whole bn. in two and threes to do odd jobs; they seem to think it is inexhaustable. Have protested that if this goes on I shall have no men to fight a battle. On the whole a busy day, paper about these operations comes pouring in – every time I go to the Orderly Room I find fresh piles. However all's well if it ends well. I hope the Boche morale is low.

The operations for which Willie's battalion was practising were those known, officially and later, as 'Third Ypres'; or, inaccur-

ately and tragically, as 'Passchendaele'. The main battle was to start at the end of July.

Haig's determination to carry out a 1917 offensive in Flanders has been much criticised. It has been said that one of the motives given – to clear the Germans from the Belgian coast in order to help the Navy – was ill founded since the principal German submarine bases were not in Belgium but Germany. It has been said that, had Haig only waited, the French Army was on the road to recovery from earlier disasters (and mutinies) and could have undertaken effective and simultaneous operations. It has been said that delay would, additionally, have enabled American weight to be felt by Germany (the United States had declared war in April); and, of course, the actual outcome of the battle, its awful cost and pitiful achievements have made of it perhaps the most potent occasion of condemnation of the High Command in the whole war.

As against all this it has been argued that there was good reason to suppose Germany near the end of her resources provided pressure was not relaxed; that French morale was in dire need of an Allied offensive success – somewhere; and that while the situation on the Russian front would probably permit Germany to transfer major forces from east to west sooner or later, she had not yet done so. Fundamentally, Haig was optimistic and so were his senior commanders. The outstanding success of the preliminary operation at Messines seemed a good augury; and the date fixed for the offensive – 31 July – appeared to allow some summer months of battle before the weather started to break. Weather, in the Ypres Salient, mattered more than in most places, so lowlying was the country and so vulnerable conditions to rain.

[DIARY) 20TH JULY 1917 Early start. Breakfast at 7 a.m.
Had a divisional show on the training area. It went very well, though there are some things which will have to be changed. Uncle Harper was there, had quite a long buck with him. He knows a lot of things. Saw Tom Holland too. Lots of redhats and things about – however they did not worry me.

*A village on the eastern rim of the Ypres Salient.

21ST JULY 1917 Parades and inspections. Went very carefully into the question of equipment and I think we cannot improve it any more. But one feels that the man has too much weight to carry all the same. A new type of carrier for L.G. ammunition is a great improvement.

Inspected B & C Coys, they are looking very fit. Then had a look at the transport.

Conference at Bde H.Q. at 12 noon.

22ND JULY 1917 Church parade in the morning and after that a day of rest, to a certain extent, though one is thinking all the time of the forthcoming operations. The men are very confident, and I think we ought to have a good show. The preparations seem complete, and our training has been satisfactory I think.

23RD JULY 1917 The battalion was photographed this morning by a fellow from St. Omer. I hope they will be good.

The trial of Methuen and Richmond for desertion also took place. The former was sentenced to death, but I do not think it will be carried out. The latter was acquitted but convicted of absence without leave.

In the afternoon we moved to the forward area. The bn. was drawn up ready to embus at 3.30 p.m. but the buses did not arrive until 5 p.m. Cannot understand why these d-ed fellows can never be in time. We left at 5.20 and got to our midway halt at 7.10. Here the men had teas. Were not allowed to leave until 9.30 on account of the light. Got to our de-bussing point at 12-midnight. There was a lot of confusion as they hurried the buses off. Result, we lost a rifle and one or two other things.

Got into our camp near St. Jan de Biezen at 1.30 a.m.

Was wandering about before we moved from Lederzeele and found a most extraordinary case of natural grafting in a tree. A pollard willow – half willow and half elm, the trunk was perfect willow and the foliage was exactly divided. The farmer knew of no intentional graft. It was a very fine tree.

24TH JULY 1917 Quite a good camp we are in, though space about it is very limited. Spent the day in inspections and cleaning.

Finished off the orders for the attack which I had started yesterday and got them out. Which occupied most of the day.

25TH JULY 1917 Z Day approaches. Tomorrow we move forward to the camp from which we assemble. The assembly is the part of this show which worries me. And it *must* go well. Today was wet. very wet which does not help our gunners at all.

Had a morning doing odd jobs such as gas helmet drill in the huts but the rain prevents much being done. It cleared about 3 p.m. and became very hot and steamy. Spoke to the battalion for a few minutes in the afternoon, and gave them a few points to remember and wished them *bon succès*. How I do wish them that, each one of them. But some must be killed, that is the sad part of it all. One cannot make omelettes without breaking eggs, and they are fine fellows.

Fleming came in after dinner and we played a game of bridge, the first for a very long time.

In the evening heard that Z day is put off as the gunners are not ready. The weather has been against them. So we do not move tomorrow.

26TH JULY 1917 Today is fine again, but stuffy. The ground is drying up. Had a route march by companies in the morning to give the men exercise.

Both H.P.B. and Uncle came over this afternoon and we heard the news.

1. The Boche is gassing the canal badly every night, which increases the difficulty of assembly enormously. Have gone into the question with great care, of how to get these masks on quickly when a man is in full equipment, and I don't think we can do any more.

2. The trench bombardments and more especially the counter-battery work has been made very hard by the weather, so Z day is put off for a bit.

3. Our assembly trenches have been greatly improved which is the best news I have heard yet.

I believe the Boche will relieve the division on our front before we go over, which means harder fighting for us probably, but should be an advantage in the end.

Walked down to see the C.O. of the battalion attacking on my right, in the evening, but found he wasn't at the place I thought.

Hutcheson and Patterson came to dinner, and we had quite an amusing evening and bucked them up I think. Not that old Hutch needs much bucking up.

27TH JULY 1917 Fine day. In the early morning a British aeroplane came down here, just missing our tents and by the most extraordinary piece of luck landed in a ploughed field or rather a turnip field. If it had been crop the machine would have turned over going 80 miles an hour and then goodbye to the two fellows inside it. They were both good chaps, Pratt and Owen, and had been shot at an altitude of 16000 feet by a French machine, which was rather bad luck. They came from the coast.

In the morning we did very careful gas helmet drill and other preparations, and found out all we could about the new gas the Boche is using. It is not very deadly but the first whiff makes you sneeze and choke and it becomes very hard to adjust the box respirator. In addition it deadens one's sense of smell and one cannot detect the gas after the first whiff. The effect on the eyes is very bad too. Also it hangs about for days in vegetation in the form of a powder, and as you pass through you kick it up and get gassed. To touch a piece of shell produces blisters on the hands, to rub your face with the affected hand produces blisters on your face – so altogether its unpleasant stuff.

Had to go to Bde H.Q. in the afternoon to see the Corps. Commander. He told us that the latest idea is that the Boche has gone out of his whole front system. Perhaps, and if so things are more complicated. Apart from that he talked rot – the standard of intelligence in his division must have been very low indeed.

Clark and Fleming came to dinner. Search lights were going hard, so probably some Boche aeroplanes were up.

28TH JULY 1917 Spent the morning training. An unexciting day. Tomorrow we move to A30 central. This was originally 'Z' day – now put off. I'm sorry it's been put off.

29TH JULY 1917 Moved off at 5 a.m. and got to A.30 Central at 7.20, where we went into huts. For some reason was very tired. Did what work there was to do and then lay down till lunch time.

In the afternoon got into touch with C.O.'s of bns on my right. Coke in the R.Bde is one of them. He seems all right I think.

The noise of the guns in the morning surpassed anything I've ever heard, and to make it even more so, there was a thunder storm and torrents of rain. That is the worst thing that could happen, because it means mud. Turned in early.

July 30 – 1917

Dear Father,

We begin the great battle and it falls to us to do the first few days work. By the time this starts on its way to you we shall be in it – by the time it arrives we shall, if all goes well, be out of it again. So there will be no cause to worry when you get this. But I don't write to Mother because she might worry needlessly. The men are in great heart, and we are all looking forward to it in a way. Though this is the worst time, when you have finished the preparations and are waiting for the shots to begin. It's like waiting to go in at cricket, and after the first ball one is fit for whatever may arrive. But, as at cricket, the first ball is the worst. You never heard anything like the noise this morning – added to the increasing thunder of the guns we had a thunder storm. If hell let loose is anything like it, one should certainly lead a virtuous life.

The worst part for me is the good fellows one must lose – one has to break an awful lot of eggs to make an omelette these days.

I was awfully glad to see about the prisoners of war in the Times. At last Master will get out of Germany and Mother will be happy about him.

The news from now on you will see in the papers, but its a more wearing game this than one believes, when one reads that we have inflicted a crushing defeat on the Boche. Goodbye and love to Mother.

Your affectionate son
WILLIE

[DIARY] 30TH JULY 1917 The weather is better, but there is no sun. Final preparations are now made and all we have to do is to wait our starting time. The men are looking splendid, and we must succeed. This time tomorrow we shall know more about it. Anyway it will be a few days before I can finish the account of this day. Orders came this morning for Adams to go to a job down the line. He is sorry about it.

The battalion left A30 Central at 7.30 p.m. en route for the assembly trenches.

Our H.Q. were in the front line, small and very stuffy. The worst time is the waiting for zero hour. The Boche started intermittent shelling in the night, but did little harm.

31ST JULY 1917 Z Day, zero hour 3.50 a.m. and at that moment hell broke loose. The noise was infernal. Our lads going to the further objectives did not start until 4.20 a.m. and the Boche shelled the assembly position before we got away. However we were fortunate and had few casualties.

The men were splendid, didn't care a damn, anxious only to get forward.

After C. Coy had gone through I moved H.Q. forward. It was a long time though before we got any news back. Then it came in and I moved H.Q. up to Minty's Fm.

In the afternoon the rain came on and the ground became awful.

I heard Fleming had been killed in the Blue Line – poor chap. He was a most capable fellow. The funny thing is he thought something was going to happen to him.

Hutcheson was splendid, did awfully well.

The Boche massed for a counter-attack in the evening but we caught him with guns and machine guns.

1ST AUGUST 1917 Still holding our position. The Boche shelling was pretty heavy all day and increased in the evening when we were being relieved. We had some casualties during relief. The mud was beyond description. During the relief we heard the enemy had broken through on the left, but decided to disbelieve it. Later we found it was untrue.

Relief went off all right and we got back to A.30 central at 3.30 a.m. Aug 2nd, where the men had soup and rum punch, and we all turned in.

2ND AUGUST 1917 Slept till 1.30 p.m. and got up about 2.30. It's an awful wet day. When I got back last night I found Adams departed, and Duff, brother of Fetteresso, in his place. He is a very good fellow.

Did a bit of writing. The worst part of a battle is the amount of writing connected with it. Before, orders and instructions by the thousand; afterwards account of the battle, recommendations etc. etc.

Aug 2nd 1917

Dear Mother,

I have just got your letter. We have finished our first part of the battle about which you will have read. This battalion had to go 3000 yards and take the second enemy system en route. They did exactly what they were asked to and got a lot of machine guns etc. on the way. The men were absolutely magnificent and all the generals who sit behind are pleased. But, what is more important, we feel we did our job properly. Of course as far down as us and indeed a bit further south too, the show went very well, but beyond that not so well.

The ground we had to traverse was perfectly awful, one mass of shell craters for thousands of yards. And the mud is quite inconceivable to one who has not seen it. I was very fortunate and came through without a scratch at all, and all the arangements worked like clockwork in spite of the awful weather. The hardest thing is to keep direction, the ground is so changed by the shelling. However, I had made every platoon in the battalion make a model of the ground which they had to traverse, with the help of maps and aeroplane photographs, and this worked well as all kept direction the whole way.

One comes out of these shows very tired and the camp we are in now is the worst I've ever seen. It's quite impossible for the men to get clean or dry. Tents are awful in this weather, they ought to build more huts.

The rain of course has just come at the wrong time – but I have never known an attack by us favoured by the weather yet. The artillery for the moment can do nothing, and the conditions in the line are indescribable. However, the Boche will be equally uncomfortable there.

I'm awfully glad to hear Master is all right, and surely he should be one of the first to be sent to a neutral country, because he has been there as long as anyone.

I'm glad you and Father are pretty well. I had hoped that Simon's grave would be behind our lines after this push, but as you will see by the Times map of Tuesday, Aug 2, they did not get along very far at that point. However it can't be helped for the moment. Love to Father.

Your loving son
WILLIE

Willie stuck into the diary an account of the battalion's operations. To the factual narratives of events for the first hours and days of Third Ypres he appended – by request – some comments. The picture conveyed is more encouraging than might have been anticipated and gives a clear and unexaggerated impression of the efficiency of the artillery, the competence of the preparations and arrangements, the dreadful nature of the ground, and the successful outcome – at first.

(I) The arrangements for the assembly were practical, and as far as the front line very good indeed. The two front Companies of the Battalion moved off from A.30 Central by PERTH ROAD at 7.30 p.m. in sections in single file, with 25 paces between each section. A halt was made near ELVERDINGHE CHÂTEAU, and Lewis Gun drums and Lewis Guns were issued. As it was still light, movement was continued in same formation from this point, but sections in rear were ordered to gradually close up upon those in front. As a result, when the Companies entered STIRLING LANE they were in close touch throughout their length. No difficulty was experienced in STIRLING and BOAR LANES, but on arrival in the assembly trench congestion was very great as the passage trench, which had been reported dug, was only existent in parts.

The difficulty was overcome by the fact that the men all kept touch with their own Section Commanders, and that all the men, both of this Battalion and of 1/5th Seaforth Highlanders, knew the time at which to go forward. Thus after ZERO hour small difficulty was experienced in getting the men formed up correctly.

The two Companies going to HARDY'S TRENCH moved off from A.30 Central in rear of 1/6th Seaforth Highlanders, and arrived at HARDY'S TRENCH without incident. Hot tea was issued to the men before the attack.

(II) ZERO hour was too early owing to the fact that the morning was very dark. At 4.30 a.m. it was still too dark to see across 'No Man's Land'.

(III) The accuracy and density of the barrage were beyond praise, and the pace was excellent. Both the BLACK AND GREEN LINES were captured under the barrage. The pauses were sufficient to enable the Companies going to further objectives to go forward and form up under the barrage without getting mixed up in the fighting in positions already captured.

All objectives were captured close under the barrage with the exception of VON WERDER'S HOUSE and ADAM'S FARM.

(IV) The state of the ground, particularly the BLACK LINE and beyond it was indescribable. Shell holes were touching one another across the whole front for a depth of over 2500 yards. Farms had been damaged, but in every farm were dugouts which were still habitable.

(V) The strength of waves was sufficient. Mopping up parties were sufficient and successfully employed. This was largely due to the fact that all men had been practised in attack on isolated machine guns, and lost no time in getting round both flanks and bringing rifle grenade fire to bear on them.

(VI) Communications worked excellently throughout the battle, although communication by orderly was slow owing to the state of the ground. On two occasions only was communication broken between Battalion and Brigade Headquarters, and then only for short periods. It was at times difficult to get through quickly, owing to the large number of units working on one line, but this was probably unavoidable.

(VII) Dump arrangements were excellent, and the pack transport train did excellent work. A large dump of S.A.A. was formed at MINTY'S FARM on the afternoon of 'Z' day, and soon after a large supply of water also arrived.

The carrying parties with Yukon Packs were extremely useful for getting up rations to MINTY'S FARM, and for carrying back rifles, equipment, captured material etc.

(VIII) A large number of our aeroplanes were up, but whether their reports were of value is unknown. No signals were sent to aeroplanes by panel.

No flares were called for after the BLACK LINE was captured, but flares were lit in response to calls on reaching the GREEN LINE.

(IX) In certain cases tanks* were of great value. A machine gun was in action in a house near English Trees (probably BRITANNIA FARM). A tank was directed to this point and silenced the gun with two rounds.

Two machine guns were active in neighbourhood of MACDON-ALD'S WOOD. These were dealt with by a tank.

No tanks were seen near BOCHCASTLE or KITCHENER'S WOOD, but it is thought that two tanks did assist in clearing the wood.

(X) The number of Officers (19) with this Battalion was sufficient.

(XI) In all, 9 machine guns were accounted for by this Battalion, three being captured and six destroyed. Two trench mortars were captured near KITCHENER'S HOUSE, but could not be removed.

Two light guns (anti-tank probably) were captured between BLACK and GREEN LINES at G.10.b.3.2. (approximately), but these were subsequently removed by some other unit.

Number of prisoners captured by this Battalion was approximately:-

4 Officers 130 other ranks.

(XII) Bombs were little used, but I consider it advisable to carry one per man.

Rifle Grenades were used with great success in dealing with isolated machine guns.

(XIII) Dress and equipment of the men was satisfactory.

(XIV) Direction was well kept on the whole, and although lost at times by small parties, was in every case regained. Compasses where used were very useful. The fact that each platoon had made

---

*Tanks had first been employed in the latter stages of the Somme fighting.

a model of the ground over which they were to attack enabled both N.C.O.'s and men to recognise landmarks, and they at all times realised where they were.

(XV) The Stokes Guns attached to this Battalion did not come into action, but they were in position on the BLACK LINE. The carrying party attached to them formed a sufficient dump of ammunition and then rejoined the carrying platoon of the Battalion.

(XVI) The work of the machine guns was excellent at all times. They were brought forward at the right time, and gave great security to the line.

(XVII) The medical arrangements were good. The Medical Officer of this Battalion established his Aid Post at MINTY'S FARM at about 8 a.m. some hours before any other Aid Post moved forward. The result was considerable congestion at this point, as men of many units in advance of this from both flanks came here to be dressed.

The work of stretcher bearers, both of the Battalion and R.A.M.C. was satisfactory.

(XVIII) The Battalion reached A.30 Central after relief on the morning of August 2nd.

Accommodation was in tents, many of which were wet inside, and as the camp had apparently been pitched without system, and there were no duckboards, the surrounding mud was indescribable. The men were soaking wet, and are so still, and it is quite impossible to get them dry or clean under existing circumstances.

In addition these conditions have a very depressing effect both upon the spirits and health of the men, and should it be the intention to undertake further operations I consider it absolutely necessary to produce accommodation as soon as possible where reorganisation and re-equipping can be carried out.

W. FRASER
Lieut Colonel

3rd August, 1917   Commanding 6th Gordon Highlanders

6th Gordons had attacked in the northern part of the British offensive line, and matters had gone well – and significantly

*better than in the south, south-east of Ypres. Willie's references to
Simon's grave concerned the latter sector, near where the 92nd
had been at First Ypres. But Simon's name is on the Menin Gate
Memorial at Ypres, one of the many thousands, 'having no
known grave'. No grave from First Ypres could have survived the
later battles and shellfire.*

*6th Gordons casualties were light. Tribute was paid to their
training and preparation.*

[DIARY] 5TH AUGUST 1917 Fine day – the ground is drying up.
Church parade by companies in the morning and the rest of the
day was spent cleaning up. It's the first chance we've had.

In the afternoon Duff and I went for a walk to Vlamertinghe
Chateau. It is hardly damaged at all, and there are still some nice
spots in the garden. Rumour of course has it that it belongs to von
Bissing and is therefore not shelled.

We were bombed by aeroplanes after dinner; they got the
Argylls' camp next door and killed 1 man and wounded 6. It's
bad luck to be knocked out back. We were playing bridge in the
mess and we put the lights out (not that they could have showed
up) and lay down to the ground. The only thing to do.

7TH AUGUST 1917 Fine day. In the morning walked about the
country with Duff watching the companies doing the attack
practice. In the afternoon we went off to hit a golf ball about, but
failed to find a suitable field and lost two golf balls. I nearly lost
my belt too – left on the ground for a few minutes and it was
pinched by a gunner.

Luckily we caught the fellow. After dinner there was very
heavy bombardment by our field guns, seemingly on our front
and to the north. However a message from the Brigade said that it
was all to the north.

8TH AUGUST 1917 Marched off on a misty morning back to St.
Jan de Biezen where we were in camp before the attack. Left at
5.40 and got in about 9 o'clock. Not a good camp – the staff
officers responsible for these places should be made to live in
them.

Was thinking about poor Fleming today. It's odd – some shells (one in a thousand perhaps) are forged to kill, destined to become not mere pieces of metal, but servants of destiny with power over the destiny of a man. Do they look any different in the furnace, I wonder?

Went for a longish ride with Duff in the evening and my new horse cast a shoe. So we had to walk the whole way home – in the pouring rain.

We had very heavy rain in the evening – which turned the dust to mud again and made our camp very messy.

Aug 9th 1917

Dear Mother,

I had a letter from Father yesterday asking me about the battle but the answer is in the letter I wrote you last[*] which must have crossed his. The men are very fit and well. The spirit is splendid; for instance one man fell into a shell hole full of mud on the way back. He was dead tired at the time having fought hard for two days but instead of being discouraged he began to quack like a duck – after which the whole company waded back through the awful mud quacking like ducks!

But I would like to see an end all the same, we can't go on for ever, and Scotland has been terribly bled already. And of course the Scottish divisions are in every battle. I'm afraid I can't get any leave yet, I could have gone to Paris for a few days now, but on second thoughts I decided not to leave the battalion. There is a lot to do always and one isn't too happy away.

I have now got Arthur Duff, brother of Fetteresso, as my second-in-command. He is an excellent fellow and it makes a wonderful difference having someone to talk to in the mess. Funny state of things though – he was Pelham Burn's captain when he joined the militia. And I was Pelham's subaltern, and now Pelham is my general and Arthur Duff is my second in command.

Father says tell him any good I can of the battalion – well I don't think there is a better battalion, not even of Gordon

---

[*] On 2 August.

Highlanders in France. But I wish we had more of the original men left.

Your loving son
WILLIE

[DIARY] 12TH AUGUST 1917 In the morning the Kirk – after which I inspected the camps and found fault with many things. Met a fellow called Levy who was in the Scots Guards and who was comdg. a bn. in the 39th division in the recent battle. His story of the show absolutely appalled me, its the worst thing I have ever heard and that commanders of such awful incapacity should exist in the army, still, as his late Brigadier and Divisional commander, is a guarantee of failure in every show. And the men are magnificent. It is such waste.

13TH AUGUST 1917 Usual training in the morning. We had a battalion parade, the first I've had in France I think. The men looked well. In the afternoon had a demonstration of how to run a platoon attack practice for officers and N.C.O.'s and it went very well. The great thing is to teach them to put life into their parades. Then we shall get really good instruction.

Duff and I rode up early to the Mont des Cats after tea. The evening was glorious and the view from there is magnificent. But it hurts to see those places again, they bring back the old days before the war had become quite so terrible.

Uncle Harper and Dick-C and H.P.B. came to dinner and we had quite a successful party. Uncle had his game of bridge afterwards.

Have got a car to take me to Calais tomorrow.

Between 14 and 18 August, Willie took a few days' leave in England. His parents had taken a house, Newlands Park, near Rickmansworth, and he divided his days between there and the London house, No. 1 Bryanston Square. By the evening of 18 August he was back with his battalion.

[DIARY] 18TH AUGUST 1917 It's really a delightful drive from Boulogne but one is not always in a mood to appreciate it. Not that one really minds coming back. '*Pour le moment la guerre c'est la vie*', and there is little outside it. Got back to find the battalion where I had left it, which was unexpected.

19TH AUGUST 1917 Church parade at 10 a.m. after which I did some office work. The war has not really progressed much since I have been away. The big attack was 3 parts failure – they got forward a bit on our front but from St. Julien southwards it was a fiasco, with the losses and depreciation in morale that such an affair entails. However these things are in the hands of the Gods who make incapable commanders who know not the principles of war. And at present it is war to the knife, and errors of judgement meet with their reward.

After lunch Duff and I rode over to Proven and called on the Guards Div. whence Duff extracted a friend of his (nomine George Lane) and he guided us round to the 1st Grenadiers where I found Mark Maitland in great form as usual. He had just heard from Freddy[*] who is in command of the 92nd, P.W.B. having got a Brigade. He challenged us at tug 'o war so we accepted and fixed it for Wednesday. But I fear me we shall be beaten as we have had no practice.

On the way home went to see Ally Boyd, who had just returned from Paris, where he had enjoyed himself.

Pelham and McDonald came to dinner and ate grouse and drank champagne.

20TH AUGUST 1917 Usual training in the morning. In the afternoon we had a practice parade for the presentation of medals parade by the Corps Commander, which comes off tomorrow.

Caryl Hargreaves, Legh and Johnstone came to dine, and we played a game of bridge afterwards and were duly bombed by the bold bad Boche after dinner. These days he comes over every night about 10.30 and drops bombs about the place. I believe our Archies hit one of his aeroplanes on this occasion.

[*]Maitland.

21ST AUGUST 1917 Spent the morning in the office writing and thinking. It's harder work than it sounds. The parade for the Corps commander was changed to 1.45 as the C-in-C[*] was to come later. Which meant parade at 1 p.m. for us – a nasty awkward hour. The medal presentation was over by 2.30 and from that time until 4.15 we stood on parade waiting for the C-in-C. When he did turn up he was very gracious – he's a nice fellow of course. It was a good parade and I think perhaps the 6th G.H. were just the best part of it, but there was not much to choose between the 4 battalions. They were all jolly good. However it was a relief to get away in the end. I liked the C-in-C but my opinion of the Corps Commander did not improve. I'm certain he's efficient, but in a nasty hole and corner sort of way. Would not trust him a yard, and he hasn't got an eighth of Uncle's brains.

These strictures on the corps commander, Lieutenant-General Sir Ivor Maxse, are surprising in that Willie later took the view that he was among the best, if not the best, corps commanders on the Western Front; and came to work with him very closely, and to like him very much.

[DIARY] 22ND AUGUST 1917 Rode out in the morning to a training area where one company of each battalion was to do an attack practice for criticism by mon Oncle. I left my Company commander to himself and he made a thorough mess of it. Good thing, more is learnt by failure than success.

Had a great argument with Uncle[†] during which he got very heated. I must be an awfully annoying fellow to argue with – don't know why. When we got on a bit I found we were both making for the same place by different roads. And that's why he has not got a Corps.[‡] He has things clear in his head, but he sees all things from a different view-point than the ordinary man, and

[*]General Sir Douglas Haig.
[†]Harper.
[‡]He got one later.

his brain goes either straighter or less straight to a point than that of another. Anyway it gets there just as quick but by a different road. Result is that he cannot explain to anyone else what he means and vice versa. At least it takes time, and you have to know him well to understand.

Rode home in time for lunch. Was a bit off colour in the afternoon and lay down.

In the evening the Grenadiers arrived to pull us at tug 'o war and they did it too, with ease. I feared it.

Mark has gone to Paris and was represented by Lascelles. Fisher – Rowe and Denison also came, and several youngsters.

23RD AUGUST 1917 Drill competition in the morning. We did not do too badly. The day was showery and the showers were very heavy. Big drops of rain that beat right through one's clothes at once.

In the afternoon wandered round the various bits of training going on, and then delivered an oration on modern war for the benefit of officers and N.C.O.'s. Hope they benefitted by it, thought it rather good myself! Then had a meeting of Coy Commanders and damned them into heaps for various delinquencies. *Et voila tout.* Dined with H.P.B. at Bde H.Q. – where also were dining Fuller[*] of the Oxford and Bucks L.I. and young Stewart in the A & S.H. We had quite an amusing dinner. Fuller is a clever devil and one of the few Staff Officers who knows anything at all about the war. We decided that the C.G.S.[†] had the mind without the personal attractions of a kitchen-maid.

29TH AUGUST 1917 Moved by train from Poperinghe to Riegersburg. Thence marched to the canal bank when we were accommodated in dugouts until 7 p.m. at which out we marched off to relieve the front line.

Passed the old landmarks on our battlefield of July 31. Guides met us at Minty's House which was my final H.Q. on that day. Arrived to find I had to relieve two battalions which were all mixed up.

[*] Major-General J.F.C. Fuller, as he later became: the 'prophet' of armoured warfare.
[†] Of the British Expeditionary Force, Lieutenant-General Sir Launcelot Kiggell.

They had carried out an attack which had failed, because it had never contained any of the elements of success. Men had been asked to attack across a sea of mud and water and they had tried and suffered in proportion. Poor devils, murdered by incapable commanders.

So the atmosphere at bn. H.Q. when we took over was somewhat depressing. However the relief went all right and the depressed elements departed and I went up to the line with Duff. Found all more or less serene – the ground was very bad indeed. Also one apparently has to walk through a barrage on the Langemarck-St. Julien road to get forward.

Bn. H.Q. a concrete shelter facing the wrong way. However we have improved it a bit.

30TH AUGUST 1917 It's a dull life. At H.Q. we are in direct view of the Boche and have to lie doggo all day, which gets very boring. In the evening the sky became full of Boche aeroplanes flying at from 500–1000 feet, and as far back as the Stienbeck, i.e. 1500^x behind our line. So much for our command of the air. The shelling has been very heavy all day, but fortunately behind our Front line.

Went round all the posts during the night and found many things not as they should be. Company and platoon Commanders have an awful lot to learn.

But the Boche is not going to attack – he could not if he wished – the ground is so bad. The right sector of my front is protected by great lakes of water.

31ST AUGUST 1917 Another day doing nothing and getting shelled. Night brings activity and some interest. Spent it nosing about the front line, finding fault a lot I fear. One does get so tired of saying 'this parapet is not bullet-proof' or 'these men are too crowded' etc. etc. – but there it is. It has to be done.

1ST SEPTEMBER 1917 The same day with the added excitement of being shelled more accurately than usual. We had a direct hit on our H.Q. but no damage done fortunately.

Gen. Harper came up to see us and made some criticisms for which I took him to task later on.

This night I walked the Bde. Major round the line. It was very quiet indeed. We were not even shelled on the Langemarck[*] road.

2ND SEPTEMBER 1917 Our last day. We had a great clearing up at H.Q. and made shelves and pigeon holes and generally improved things for Campbell who takes over from us.

With dusk came the relief and it went through without hitch and I left with Duff about 11.30 p.m.

We walked back to dugouts in the canal bank to find the battalion settled in. No casualties in the relief.

Our tour cost us 17 casualties in all, mostly in carrying parties.

4TH SEPTEMBER 1917 A lazy day. Dined with Uncle and read some notes he has been compiling on organisation and battle. We had a very good dinner. Also arranged for a car to take me to Boulogne on the 6th which is the day I go on leave.

After dinner we played bridge.

Bombs were dropped all over the country by enemy aeroplanes. This happens every night. It is a fairly recent development and has reached a pitch at present never attained before.

On 7 September Willie began a longer spell of leave. 'It's nice', he wrote in his diary on that day, 'to be in a quiet place, but it makes one hate the war more than one does in France.'

Lord Saltoun had been lent some fishing on the River Chess and Willie spent a good deal of the days with a rod in his hand. 'It was wonderful beside the water,' he wrote on 11 September, 'but the war is a nightmare all the time. How I hate it.' 'One's life is the war,' he wrote a few days later. 'These quiet days are brands snatched from the fire – and even they have the dark red mantle round about them. One reads of other wars – what child's play they seem in comparison to a world struggling to free itself. I wonder if anyone is tired of the war as I am tired. I dread the going back, the noise, the awful sights and smells. But there it is. We must see it through.'

On 19 September he was back at the front.

[152]

[DIARY] 20TH SEPTEMBER 1917 In camp at A.30 Central. A Company and one platoon are away carrying shells for the heavy gunners. The remainder spent the day on the range and the shooting is improving. We also completed the firing point on the Siege Camp Range.

Long came to dinner. The day was full of various rumours about the attack by the 154 Bde[*] which took place this morning. It was quite successful, but the division on our left did not get on and that left our flank exposed. The defensive flank which we formed was later on shelled out by the guns of the division on our left.

The G.O.C. 154 Bde seems to have mishandled his reserves pretty thoroughly, frittering them away by reinforcing the front line in driblets. However on the whole the Boche counter-attacks have met with no success and he has had very heavy casualties, which is satisfactory. But I think we shall have to go up to the line, which is a pity. We have orders to move to the canal bank tomorrow morning.

21ST SEPTEMBER 1917 Left for the canal[†] bank at 8.30 a.m. and arrived at 10.30 a.m., and were located in dugouts in the bank. The day was spent issuing extra S.A.A. rations, rockets and lights, and the various things which the soldier requires in these complicated days.

In the afternoon the men rested. The company which had been with the heavy gunners rejoined – they had been working very hard and were somewhat tired.

About 3 p.m. we got orders to move up to the line, where we shall be in a support position, leaving canal at 6.30 p.m. I also got orders to send the battalion up under command of Duff – because I have to go off to chaperone some Americans. Had a meeting of

---

[*] One of 51st Highland Division's brigades. The brigade attack had been supported by no less than forty-seven batteries of artillery, including large numbers of 'heavies': and by the firing of nearly 90,000 artillery rounds on the first day of the attack, in addition to twenty-four hours' intensive bombardment the preceding day. The attack was towards Poelcappelle near Langemarck in spite of Willie's strictures (in the diary only and from initial rumour) on the handling of some aspects of the attack, it was described later as a model of its kind; although over 900 officers and men were lost.

[†] The Ypres-Comines Canal, often referred to. It runs north from Ypres to the River Yser.

[153]

company commanders and went through the orders and the battalion left at 6.30. I rode back and dined with division. It's all very well, but don't like being away from the bn. on these occasions.

The general asked me to stop at Div. H.Q. until I go off to the Americans. I had my things at the transport, so went back there for the night and found myself fixed up very comfortably in a tent.

22ND SEPTEMBER 1917 While I was at breakfast the Boche came over and bombed the neighbourhood. They put one rather close. However it did no harm. Rode down to the division after breakfast, and found myself very comfortable in a hut. I must say it is a pleasant change.

In the afternoon motored over to see Divisional reinforcement camp at Houtkerque. Found the drafts for the battalion were very good, and the training is going on well under Battalion instructors.

23RD SEPTEMBER 1917 Spent the morning writing out a paper on defence of a position for the general.

Heard that the Americans have failed to materialise, or rather that they have got someone else to trot them round – and I am not sorry.

Wrote some letters in the afternoon and did little else. The Boche put a very heavy barrage behind our front line in the evening and it seemed as if he might attack, but if he intended to our artillery reply dealt with him all right, as no infantry action followed.

Played bridge after dinner.

24TH SEPTEMBER 1917 Managed to get a new mare from DADVS[*] through Weston's good offices. A very nice mare – a bit gone in the wind perhaps. Rode her up to Trois Tours to see Finlay. The battalion comes out of the line tonight.

In the evening wrote a good deal of the Divisional book on the offensive and got it ready for typing.

After dinner played a game of bridge with the general.

[*]Deputy Assistant Director of Vetinary Services.

Dear Father,

How goes it at Philorth? If you are having weather like us it should be glorious. The attack the other day was a real success after all, and on this divisional front the number of dead Boche is very large indeed. They were very thick in their front line – in one piece 100 yards long they counted 150 dead. The counter-attacked with 7 battalions of a new storm division against the front of the Bde we had in the line and did no good and must have suffered very heavily indeed. I am quite optimistic after this show – I think we can beat the Boche next year. There's no doubt he is not as good as he was, by a long way.

The bombing behind the line is really unpleasant, though not productive of very great results. He dropped one close to my tent when I was having breakfast the other day.

I was to have taken some Americans round the country – but now they have selected a fellow in the Guards Division for the job. I am not sorry because they are not sending them up to the front line, which is the only place they would learn anything and it is sure to develop into a sort of joy-ride – and I am no good at drinking cocktails. The battalion is up in the line, but come out tonight – I was not allowed to go up on account of this American stunt, so Arthur Duff has taken them up. There has been nothing doing so far except very heavy shelling.

I have at last managed to get hold of a really nice mare. Her present owner won't ride her, as he says she is bobbery, but she's quite quiet really. It's a joy to feel a decent horse under one again.

I have been stopping at divisional H.Q. for a few days, and it has been very nice; tomorrow I go back to the battalion. I suppose you did not see George in Edinburgh, did you?

There are an extraordinary number of wasps about, and one had the cheek to sting me this morning. However the damage done is slight.

Have you seen McDonald yet? How is Brown, and McKechnie and McIntyre, and how is Bruce and my new dog Billy?

Your affectionate son
WILLIE

[DIARY] 25TH SEPTEMBER 1917 The division handed over to the 11th div. about 9.30 and the general left at 10 for Wormhoudt. I rode up to the battalion at Siege Camp. Found everyone still asleep. However they woke up presently and I heard the news.

They had a pretty rocky time in the line – the Boche shelling was very heavy indeed at times. Our total casualties for this tour are 54. Duncan, 'D' Coy's new officer was killed – he was a very stout hearted fellow and is a great loss. Young Henry was wounded, I hope he is not bad. He was not efficient and I might have had to report badly on him so perhaps it's a way out.

27TH SEPTEMBER 1917 Inspected all companies in the morning in full marching order. Turnout fair.

After lunch rode over to 14th Corps H.Q. with Arthur Duff to see Claud Hamilton, but he was out – so rode back again. My new mare is quite a good mount and a ride becomes more of pleasure·than it used to be.

Pelham goes on leave tomorrow and Scott and I dined with him at Trois Tours. It was a brilliant moonlight night and the Boche made full use of it. His bombing aeroplanes were over in scores, and dropped a lot of bombs – some very big ones, some not too far from our camp either. I wish the authorities would move us right back now we are out of the line – we are doing no good here, and its asking for casualties to crowd men into these camps.

29TH SEPTEMBER 1917 Usual parades all day. It was a wonderful moonlight night and the Boche took every advantage of it. His bombing aeroplanes started at 8 and continued until 2 a.m. almost without intermission. By the grace of God they missed our camps dropping them all round us and we had no casualties.

VI
Cambrai
1917

[DIARY] 30TH SEPTEMBER 1917 Marched off from Siege Camp at 7.20 a.m. except A. Company which left earlier. Entrained at Hopoutre and left there at 11.30. The train was very much delayed – we were ten hours late at our destination – Bapaume.*
The line had been damaged by bombs and a train which had got derailed. It was a glorious day and it was real joy to pass through a country untouched by war – at any rate to the outward eye. The woods are turning brown, except where the poplars still keep their green. One passed quiet unhurrying people wandering along country lanes, I wonder if they know what joy they give to travellers hurrying through a dusty smoky world.

It got very cold in the evening and we had no windows to our carriage. Tried to rig up newspapers to replace them, with only partial success.

Sgt. Begg had provided a splendid rabbit pie for the journey, so we did not starve. We were due at 8.40 at Bapaume, but midnight found us still in the train.

1ST OCTOBER 1917 It was nearly 6 a.m. when we got to Bapaume. We soon got the train unloaded and the battalion marched off. Our camp was near Achiet-le-petit – five miles distant. The guide lost his way, which made me very angry as the men were very tired. However eventually we arrived and after a dish of tea, all turned in and slept. The camp is not a good one, most of it bivouacs rigged up by the advance party. But it's all right in dry weather.

A wonderful country this – rolling downs as far as the eye can reach. It has not been cultivated for three years. This is where the Boche retired last year, and the thorough way in which he does

*At long last 51st Highland Division and 6th Gordons were leaving the Ypres sector and returning to the area of Arras – Bapaume. Another great battle was planned in Picardy, although first there would be a spell of trench routine.

things is fully in evidence. Every house in every village is a ruin, even his dugouts he has mostly destroyed. He is a wonderful barbarian. Arthur and I went for a walk in the evening.

2ND OCTOBER 1917 Usual training and parades in the morning. In the evening the massed drums and pipes of the Brigade played at Div. H.Q. Our Corps Commander here is Haldane,[*] to whom one can apply the epithet 'sticky' and his staff one of the obstructionist order. Very different from the XVIII Corps. However we have got Bungo[†] for our Army Commander, which should make up for a lot. I can't really like the A.B.[‡] somehow. Wrote some letters.

I'm afraid I shan't be able to stand Archibald as adjutant – he is so awfully worthy and has absolutely no imagination. Nothing is done that one does not order him to do. Hope I shall manage to get Mitchell from Aberdeen.

4TH OCTOBER 1917 Training. Two companies Field Firing. Section rushes – quite a good show on the whole.

Arthur Duff and I reconnoitred route to our next area where we go on the 6th.

Had quite a good gallop coming home.

5th October 1917

Dear Mother,

I think really it must have been rather lonely down at Newlands – but I'm not at all sure London is a very healthy place yet. The moon will be up again next month and we may get some more fine weather yet. The weather has broken here now, and its very cold with heavy showers. I can tell you all about bombing raids now; one night before we moved the Boche started at 8 p.m. and his aeroplanes came over in a continuous stream until 2 a.m. dropping bombs of all sizes. How they missed us I don't know, but they did. But we are out of that for the moment. I can't tell you much about the last show because we get the news very slowly

---

[*] Lieutenant-General Sir Aylmer Haldane, formerly Gordon Highlanders, commanding VI Corps.
[†] General. The Hon. Sir Julian Byng, later Field-Marshal Viscount Byng of Vimy.
[‡] Haldane.

unless we are near the scene of the battle, but I think it was what one can call a partial success.

There is an old saying that whoever holds Houthoulst Forest holds Belgium. At present the Boche holds it and I should think it would be a hard nut to crack.

The men are very fit indeed, but the winter is approaching again – one has realised it the last few days – and a winter campaign is never much to look forward to.

I have chucked Fortnum & Mason for parcels – they have never done me very well. Would it be possible to order me some things at Cooper's? He would not mind putting them down to me. I only want kippers – findon haddocks and fresh sausages, a weekly consignment. They keep perfectly all right at this time of year and make a great addition to the mess. There are no special formalities in sending them out, he can just address them to me and they will arrive. The cake from Buzzard comes regularly and is very good indeed.

I heard from Father who seems to be quite fit at home. I must say I wish that they would send Master to a neutral country – Switzerland for choice. I saw a photograph of Lord Stair in some paper and I must say he did not look very fit. Did I tell you I saw Simpson in London the day before I came out here? He was going up to Aberdeen and I told Father, so they have probably met. It's bad luck George having to go off north again, but I expect he will be down again shortly and get a bit of leave.

The division did very well indeed in its second show the other day,* and our general has now got a great reputation – thoroughly well deserved. They have thought of getting rid of him before now, I believe, because he won't kow-tow to anyone, but he's always been too strong for them, as he knows three times as much about the war as anyone else in France.

Your loving son
WILLIE

[DIARY] 6TH OCTOBER 1917 Marched off at 9 a.m. to Reserve Bde. area of division in the line. Very heavy rain on the march.

*The last participation in Third Ypres.

Camp looked very desolate when we arrived. Huts very badly built, neither wind nor water tight and no means of getting fires going. Bitterly cold too. Shall have to get busy on the place or we shall have all the men sick.

Walked over to transport lines 2 miles away – they are pretty good. Saw the range – fairly good, and called on the Brigade and put in a large indent for material.

9th October 1917

Dear Father,

Many thanks for your letter. So you saw MacDonald – you seem to have had quite a cheery gathering and I'm glad you gave him a pat on the back because he deserves it. I daresay you will be back in London by now.

I have come to the conclusion we do things the wrong way in Scotland – we ought to go in strongly for Home Rule, organise a Land League and have a Society for the Shooting of Englishmen from behind hedges.

Listen to my tale and you will see why. There are two divisions, one a Highland and one an Irish division. The former has in the last 14 months fought seven battles, all of them successes, and bears the reputation of having killed more Boches than any division in France. It heads the Boche black list in fact.

The Irish division has fought three battles, two of them were very much written up in the papers, but were really complete walkovers and there was no resistance – the third was a complete failure.

During all the time it was in the present fighting area, it got 20 places *a day* for leave per Brigade, as soon as it left it got 43 per Brigade, and for the last fifteen days it has had 73 per Brigade per day.

During this same period the Highland division got never more than 60 and more often 20 places *per week* per Brigade. And this in spite of the fact that it (although suffering more severely) has got its battalions up to strength, whereas those of the Irish division number about a third of that number.

I saw in the paper today that Lord Derby states that now all men over 18 months in France have had leave. This is true I believe, but only just. A few weeks ago I had men who had been out since

December 1915 without leave. In addition the Irish division got recently a special allotment of French honours – the only qualification required was an Irish name. The allotment was about equal to what is given to the *Army* as a rule. So you see we should start sedition in Scotland, and in the next war our men may get a fair leave allotment. The whole thing is a perfect scandal, and I think some very awkward questions might be asked on the subject.

The battle N. of Ypres seems to have gone well. There was another today about which we have no definite information as yet, but what news there is seems to be good.

We had a glorious September, but October is making us pay for it with interest, the cold has been chronic. I have lost my adjutant who has been sent as second-in-command to another battalion, and his successor, although hard-working and conscientious, lacks originality and will never make an adjutant. I hope you are really fit.

Your affectionate son
WILLIE

Oct 9th 1917

Dear Mother,

Thank you very much for your letter. I must say you are a perfect marvel to make her go 50 miles to the gallon – it just shows what a lot of petrol is wasted.

I think London ought to be fairly safe as long as this weather lasts – one can't fly much in a gale of wind with rain-storms. The rain is worse than the wind. But there is no doubt that the best way to protect London is to bomb German towns – it's a nasty thing to have to do, but it's the sound way of protecting ourselves.

I think this last battle has gone well, we have got more details now and there is no doubt that the Boche has suffered very heavily. We have had no excitements lately. The division is in the line but we are in reserve at the moment.

It has been most bitterly cold with a gale of wind and the huts which we are occupying were thrown up very badly and are neither wind nor rain proof. However we are gradually improving them, though it's a slow job. One great difficulty one has as the evenings close in is to give the men amusement and occupation after dark, and it's very dull in a badly lighted hut if one has nothing to do at all. However when one thinks of the first winter of the war one realises how well off we are. I remember the battalion coming back from awfully muddy trenches where they had been for twelve days, for four days rest. We were shown an exposed open field and it was pouring and blowing a gale. However we settled down somehow and when the rain stopped were more or less happy. Things are a bit better than that now.

If you happen to come across any good books now and again I should be grateful for them – only I intensely dislike the general run of modern novels.

I'm going off for a joy-ride this afternoon, as least it's really on business to get myself a warm coat. One gets a most excellent coat lined with sheepskin from the Ordnance Stores, and made of cloth which will keep out anything almost. And all for £2.10/-I think. And the last few days have brought home to one that winter is upon us.

This has been an odd year, spring and autumn seem to have got lost. It was winter until the end of April when it suddenly became summer – summer lasted until a few days ago and now it's become winter again. I'm not sure I like it, one prefers to be let down gently as far as winter is concerned anyway.

What dull letters one does write – but except when one is battle-fighting life is very much a routine – training and holding trenches and training again. And all one's interests are more or less technical, and would lack interest in a letter.

Arthur Duff is away for a week doing a course at the Third Army School.

Give Father my love – he ought to arrive about the same time as this.

Your loving son
WILLIE

[DIARY] 13TH OCTOBER 1917 H.P.B. got back from leave last night. It was a fine day for a change. Got orders for a demonstration attack to be carried out for the instruction of an

American general man. Wrote the orders for the show and went over them with my Coy Commanders.

In the evening got fresh orders about it and had to do the things over again. It's a way we have in the army – don't know about the navy, but it's probably the same.

Conference of C.O.'s at Bde. H.Q. at 2.30. H.P.B. was looking the better for his leave. He had brought back the new set of pipes he promised us. They are very fine ones, and the old pipe-major was absolutely jumping with delight when he saw them.

14TH OCTOBER 1917 Had no time to go to Church. Marked out the ground for our attack* and went over it with Coy Commanders. It's a very good bit of ground. At 3 p.m. we had a rehearsal with the men and it went very well. Had a lot of work to do in addition in connection with our move to the trenches on Tuesday.

15th October 1917

Dear Father,

Many thanks for your letter. It's rotten luck not being able to see a bit more of George. The Division is in the trenches and we ourselves go in tomorrow.

I don't know that anything very exciting has been happening, we have been training and doing a great lot of work on our Camp, which needed it badly, and have made it more comfortable than it was. This morning we had a practice or rather a demonstration of our attack formation for the benefit of an American General who is visiting the division. He was greatly impressed and it was rather a fine sight – the men did it extraordinarily well considering it was practically an unrehearsed show.

This is a grand training country, all open and you can go anywhere, and if we are here for a few months one should be able to get the battalion really handy and fit to tackle anything humanly possible; but I misdoubt me. I don't think they will ever leave the Highland Division out of a show if they can help it.

The American general man was quite a nice old boy and very anxious to learn all about it and I think he learnt a bit this morning. He saw two battalions on parade and then saw my lads

*The demonstration.

do the attack, and then went off to a trench mortar demonstration. After a hurried lunch they switched him off in a motor car to go and see battery positions.

Pelham Burn is back from leave – he told me he met you in the train and that you had a crack together. McDonald is also back again, but I have not seen him to talk to yet. I hear you got 68 brace the other day when Simpson and Hugh Ross were out. That's not bad, is it! It would be a great thing if McKechnie could send me out two or three brace of partridges now and again. They keep best cooked, and they will travel quite well in this weather. Anything in that line is a change from beef.

This has been a busy day – there are always a lot of things to see to before going to the line. I'm afraid the last show up at Ypres was rather a wash-out, the weather was very bad – far too bad to make the attempt, I think. I hope the casualties weren't big, but failure costs more men than success. Arthur Duff came back today – he was away for a week on a course of sorts, and it really was a bit lonely at times.

Love to Mother – I am very fit.

Your affectionate son
WILLIE

[DIARY] 16TH OCTOBER 1917 An early rise. Battalion marched off by platoons at 7.30 a.m. Relief went off without incident. A few shells near entrance to Hindenburg line, but no accidents. Saw Long and Newson en route. The relief was finished about 1 p.m. Asked Campbell (6th B.W. Colonel whom we relieved) to lunch. He refused till he saw our lunch (roast grouse) after which he decided to stop.

Went round the trenches in the afternoon and fixed up about work etc. The Right Company sector is very unsatisfactory. Our trenches never seem to be dug on a system somehow – they just happen, no one plans them. The Corps Staff seem to have plenty of time to interfere with the administration of battalion – none to plan a decent defensive system on the Corps front. And yet we *are* winning the war.

18TH OCTOBER 1917 Trenches – they are most monotonous

things in a way, but with points of interest. There is plenty to do – the work of construction never ends and never yet have I taken over a good show in trenches. The lack of exercise is the worst part of them, walking round trenches isn't really exercise although one walks miles.

It's very quiet here on the whole – a certain number of T.M.'s[*] and a few shells – but we throw much more at the Boche than he does at us. We had a strafe on the left at 6.30 and threw a lot of T.M.'s and shells at one place – the Boche made no particular reply.

21ST OCTOBER 1917 Sunday and a glorious morning. There are partridges about here, one can here them saying goodnight in No Man's Land any evening.

Thick fog as a rule in the mornings now and one can go for an ante-prandial walk outside trenches, which assists the appetite. Because our dugout is deep and dark – though marvellously well-aired, I must say.

Spent a busy morning doing orders for the relief and various other things. Spent the afternoon and evening wandering about the trenches.

22ND OCTOBER 1917 Dull wet morning. Walked round the trenches. They are not quite so nice on a wet day. Tore my breeks on some revetment, which is a nuisance. We were relieved by the 8th A. & S.H. – the relief went well and finished about 4 p.m.

On the whole the Boche was more active than usual with his guns and T.M.'s and he threw some gas at the people on our left. But the wind was wrong and it all blew back into his own trenches, where there was much excitement and running about. There was an attack up at Ypres this morning. Bad weather for it. No news yet of how it went.

We moved back into support, three companies in the Hindenburg line, or rather the Hindenburg Tunnel. It's not a bad place, but it's not been looked after properly in the past. Also there are beams all over the place and one is always banging one's head.

[*]Trench mortars.

[167]

Wrote two letters – have been rather lax with correspondence lately.

Water is the great difficulty here – for washing purposes. One can only wash once a day, and by the end of the day one's hands are awful.

It cleared up in the afternoon and we had a glorious sunset, but the weather has broken, I fear.

In Russia, on 22 October, the Petrograd Soviet attacked the Kerensky Government and Trotsky demanded that Russia make peace with Germany. On the same day a series of attacks began at Ypres, inching forward in deplorable conditions to the ultimate capture on 6 November of the Passchendaele ridge. Meanwhile, and mercifully, 6th Gordons were still in the Somme sector near Bapaume, in and out of the trenches, but comparatively quiet.

Oct 22 1917

Dear Mother,

Many thanks for your letters and the trouble about the parcels. One has arrived very well.

I have not had much time for writing lately as we have been holding the line – or at least one has time, but I never can apply myself to anything when I am in the trenches, apart from the job in hand. We are still in, but are now back in support, which means one has not immediate responsibility, which is quite a different thing. We have just finished our relief, and are not yet settled down here, and so far as I can see there is not a vast deal to do, as most of the men are away working and one has not much left to command. We've been having glorious weather – this morning I was afraid it had broken but it cleared up in the afternoon and we had a sunset worthy of the desert itself.

There is awfully little to write about in trenches – we throw things at the Boche and he throws things back at us, which keeps us both busy mending the trenches the other fellow destroys.

It's a quiet part of the front as things go at present but we contrive to put over a thousand or two projectiles of various sizes and sorts in the 24 hours. The country is all waste – it's where the

[168]

Boche retired, – the place is full of partridges, you hear them calling in the evening between the lines. It's rather weird. One thinks of past October evenings walking down from Witch Hill with a gun on one's arm and a dog (Bruce) at one's heels. Isn't that ages ago!

There seems to be a chance that I may get a month's leave sometime after Xmas, but so often these things don't materialise, that I am not counting on it. But they more or less offer it to all C.O.'s and if it happens along I shall take it. It just depends on the war. I am going to let Arthur Duff go first though – he wants to do a bit of shooting in December I think, and I don't care if I go then or later.

The old Russky seems pretty well in the soup doesn't he – we are now getting our own shells thrown at us, which we laboured so hard to get out for the Russians – which has its comic side – especially from the Boche point of view. Gas is an awfully common weapon now, and the precautions one has to take against it are an awful nuisance. However, I think we have made the Boche regret that he ever used it. He made war more horrible than it need be and he has paid the price and no mistake. I believe by this time next year we shall have him on his knees.

The battalion had to do a demonstration attack for an American general the other day, and fortunately they did it well. He was a nice old boy and learnt a lot I think.

Love to Father. I wish you weren't in London, they'll start bombing again with this moon and the fine weather.

Your loving son
WILLIE

[DIARY] 23RD OCTOBER 1917 Another wet morning. Started the day with a bath in a basin, a slow operation, but *faute de mieux* very refreshing. Breakfast and paper work and then walked over to see D Coy which is a long way away in a place called 'The Nest'. It's an old nest of machine guns, made by the Boche – deep dugouts with concrete machine gun emplacements at the top of each stairway. The place is pretty messy on the whole, as is this place too.

Walked back to lunch and then went down to see how the

mining platoon is getting on with their deep dugout. Not very badly, but not very well. We had a bit of a shoot at the Boche this afternoon and threw about 2000 odd projectiles at him, with some effect we hope.

It cleared up again in the evening – but it's pretty cold. Played picquet with the doctor after tea – really I haven't enough to do here.

25TH OCTOBER 1917 Fine morning. The Boche spent it shelling round about here, but nothing to worry us. Walked down to see the mining platoon after Orderly Room. They are getting on well. Then went on to the Lovat Scouts O.P. It's a wonderful view of the country behind the Boche lines. One saw Boche walking about. It is odd looking at men through a telescope. You see them in the most private moments when they think they are alone.

26TH OCTOBER 1917 We are to be relieved by the 153 Bde on Sunday and personally I shall not be sorry to get away from here for a bit. One gets no exercise – and I long to get on a horse again. H.P.B. turned up in the morning and we went down to see our miners. They are getting on very well with their dugout. It came on to rain when we were out, and Arthur Duff and I – we walked on to see D. Coy – got absolutely soaked to the skin. It makes one realise the beauties of Egypt as a country to winter in. Couldn't go out again in the afternoon as one's clothes were being dried – in any case there was no reason to do so.

The Boche chucks a few shells at us here every day – usually in the morning. Have finished the only readable book here – Harry Lorreques by Lever. It's very well written and gives one a very good picture of a subaltern's life just after Waterloo.

27TH OCTOBER 1917 The Boche seem to have given the Italians a pretty bad knock on the Isonzo and I think there is worse to come. In fact on all fronts except this one he is still top dog. It takes a very lenient and understanding mind to forgive the Russian – he has cost our country thousands of good lives already and will cost us many more in the future.

Dear Father,

I am sorry to hear that you and Mother have both been laid up. We are still in the trenches. Owing to one thing and another we have had rather a long spell this time. The worst part of it is the lack of exercise – for walking about in trenches is not really exercise. It's bad news about Master I'm afraid, but I hope they will send him to Holland all the same – I can't believe that the fact of trying to escape* will count against him there. Also he must be a bit of a nuisance to look after, so perhaps they will be glad to be rid of him.

We're having rotten weather again now, I got absolutely soaked on Friday, right through everything. It was an awful day. This is a most uneventful place, we are not actually in the front line, and it's very hard to find enough to do to keep one occupied. So one's brain stagnates with one's body rather. The Boche seems to have given the Italians a proper knock. How the time does run away – we're almost at the 4th Christmas of the war, and I can see no reason why there shouldn't be a fifth. A great thing is that we get the papers only one day late now, so that one keeps more or less in touch with things and sees all about Lord Northcliffe in America and other points of interest only one day late. The national candidate got a proper knock at Islington didn't he, in spite of the prophesy of the Morning Post. I think it was very ill advised to stand.

They have now increased our leave allotment greatly, but we want to fight the point that our men only get ten days, of which at least four are spent in travelling. *Sub rosa* I have taken to increasing it according to the place they are going to, but it's against the law. But a man is out here for eighteen months and then to go home for 6 days is a bit hard, isn't it. They ought to get ten days at home. However I believe that the matter is being taken up now.

One beauty of this place here is that one can see for a very long way behind the Boche lines, and know to a certain extent what he is up to. It's rather amusing looking at Boche through a telescope, the only disadvantage being that one can't get at them to kill

*The Master of Saltoun was an inveterate and ingenious escaper, but never with lasting success.

them. But in the old original trench line, you could go from end to end and find no place where we overlooked the Boche, whereas he overlooked us everywhere.

Goodbye and love to Mother.

Your affectionate son
WILLIE

[DIARY] 29TH OCTOBER 1917 A comparatively fine day. A fortnight tomorrow since we came in to the line – and 8 days since we came to the Hindenburg line. It's an odd place this Hindenburg Tunnel. Five miles long they say, and we hold 3 and the Boche two. It's about 4 feet wide and 5'10 high and lit by electric light. Off it at intervals there are little rooms and entrances (43 steps down) at intervals of about 30 yards. The whole thing constructed by civilian contract employing Russian prisoner labour. The trench itself is about 10–12 feet deep and about 15 feet wide at the top – but now it's in very dilapidated condition and will all fall in in the winter.

We are to be relieved the day after tomorrow and go back into Army Reserve. Another chapter finished in the history of the 51st Div. as Uncle said this afternoon. Spent the morning trying to shoot partridges but they were very wild and the only one I got we couldn't find. Had lunch at Bde H.Q. which is where I met Uncle as he turned up after lunch. The Brigade on our right had a raid this afternoon, which was a success, they say – but the retaliation got several of the Argylls unfortunately. The barrage looked all right, but I did not watch it very long and the Boche retaliation comes around here – and the tunnel is the best place then.

30TH OCTOBER 1917 Had to get up early this morning as the C.O. of the bn. which takes over from us arrived at 7 a.m. Sent him for a walk and then got up. After breakfast showed him the country and took him for a good long walk round about. He went away before lunch. The day was uneventful – the Boche shelling the batteries behind us continuously during daylight – in fact right up to 6 o'clock.

1ST NOVEMBER 1917 The Bn. which relieved us yesterday was made up of fine men. But no discipline and as far as one could see, no leadership of any kind by the officers. It is sad to see it. The 34th Div. – made up of north country men – gamekeepers, miners, farmers, and it's never done any good. And the C.O. who relieved me spoke of being a 'used-up division'. And he had 500 d-ed good men in the line, which means a battalion 700 strong. And there seems to be no one to put them on the right lines. It's sad to see the waste of every sort of material out here, but the waste of human material is the saddest thing of all. Lack of knowledge is mainly to blame. Well, it's no good grousing – one must hope we are winning the war in spite of our leaders.

Here we are in Dainville – the billets are fairly good, but not too clean. Personally I hate billets and would far prefer even a moderately good camp. Office work mainly in the morning – in the afternoon reconnoitres for training ground with A.D. and then we walked on to the Brigade. It's looking awful like rain the nicht. I've an awful good billet with some amiable people, a fire and sheets on the bed. I prefer it to the Hindenburg Tunnel.

4TH NOVEMBER 1917 Church Parade. Rode over later to near Mercatel with Arthur D. to see a demonstration by tanks. It was quite interesting and the number of red hats about was amazing. Saw several fellows in the regiment, in fact we were quite a collection. Craufurd and P.W. Brown, Pelham, Dick-C, Long, Arthur D and self. Asked them all to dine on Friday evening. Shall also ask Drummond.

Also saw Bernard Paget,[*] whom I haven't seen for years and years. In India was the last time. One loses touch with one's friends and then they crop up again. Saw little Loch and Duncan in the Royal Scots, both brigadiers, and our Army Commander, Bungo.[†] And I don't know who else.

As we started back, Arthur's horse got away as he was mounting and he fell back. The brute bolted and mine followed and it was ¼ mile before I got her pulled up. His had disappeared and he got a car home. His groom caught it eventually. I rode home alone.

[*] In a later war, General Sir Bernard Paget.
[†] Byng.

5TH NOVEMBER 1917 Parades of various sorts and no excitements. It's very showery but not cold.

Bernard came to dine and we had a long buck about attacks and attack formations.

9TH NOVEMBER 1917 Had to get up early. Breakfast at 7 a.m. Brigade attack practice about 4 miles away. The weather left much to be desired – cold with heavy showers. The ground we had to traverse was very bad indeed, and the tanks were not entirely a success. Had dinners on the ground and the bn. then marched home by companies.

We had our dinner in the evening and it was quite a success. The menus were drawn by Mackie, bootmaker from Aberlour, who used to make boots for Pelham in the past and is now Arthur's servant. All had left by midnight and we turned in. It was a great pity Hammy could not come, I would like to have seen him again.

Heard a rumour last Sunday that John Mackie was missing, but now hear it was untrue. Which is a great relief. Old John could ill be spared by the regiment.

Jumbo Hope turned up in the afternoon, looking very fit for him and we had the devil of an argument as usual. He's a right good fellow.

The menu reads pretty well for the Western Front in November 1917:

MENU

November 9th 1917

Dainville

Oysters

Turtle Soup

Fillet of Plaice

Grilled Cutlets

Roast Pheasant

Cherry Tart

Scotch Woodcock

[174]

Reference to tanks indicated the immediate future. The Battle of Cambrai, including the first use of massed tanks, was about to begin and the next weeks were again a time of preparation.

[DIARY] 11TH NOVEMBER 1917 Went to church and afterwards to Communion Service. It was Presbyterian. Does it matter – I belong to the Church of England I suppose, but the sacrament is to honour Christ's sacrifice and draw from Him strength to sacrifice ourselves. Does it matter, then, the exact form it takes?

Did a lot of paper work and after lunch went for a canter across country for half-an-hour and then did some more work.

Pelham lectured to all officers at 4 o'clock, and when I got back to tea I found Jumbo Hope there, on his way back to his school. Bernard came to dinner, which was very pleasant – it's good to see one's old friends and find they are still friends.

13TH NOVEMBER 1917 The anniversary of Beaumont Hamel. We had a holiday and played some matches of the inter-company league (football) amid great enthusiasm.

The men had a special dinner. Bde sports in the afternoon, but the lorries we had been promised, to take the men to the ground never arrived, which rather spoilt things. We were beaten in the final of the tug o'war. Bn. Concert in the evening, but the minister is quite hopeless at getting up these things and as usual it went rather flatly.

Said a few words to the men at the end but forgot most of what I had meant to say. The spirit of the Highland Division is the spirit of Scotland – yes I think it is. Are we as tough men as our fathers were I wonder – I wonder? Because the trial is coming and if we are found wanting, we shall have a bitter draught to swallow. God give us strength to endure. From now on we must bear the whole brunt of this war.

17TH NOVEMBER 1917 Up at 4.15, on the march at 5.20 a.m. We had a five mile trek to entraining station and then 2½ hours in the train and a 6 mile march the other end to huts at R. – a ruined village, destroyed by the Boche when he retired.[*] A very thorough

---

[*] At the end of the Somme battle, November 1916.

job he made of it too. It is close to Le Transloy, which was a scene of very bitter fighting at one time. We have got far more comfortable quarters here than I expected. Brigade conference in the evening, but nothing much new came up.

20TH NOVEMBER 1917 Awoken in the cold of the early morning at 2 a.m. and dressed and had some coffee and an egg. The bn. moved off by companies at 3 a.m. and moved into position of assembly for the attack without incident. H.P.B. had asked me to look him up at Bde. H.Q. and I went off to do it and got lost and was wandering about the country for an hour and a half.

Zero hour was at 6.20 a.m. and the tanks which were to precede the infantry in the attack were moving forward in No Man's Land like hosts of dead leviathans. Then the barrage opened. It was a most wonderful spectacle of smoke and flame, and then the infantry went forward.

Then came the long hour waiting for news. My lads did not go forward until an hour and a half later, but Scott (5th S.H.) and I had a joint H.Q. When the news came it was good. We stood watching the battle for a long time, one got a wonderful view from where we were. Then at 10 a.m. I got orders to move up my reserve companies and my H.Q. moved forward. When I got up I found things not going quite well – but the story of this and succeeding days will be found at the beginning of my diary.[*]

21ST NOVEMBER 1917 A wonderful place this H.Q. – once the Boche bn. H.Q. and now mine. Very comfortable and strong enough to defy the heaviest shell. We have got his food too and my breakfast this morning was the best of veal and ham and coffee. Last night I fed the bn. on Boche rations. Very early this morning I got orders to carry out a further attack at dawn, and A & C Coys had it to do, aided by part of D. So Company Comds arrived and we went through the plan and made all arrangements. At 6.15 they went over and did their job almost without casualties, and very soon after I knew all about it. Just before Zero hour, all arrangements being made, I had a wash and a shave which were amazingly refreshing.

[*]Typed and stuck inside the cover.

I had sent down to Scott to tell him to make use of my H.Q. on his way forward and he arrived soon after the battle commenced, and shared my breakfast after we had heard the result. His leading companies then passed through me and we went forward together to see how things were going. The men were very elated. Soon after I again moved my H.Q. forward. It's tiring work this but exciting.

The opening stages of Cambrai were a considerable success and Willie's detailed account of operations (stuck into his diary) has at its penultimate paragraph: 'The men were very tired but very keen and pleased that the advance which had been held up the previous day had eventually been accomplished.'

Nov 22. 1917

Dear Father,

In the midst of the battle we are at the moment and in open warfare too. We started on the 20th and the barrage was a magnificent sight. Of course the chief difficulty was the wire, but the tanks made lanes through it. We had to take the 2nd objective about 4000 yards from our old line. However the tanks got knocked out by Boche Field Guns on my front just as they were reaching the wire in front of the first trench – which we had to take and my fellows came under very heavy machine gun fire and had to push off to the right. They took the trench further along but could not get all of it as the people on our left were still held up and the Boche machine guns going strong behind wire 20 yards broad. However we dug in where we were and pushed forward yesterday morning and got on well. Some more troops then went through us and we dug in again. So at present we are behind the actual fighting and preparing for another go.

It's tiring work but the men got a good sleep last night and hot food. I managed to get up the cookers yesterday and it makes a lot of difference. I was rather tired yesterday but managed to get a good sleep last night and was fresh again this morning. It seems an awful long time since the battle started. The Boche knew it was coming, he caught some Irishmen the day before and they gave it away. But he thought his wire was impregnable and never thought of tanks. However he will be counter-attacking heavily very soon. By the way I don't mean to imply that they gave it away because they were Irish; but it needs a very determined fellow to give nothing away to a good cross-examiner.

My first H.Q. at the Boche lines was the battalion commander's dugout – very strong and roomy and well-furnished. They are masters of trench construction and take the trouble to make their men and officers comfortable, and avoid a lot of sickness thereby. We got quite a lot of food and lived on excellent veal and ham and coffee and rationed the whole battalion with preserved meat. Also we got glasses and plates and knives etc. so were very comfortable.

However that is behind us now and here we are not quite so well off but not so bad all the same. It's just dark now and daresay we shall be pushed forward before very long.

I hope your cold is all right now. By the way my doctor was quite amusing on the first day. He pushed on to find a place for his aid-post and found quite a good cellar, out of which he captured nine Boche, who had been over-looked. When he was marshalling them he was sniped from a house. So surrounding himself with his nine prisoners – he is of ample habit and it took the whole nine – he advanced on the sniper, who thought discretion the better part of valour and decamped.

Well, well I must stop – so far the battle has gone pretty well, but it's not finished yet.

Love to Mother,

Your affectionate son

WILLIE

[DIARY] 22ND NOVEMBER 1917 So we are resting – in captured positions ready to go on. The men have made themselves pretty comfortable and we are re-organising after our losses. Mackay (D Coy) has lost two officers, but he has some good N.C.O.'s and we have made his coy into three platoons.

I ought to have got some sleep today, but it did not pan out quite.

We have captured some guns, the gunners of which we slew yesterday with Lewis guns.

[178]

We were offered billets in Flesquieres[*] but I thought the men were more comfortable where they were and far safer, so we did not accept the offer.

23RD NOVEMBER 1917 At about 12.15 a.m. received orders to carry out an attack on Fontaine village[†] which the 154 Bde had captured and lost again. It was not their fault they lost it – the position there was untenable with both flanks exposed.

I did not like the plan of attack at all, but the division had been ordered to carry it out, and it had to be done. But we were to be on the right and the right flank was entirely exposed, and the protective measures I suggested could not be carried out owing to lack of shells. Got company commanders together, issued orders and told them all about it. We had not much time as we had to be in position some miles away at 6.30 a.m.

One had to tell them it was a good show, but they knew too much of war to believe it. However they took it well like the good fellows they are, and I found no sign of discouragement amongst the men, when I saw them in the assembly position. We formed up in a sunken road and waited there until 10.30, when the advance commenced. It went well at first except for one unfortunate shell which got 8 men in the assembly position. Then the critical time arrived, and we came under very intense machine gun fire from front and from both flanks and the advance was held up, and it soon became apparent that further progress was impossible, owing to the exposed right flank and the great number of machine guns in the village itself. Poor old Minty was killed and many other officers wounded.

It was on the whole one of the worst days I have ever spent, we lost many a good lad to no purpose whatever. It's a sad and weary business, this war, to those who are in personal touch with the sacrificed.

In the evening we were relieved and moved back to the place which we had quitted that morning. We were relieved by the Irish Guards who had marched 20 miles that day. I hope we handed over a good show under the cirumstances. I think I did my best to make it so.

[*]About six miles south-west of Cambrai.
[†]West of Cambrai, north-east of Flesquieres.

Willie's concluding paragraphs of his account of this latter action run:

Considerable casualties had been sustained more especially in officers. All ranks were very tired and a little depressed that the operation had not been attended with greater success. It is considered that the ill success which attended this attack was due to insufficient time available for preparation, in consequence of which no reconnaissance was possible before the plan of attack was formed. In addition the necessary number of shells, and more especially of smoke shells, were not forthcoming.

After reiterating the points given in his diary entry, he ends: 'The success of the operation appeared to depend upon the enemy retiring without fighting – in the face of stubborn resistance it was doomed to failure.'

6th Gordons had been launched, with inadequate artillery support and with a right flank enfiladed by German machine guns against a defended village (Fontaine). It was an expensive and unsuccessful operation.

Failure at Cambrai after the initial success has been attributed, as at Loos, to lack of reserves in the right place. Reserves should be not only ready but fresh.

Willie consistently deplored two facets of the British attacks. First was the tendency to set over-ambitious ultimate objectives, to hope for breakthrough. Even at Cambrai, where the tanks had achieved a certain tactical surprise, this applied. Willie's experience led him to believe that limited attacks, well rehearsed and prepared and accompanied by intensive (but not protracted) artillery support, could almost always achieve initial and comparatively inexpensive success. He believed that then was the time to pause – the enemy's losses had greatly exceeded the attackers', his line was strained, and the same operation could be repeated, probably elsewhere. He criticised the continuance of attacks beyond this initial stage because preparation and planning were necessarily inadequate and because the conditions of the ground almost invariably favoured the defenders' power to concentrate rather than the attackers' ability to exploit.

But secondly, Willie also strongly objected to the pushing of troops on when they were no longer fresh. Reserves should be available for further effort if it were to be made, and reserves should be fresh; and the operations to which they were committed should be as well planned as those which preceded them.

Willie misjudged the potential of tanks. 'Useless', he was to write, 'against a good defence.' There was more in this than the tank enthusiasts were generally to admit but it overlooked the exploitation potential of the tanks – even the primitive tanks of 1917 – once the shell of the defences was really cracked. As an assault weapon against suitable and well-sited defences the tank had – and has continued to have – predictable limitations; as a means of rapidly and securely moving firepower in a fluid situation it presaged a new era in warfare.

[DIARY] 24TH NOVEMBER 1917 Our relief started yesterday, but finished today. It was 5 a.m. before we were back in our old place, and a dark wet night had not made things any more pleasant. I turned in about 5.30 a.m. and slept till 8 a.m. when the cold woke me up. Still very tired too. Later on I had a wash and a shave. Arthur Duff turned up and helped with the arrangements for our move. We were to get buses at Metz, 6½ miles away at 8 p.m. So we moved off at 3.30 and halted for tea at Havrincourt Wood. I saw Crawfurd on the way down.

When we got to Metz there were no buses, so we walked on to where we were to entrain. The men were so tired I did not dare to let them halt, so we went on slowly through the rain and cold. When we got to the station there was no train and no proper shelters for the men. It was very cold. Arthur Duff and I spent the night sitting on a biscuit tin beside a fire we had made.

25TH NOVEMBER 1917 Dawn came at last and we had a cup of tea, and had some made for the soldiers. The train eventually turned up at 10.30 – 12½ hours late – we had been waiting for it for 14 hours. It did not take long to get the men in and we left soon after. A three hours journey took us to ? where we detrained and marched to Mellincourt where the battalion is to be billeted. Got in about five o'clock; just about the limit of endurance had been reached by then.

The billets are not so bad, but not very good. A hot meal was soon ready and the whole bn. turned in and slept. I had a hot bath and a meal and eventually to a nice clean bed in a good billet at 10 p.m. My landlady is a good soul but a great talker.

26TH NOVEMBER 1917 Got up at 10 a.m. having slept for 12 hours and felt all the better for it. Breakfast at 10.30. Its a fine cold day. Had orders last night to go on a month's leave tomorrow but H.P.B. turned up during the morning and I pointed out that I must stop here and get the bn. fit again. So Arthur Duff is going instead – is gone in fact. He left this evening. Spent the afternoon and evening writing letters and the account of the battle. And after dinner brought my diary up to date.

Nov 26th 1917

Dear Mother,

A very hurried letter. We are out of it for the moment after five hard fighting days, which is about all the men could have stood. We had a great success, and a failure which cost us a lot. It was a failure because we were asked to do the impossible and a miracle did not happen, and the result cost us some splendid fellows. I was very tired yesterday evening after a week almost without sleep, but 12 hours last night have put me right again.

The general wanted me to go on a month's leave tomorrow, but I have much to do here, so I have persuaded him to send Arthur Duff instead and he went off tonight. I can't leave the bn. just when it wants bucking up and I can take my leave after Xmas instead. But it would have been nice to be starting tomorrow all the same.

I have been very busy all day – the writing after a show is always the worst part of it – accounts of the battle, recommendations for rewards etc. etc. and all the work that has accummulated during it.

It is a sad business this war when one is in personal touch with the men who die. Arthur Duff will be in London for a few days and I asked him to go and lunch or dine with you and give you all the news. I thought you would like to see him.

[182]

I think that you really can expect me home about the end of December if all is well.

Your loving son
WILLIE

[DIARY] 27TH NOVEMBER 1917 Nothing much doing. The soldiers are still resting but we are rather handicapped by non-arrival of any of the men's packs and cleaning kits. However they are all looking happier and less pinched in the face today. Rode over to Brigade in the afternoon for exercise and found Uncle and Dick there. Stopped for tea and rode home in the dark.

The billets aren't up to much, they need a lot of patching to keep out the wind and the ground all around is very filthy. Also with one or two exceptions the people don't compare with those in the majority of French villages. Have finished the reports on the battle and started on the recommendations. The outstanding feature was the really splendid work of the section commanders who have fully justified their training. But it's sad the good lads we have lost, and Minty and Crichton are difficult fellows to replace. One misses them at every turn.

28TH NOVEMBER 1917 Another day of rest for the men and they need it. But the cleaning kit only arrived this evening and then only a part of it.

Did a lot more writing and finished the recommendations, am glad to say. Rode into Albert in the afternoon and saw the wonderful Madonna on the cathedral spire leaning over the city with the Infant Christ in her arms. It is a most wonderful sight. But she seems to be kept in place by iron girders which have only been bent by the shell, and if the war is to last until she falls, then I fear there is a long time to wait for the end.

30TH NOVEMBER 1917 Parades all the morning. Started with a short talk to the bn. and then we did arms drill etc. They need a lot of that now. Got back to lunch to find Gen. Oldfield had turned up with Jack, to see the Boche director we got in the battle, which I promised him. He was awfully pleased with it. He said the Boche had been attacking very violently near the scene of our late fighting, which made me think the order we got just before lunch to be ready to move at short notice may mean something.

Had a short talk to all N.C.O.'s after lunch, and had hardly finished when we got orders to move. We had barely time to get packed up so quickly we had to go. Back to the battle again. So much for our rest.

The German counter-attacks that followed at Cambrai had a considerable measure of success. The enemy infantry were handled boldly, concentrating against tired troops and recovering much of the ground won by the British a few days before. The Highland Division was ordered (on St Andrew's Day, unfortunately) to relieve 56th Division in the line as a matter of urgency. Willie's battalion was initially in reserve, but only for five days; and rest, much needed after the gruelling battles in November, had been denied. It was a sour conclusion to the early triumphs of Cambrai. Sadly, Willie was to refer to Cambrai as 'the biggest disaster since Loos' – a pardonable exaggeration in the aftermath of disappointment and loss. In the following year, however, after further discussion of Cambrai he was to write: 'The balance remained very substantially in our favour.'

[DIARY] 1ST DECEMBER 1917 Rather unsettled as we did not know how long we were to be here. It was very cold. Also we all rose late after a late night yesterday. In the afternoon we heard we were going into the line to the north – rather a bad bit I fear. The orders for our move came late at night – we march to a village about 3 miles away starting at 9.45 a.m. Very heavy gunning to the north this evening.

2ND DECEMBER 1917 Marched off at 9.45 a.m. It was a glorious morning, but a most bitter cold wind. We got to our destination rather before 11 a.m. – two companies in huts and two in tents. The tents are pitched on a bare slope in the wind's eye. They are awfully cold and the men have no means of getting warm as you cannot light braziers in tents. The whole place is very dirty and disorganised. Every sort of little unit all over the place.

In the afternoon cut up some firewood with an axe for exercise and to get warm. We are the last Brigade for the line, but its a bad place I'm afraid and this winter campaigning is killing for the men.

Dec 2. 1917

Dear Father,

We have been much on the move the last few days. We had five days in that battle and the battalion did well and we were promised a rest. But it hasn't come off, and we are back into it again, which is a pity. I don't think there is going to be much more rest for anybody this war. What is going to happen? The Boche has now got over many divisions from the Russian front, and I suppose the few he has left there will be over here soon. Also he will have to stop in Italy before long, unless he gets down to the plains, which means more still. And all these swine at Coventry are on strike. Things look very serious indeed I think, and it's weary work.

The cold is intense now too, a gale of wind which goes right through you. One is very seldom warm. I took an axe this afternoon and cut up a tree to get warm. This is an awful grousing letter – we are not really so bad and are all cheerful, outwardly anyway. But honestly I'm looking hard for a ray of light. I think there are very difficult times ahead of us.

There is going to be more heavy fighting down here now – they under-estimated the number of troops the Boche had about. His counter-attack very nearly succeeded the other day – he did it from both flanks of the salient made by our new advance, and got right through on the southern flank and scored a very big success of which I have seen no mention in our papers. He was held on the north luckily – if he had not been, there is no saying what might have happened. And I give him credit for something more up his sleeve. He has a great deal of artillery here. The Palestine show seems all right but those sideshows are so unimportant.

That seems to have been a most ill-advised letter of Lord Lansdowne's doesn't it, more especially as there's some truth in it? At least so one would say who only knows the facts as they appear to be. I have no faith in the starvation of Germany and no faith in revolution before the end of the war. And so great an advantage are interior lines in an age of railways, that I have no faith in her complete military defeat now that Russia is out of it. If all our divisions were like this one – well it might be possible – but they're not and that's all about it. One division in ten has a capable commander and staff and about two of the corps' on the whole front. You've only got to look at our back areas to see it. No proper organisation, and incapacity everywhere. The owner of the house in which I was billetted lately – an old soldier of the '70 campaign – said to me the other day 'Do you know what strikes us Frenchmen most about your army – that those who never go to the trenches get the softest beds and the most decorations!'

I can't tell you what the men go through these winter months – one can stick being shelled in the warm weather – but cold and shells together need a lot of sticking. Many of us are under canvas and no fires possible.

There is no one who realises what the men have to stick except those who are there with them. Corps and Army Commanders may talk about it when they're home on leave but they don't begin to realise it.

This is confidential – I wouldn't tell the men they had anything like that to put up with to save my life. They are great-hearted fellows.

You mustn't take much notice of this letter, but one must have a grouse now and again, when one's face always has to be cheery and one's tongue too. But I would be awfully obliged if you would write me your view of the situation. Absolutely honestly, now that Russia is out of it, I don't think we can beat the Boche, even in ten years. And I think that the peace we could have got last year was a better one than we could get now. In this last battle the Boche has been fighting well and one has only to capture his positions to realise how far superior his organisation is in every way to ours.

We have no discipline really – it is all a case of goodwill – he has real discipline. And it does tell. He has interior lines and can bring troops from place to place on a perfect strategic railway system. We have had to weaken this front to help Italy. And how far is the Boche exhausted? I think he can go on a long time.

While *we* have America. But she is not ready yet – she has communications thousands of miles long, and when her soldiers come, they will take 8 months at least to learn the game. And they are not disciplined. I should like awfully to hear what you think about it all.

I could have come home for a month the other day, but there was a good deal to do here one way and another, so I sent Arthur Duff instead. However I hope to after Xmas, about the 28th of December perhaps. I'm very fit and full of go really, but it's a relief to get some of one's ideas off one's chest.

Harry Burn is well but looking worried. The strain is telling on him.

I hope you and Mother are fit. Love to Mary.

Your loving son
WILLIE

The Marquess of Lansdowne had written a letter to the press[*] suggesting that negotiations for peace should be considered. He had been Foreign Secretary earlier in the century when the Conservatives were last in office. The general reception of his letter – not unnaturally, considering the emotion of the times – was indignant. The Allies were undoubtedly exhausted but there was a sense that such huge sacrifices must be attended by ultimate victory and that to win was a sacred obligation. In Allied Councils, of course, the Lansdowne letter was perceived by the French as indicating a divided and half-hearted Britain, and the Coalition Prime Minister, Lloyd George, had a good deal of consequential trouble. Many people would have later concluded that a negotiated peace in 1917 would not only have saved a large number of lives but might have preserved some sort of order in a Europe which, in the post-war era, was doomed to disintegration, revolution, fragmentation, inflation and – ultimately – another war; but such conclusions were inevitably pre-empted at the time by the force of public opinion to which governments must bow. Willie's reactions – 'a most ill-advised letter, more especially as there's some truth in it' – were moderate in tone. He

---

[*]It appeared in the *Daily Telegraph*. *The Times* and *Morning Post* refused to print it.

was depressed about the course of a war which now seemed absolutely to turn on the fighting on the Western Front.

Dec 3 1917

Dear Mother,

Very many thanks for your letter. I wrote to Father yesterday with all my pet grouses in the letter. One is just accommodating oneself to the idea that the year in front of one is the worst we have had yet and that we have got to see it through at all costs to give the Americans time to get going. But one can't forgive the Russians, they have forfeited their position in the world for all time. I believe all the same that there are some good men left over there and that one could recruit an army for this front there if one went about it the right way.

It still continues awfully cold, very bright weather and freezing hard all the time in spite of the wind. However we are settling down and I have got all the men into huts which are at any rate warmer than tents. One has been on the move ever since the battle which makes re-organisation a work of great difficulty and in a few days we go into the line, and not a peaceful part either.

The direct responsibility for a battalion is a lot. You are directly responsible for the line you hold or for what the battalion does in a fight. The authorities write orders but you have all the detail to do and the task of seeing the orders carried out. Sometimes one thinks the job is almost beyond one.

I'm looking forward awfully to my leave, but I can't help feeling glad I didn't take it the other day. One thought then we were out for a long rest, but now we are back in the line, one's job is here more than ever. And Arthur Duff is really too easy-going to command a battalion. He is a jolly brave fellow though, and he's a great companion, and I miss him a lot now that he is on leave. I must stop now, more orders have just come in that I must attend to.

Your loving son
WILLIE

[DIARY] 4TH DECEMBER 1917 Got sudden orders that car would take the general and all C.O.'s to reconnoitre the line and that the bn. would be ready to move up tonight. Also secret orders that we were going to withdraw from the advanced position in the Boche front line which was captured on the 20th and which recent events had made untenable. The fact is that the attack for which they rang so many bells at home was really a bit of a fiasco, and more than a bit to tell the truth. And why? The infantry and the tanks did all that had been asked or expected, so the answer is that the plan did not contain the elements of success.

Anyway I had to rush round today. Found that the 6th B.W. could supply me with guides, so reconnoitred the line and rushed back. The bn. moved off at 6.40 p.m.

A very cold night. I rode as my foot was twisted and very sore, and very cold it was. The relief went off without incident, in spite of a good deal of gas shelling which is nasty stuff. It was a bit slow on the right owing to bad guides. The withdrawal of the Brigades in front of us also went off all right. A sleepless night though.

5TH DECEMBER 1917 Started off with Clark, who is acting 2/in/C. while Arthur Duff is away, at 6.30 a.m. and went round the line. All was quiet and the Coys were settled in pretty comfortably, though the support coy (D) is not too well off.

About 11.30 the Boche started shelling, a considerable amount coming on to our front line. Two casualties that I know of. Then he got very busy south of us and it has continued the whole day. I think he must be attacking down there. Our guns have been going too. H.P.B. came round just as I got back to H.Q. and later on Uncle Harper turned up with Dick. We walked up to the left of the line, but I did not encourage him to go along as the Boche was on it at the time.

Did some writing, in fact have been fairly busy all day. Saw a wonderful sight in the evening, an aeroplane caught by the sunset. It suddenly sprang from the dusk into flame, it was hard to believe it was not on fire.

The frost holds, it's going to be very cold again tonight. I pray it does not turn to rain, I don't think the men are fit for it.

6TH DECEMBER 1917 The frost continues, fortunately, for although it's cold, it's dry. The front line is very bad, the trenches having been dug on no known system and being both shallow and narrow and in a very bad state of repair. There seems to be no system at all in higher formations, no one lays down what a trench is to be like, divisions do exactly as little or as much work as they please and as the majority please to do nothing – the result is inefficiency rampant everywhere. We are wasting men by needless sickness and casualties, and the final result may well be the loss of a war, which at one time promised certain victory. When one has been out here since 1914 and still sees the same old mistakes, the same old lack of organisation – one is apt to lose faith in the higher command and in our ability to win. And the men are splendid – if we win it will be in keeping with the traditions of the British Army – it will be in spite of, not because of our commanders. It is horrible to think of the public at home ringing bells over this last battle* which they have been deluded into thinking a victory, and which is in fact – as Uncle Harper says – the biggest disaster since Loos.

Our H.Q. here are fairly comfortable but by no means shell-proof. The Brigade is concentrating on constructing a new Support Trench. We had a hundred men working tonight.

Dec 6th 1917

Dear Father,

How goes it? We have been back in the line again a day or two now. Luckily the weather is fine though very cold. The wet is the worst thing for us. I suppose everyone is beginning to realise that the joy bells were rung a bit too soon. I was very surprised when I heard that the country was waving flags – there was nothing to wave about even the second day, and it was at its best then and should have stopped. We have had a hundred lessons but we never seem to learn. It's the one day show where you end up with the balance in your favour – we all know it but the authorities don't seem to. The break through is an impossibility until the Boche is demoralised, and the war will be won by killing Germans and saving our own men and no other way. Which we did not do this time. But there it is, cavalry tactics applied to a situation with which only artillery and infantry can deal are bound to end in

*Cambrai.

failure. Luckily we did not know the details of the show when we went in, so we went with high hearts.

Another thing is the authorities have gone mad on T.s.* and they are useless against a good defence. I can't write much but I will tell you more when I get home. And every T. means fewer guns and shells and mechanics for other purposes. Guns and shells and aeroplanes will win the war, nothing else. The rest is fantasy and imagination – all right once in a way for a little surprise but no help to win the war. When one has been in the show and thinks it out after, one knows. Defence is so easy against those things. The show down south, of which I told you I had seen no mention in our papers, was far worse than one knew then and was very near a catastrophe on a huge scale.† It was partially retrieved by a fortunate combination of circumstances. We still have the cards in our favour, but there is no doubt which side possesses the military talent. We are an army of civilians after all.

I am very busy and happy in the work and quite cheery really, though again this letter does not read it. But I've told you facts and we have got to face facts and we are bad at doing it. We are too apt to flatter ourselves and bury our heads in the sand.

My leave has been sanctioned and all being well I should be home about the 29th or 30th, and am looking forward to it.

Goodbye and love to Mother and Mary.

Your affectionate son
WILLIE

7th December 1917

My dear Mother,

I've been in the wars rather lately – I twisted my ankle slightly in the battle and have been so busy ever since I've had no time to rest it. However its gradually curing itself. This evening I was walking back from the trenches across country in the dark and I ran into an iron spike. It went clean through my leather boot and into my leg inside it. However it's not very serious.

I am pretty busy all day, there is a good deal of writing to do

---

*Tanks.
†The German counter-stroke at Gouzeaucourt and Gonnelieu.

one way and another, and constant supervision and application of ginger where required (which is nearly everywhere) keep one fully occupied.

We took over a sector (as usual) where practically no work had been done – and what had been done, done badly. So there is a great deal to do.

Thank you very much for the Novena – I think it is helping an awful lot. I feel full of energy and go really, and the men are doing very well under somewhat unfavourable circumstances. They have had a very hard time lately.

The frost has gone and I thought it would be rain today, but it held up. I'm hoping it won't rain while we are in the line, standing in water would be very bad for them just now.

There's a good deal of artillery activity round about here, it hasn't settled down yet after the show. I'm living in shelters behind a bank and we have a deep dugout to run to if the Boche gets too unpleasant. Only it's not completed and very uncomfortable, so that one does not take to it if one can avoid it. I'm having it made properly and when finished I'm going to make it really comfortable, and then I hope that it will be more used.

Your loving son
WILLIE

[DIARY] 7TH DECEMBER 1917 Managed to get one company, or rather most of it, back into reserve yesterday, which makes the men safer and more comfortable. We are holding 1300 yards of front with 2½ coys and I would like to do it with two companies, but the lack of a trench system properly constructed for defence makes it impossible for the present.

The thaw is coming, S.W. wind and it looks like rain. Uncle Harper and Dick were up this morning and we walked up to the support line. However the Boche was shelling the front line pretty hard and you can't allow a Divisional Commander like Uncle to poke his head into a shell. I had already been round the line in any case.

The Boche always gets more active at night here and he has started shelling the Strand, which is the road we walk up to get to the line. There are no communication trenches.

What a bleak country this is. With the ground white with frost and made whiter by the light of the moon, and over all a thick mist, it must equal the desolation of the south pole. At night the few signs of the presence of man which are visible by day, are blotted out. As one walks along one almost doubts the existence of other men. And then a line of dark figures materialises out of the mist. 'Who are you,' you ask. 'Ration party 6th Gordons', comes the reply, and the line disappears into the mist and again you are alone.

10TH DECEMBER 1917 It's not a bad day on the whole – very, very clear. The Boche was rather busy with his guns all the morning and put a few near the new support trench where we had a party working. No damage done however. We are to be relieved by the 6th B.W. in the evening.

I waited in all the morning to see H.P.B. who never turned up until lunch time. Then the Corps Commander turned up too, and between us we told him just what we thought of many things.

Campbell and his bn. turned up about 5.30 and the relief went off very well, except for A. Coy. Their guides lost their way and delayed matters 3 hours. One did not mind a bit being kept all that time, but what did make one furious was the thought of the poor devils who were to relieve us trekking about for 3 hours unnecessarily. I was very angry. Got away about 11 o'clock in the end, met the horses a short distance away and rode back to camp. It was a cold frosty night, full of stars.

Dec 12th 1917

Dear Mother,

Very many thanks for your letter. Of course I suppose the Boche is feeling the war too. And it's just as well, because there is no doubt that from a military point of view he has got everything on his side. However he may not be strong enough to take advantage of it. You know, as things are, we should be much stronger if we were fighting the Boche on this front only and had not got Italy to bolster up. It seems rather a doubtful question how much good the divisions from the Russian front will be to him. I think he had drafted most of the fit men to this front before.

If he gets back all the prisoners from Russia that will be a gain. But of course he has a huge number of Russian prisoners working for him now. Only we aren't efficient or properly organised, our trenches are bad – all our arrangements are bad except the rations, wherever you walk you see inefficiency rampant. However, I suppose it's all on the knees of the gods, and one must just do one's own bit as well as one can. But one isn't helped – one is fighting difficulties all the time that one ought not to have at all, and it uses up energy one ought to devote to other things. And the result isn't satisfactory. It's lack of organisation and system and knowledge at the top.

Personally I think, and am not the only one by any means, that it's a great error to have cavalry soldiers in supreme command everywhere.

We are out of the trenches for a few days, but have not got a proper camp and all is mud. The bn. is split up all over the place and it makes discipline and cleanliness so difficult.

There was very heavy shelling this morning and I thought the Boche was attacking our front, however it was a bit to the north as it turned out, and the final result we don't know yet. But I think there is more fighting to do here yet before Christmas. It's pretty cold but not so cold as it was. As a matter of fact that frosty weather suited us down to the ground as dried things up – but the thaw made an awful mess of things.

Jim Burnett has got a Brigade – I wish it had been in this division. Normally I ought to get away just as we finish our next tour in the trenches. We only had two men slightly wounded last time, which I ascribe directly to your Novena, because we had considerable shelling one time and another.

Love to Father and Mary.

Your loving son

WILLIE

Willie's strictures on 'Cavalry Soldiers' presumably meant Haig – although he never, in later life, joined in the criticisms of the Commander-in-Chief, whose steadfastness and strength of will he undoubtedly admired. Of the other British Army commanders, Allenby and Gough were cavalrymen (to whom Willie made no direct reference) as was Byng whom he knew well and much respected. The general sentiment, however, was widely held.

[DIARY] 13TH DECEMBER 1917 Both yesterday and today we were woken at dawn by a very heavy bombardment which continued till about 8 o'clock. In each case the Boche was attacking somewhere up at Bullecourt, but we have no real details yet. But one thing seems certain, that the Boche has got the initiative on this front at the moment and I cannot see what is to prevent him keeping it for the present. I'm afraid I have been worrying very much about the war recently, one sees the weakness and inefficiency on our side very clearly – but perhaps the Boche suffers in the same way. Though one sees no sign of it in his trenches and we have been in them often enough.

Heavy shelling at intervals all day today – personally I think the Boche will attack along the whole of this sector soon, but he has one or two minor operations to do first to give himself a favourable kicking off place.

Commanding a battalion gets harder every day, men taken away for this and that and its so difficult to keep one's organisation. However one carries on somehow. We really *need* six weeks rest and training to make the battalion really efficient again. We could do it in that, now – soon it will take far more. One gets very tired at times and one's temper is apt to be very short too.

I am looking forward to my leave, but even so, one half wants to stop with the battalion.

14TH DECEMBER 1917 Dull day with fine rain in the morning – Started parades this morning, the men are not looking too bad. Seton who is commanding B Coy is most unsatisfactory. I don't think I can keep him.

H.P.B. has gone off for a trip to the base and eventually I believe to Paris – we shan't see him back for a few days I know. Did promotions in the afternoon, it's always rather a difficult job. One's days are pretty well occupied – I must try and get out for a ride tomorrow, but the days are so short now.

There has been less gunning today than usual.

The 'Times' had a leading article on the 12th demanding an enquiry on the fiasco at Gonnelieu and demanding that those responsible be *dégommé*, and 'pon my word I think they are right, though why it should be left to a newspaper to say these things I don't know. I wonder if the country is at last growing tired of rule by second-rate politicians, as the army is of rule by incompetent idiots.'

15TH DECEMBER 1917 Was woken at dawn by the sound of bombs bursting not far away and the unmistakeable hum of the Gotha. After a bit I got up and went out to find a glorious morning, though very cold and the Hun flying quite low right over head. Fortunately he dropped no bombs very near us. A Lewis Gunner with nothing on but a shirt was firing at them frantically and the shells from the A.A. guns were bursting round them, but apparently quite harmlessly.

Parades all the morning. I found a place where we can make an excellent range with a little work, so started a party on it right away. Unfortunately they struck chalk in digging the markers gallery, which makes it slow work.

Went to a lecture by Uncle in the afternoon and he was quite amusing. Dined with the Division in the evening and we talked all sorts of heresies about the high command. True heresies all the same. I'm not sure that is not a 'contradiction in terms'. Afterwards played bridge and got home about 12 midnight.

Willie was awarded the DSO for the November fighting. He was also again mentioned in despatches.

Dec 15th 1917

Dear Mother,

It's fine frosty weather which suits us better in the trenches than out of them, because of the bombing. They were over at dawn today and dropped a lot of stuff, but fortunately did little damage. Enormous great machines they are. I was standing looking at them and they came right overhead but did not chose that moment to let go their bombs. I can't pretend to like being bombed, but prefer it in daylight to the dark. Normally we shall have just finished our next tour in the trenches when I get my leave.

I suppose you have seen the despatch, the staff part of it. It's an awful farce, I was trying to think of all the dud divisional commanders I knew of – some of whom have been sacked – but they are all mentioned – every one. I haven't been able to think of one staff officer whose name is not in that list, and they will most of them get DSO's, so you see what I mean when I say that it's not a thing of great value now.

What do you think of our battalion Xmas card – but no, you won't get it as soon as this because I haven't sent it off yet. Everyone said it was too high class and not what the men would like – but the proof of the pudding is in the eating and we are almost sold out now. I got 1500. It's sold to officers at Frs. 1.20 and to the men at Frs. 0.60, which tickles the men's fancy I think – they feel for once they are not being done down. They cost about £26. a thousand.

Arthur Duff is in London and I daresay he will roll up at No. 1 on day – he said he would anyway. There's no more news than usual, war is a dull game even when it's exciting, because it's the same sort of excitement in nearly every case. I rather enjoyed Nov 20th though, until they insisted on pushing on and made what might have been a magnificently successful show into a reverse. We knew what would happen, but the General Staff is very slow to learn. They've been too long at the back of the front, what we want is some new blood in high places, then we may get something done.

We were all glad to see that leader in the 'Times' the other day. A good many thoughtful fellows are losing – have lost! – confidence in many things.

Will you thank Father for his letter – I won't answer it today as I am writing to you. Love to him and Mary.

Your loving son

WILLIE

[DIARY] 17TH DECEMBER 1917 Woke up to find the ground white, and snow still falling, and a most bitter wind blowing.

Parades were impossible so we confined ourselves to lectures and similar pursuits.

It's awful weather to be fighting – it makes one feel they did things far better in the old days when they knocked off for the winter and started again when the fine weather came. We are in divisional reserve, which means that if there is an attack we move up right away. So let us hope there won't be an attack.

One can almost enjoy this sort of weather at home when one comes back to a house and a warm fire, – but for campaigning – well I prefer the summer. A week tomorrow is Christmas day, the 4th Christmas.

The range is finished but this is no sort of weather for musketry.

19TH DECEMBER 1917 Another day of frost and snow, but without the wind, which made it more bearable. Some parades as yesterday. Lunched with H.P.B. at the Brigade and heard the news from the base which is very little. He and Weston had gone on to Paris and had got snowed up on the way back, with the result that they had to finish the journey by train.

It's awfully hard to keep one's feet warm – one walks and they get warm, one stands for a moment and they freeze. The floors of these huts are so cold too.

Found time to destroy a lot of papers this evening which is something off my chest, and wrote some letters. Among them one to the father of a lad Duffus who was wounded on the 23rd November and died of wounds in hospital. He was a splendid chap, one of the best. How long must it go on?

Dec 19th 1917

Dear Father,

Very many thanks for your letter, which hits the nail bang on the head. The sky is black, but we've jolly well got to do our job and be damned to the Boche. I've been thinking it all out and have come to the conclusion that if we are fighting this time next year with our tails well up, we shall have cracked the hardest part of the nut. It's a sad business though, I have heard of the death from wounds of another of my officers, a fine fellow.

It's most bitterly cold, snow is on the ground and the frost is very, very hard. You open the door of your hut and an icy draft blows in. The difficulty is to keep one's feet warm. One walks and they get warm, stand for one minute and they are icicles again. The floors of all the huts are so cold.

We go in to the trenches again in a day or two and when we come out I hope to get away and join you all for Mary's wedding. I am in great hopes George will be there. He and I have not had a jaunt together for a long time now. It was most excellent news to hear that Master had been transferred to Blankenberg, especially if it's as cold in Bocheland as it is here.

There is a thick mist tonight which has its advantages as the Boche aeroplane cannot see where to drop his bombs. Otherwise with a moon and snow on the ground it's a grand bombing night. I think we may expect a very big effort by the Boche here shortly, but not just immediately as the weather is against it. To attack in this weather means exposing one's men to incredible hardships – also it's very hard to get one's guns into position with frost and snow on the ground. However we shall soon know more about it.

It will be awful good to be home again for a bit – I'm rather feeling a rest wouldn't be a bad thing – it's rather a strain when one's officers change as quickly as mine have recently.

Your affectionate son
WILLIE

[DIARY] 21ST DECEMBER 1917 Very cold and freezing hard. The morning was very misty but it cleared up later – in the afternoon. The whole battalion paraded at 9 a.m. and went off to dig trenches for instruction. They worked very well indeed and incidentally learnt a lot, which I hope we shall put to good use when we go back to the line.

Saw the men who got Military Medals for the 20th and 23rd of November, at 2 p.m. – or rather as many of them as were available, 10 out of a total of 19.

Tomorrow we go back to the trenches – not those we occupied before, but a sector a good deal further south, where I think the Boche is a bit more active.

22ND DECEMBER 1917 Fine day and very clear, which is not exactly what we wanted for the relief. We were not able to go in by daylight, which would have been an advantage. The morning of the day one goes into the line is always a rotten time because all orders have been issued and everyone is busy packing up and carrying out inspections, and a C.O. has no one to inspect and nothing much to do.

We moved off at 2.45 p.m. The march up took longer than I expected and we did not arrive until 5.15 p.m. – we were due at 5 o'clock. However there was a brilliant moon and the relief went off without a hitch and was complete by 7.30 p.m. It was very quiet fortunately.

After dinner I went round the line with the gunner liaison officer – a fellow called Frater, which he said was a corruption of Fraser, but I suggested that he was of Quaker stock and his forbears had taken that name as a token of their beliefs. However, he wouldn't have that.

The trenches were far better than I expected. Only I hope the frost holds while we are in the line – one can put up with any cold. Got back about 12.30 a.m., had a cup of cocoa and turned in.

23RD DECEMBER 1917 Breakfast about 9.15 a.m. and spent the morning doing routine work and going round the reserve line. H.P.B. turned up with the C.R.E. and Gemmel – had a word with him about one or two things. After lunch started off with Archibald and went round the line except a bit on the left. It's pretty quiet, but the Boche is more active than he was in our last sector. We are really on the battle-ground of Nov. 20th here – which explains it.[*]

There is no defensible trench system, I need hardly say – nothing but a bad front line. We are all digging like beavers or moles trying to make one. Bn. H.Q. is a fairly comfortable place and we have a dugout to run to in case of need. But the Coy. H.Q.'s in the line are not up to much. Got back about 5 p.m. It's going to freeze again all right.

[*] In the Cambrai sector.

Dear Mother,

I write from Bn. H.Q. in the line. We are in a different sector from last time, but although the trenches are a good deal better than in our last place the Boche is a bit more active with his guns. However I am trusting in the staying power of the Novena.

It's most wonderful weather, very cold but dry. Yesterday and today were wonderful days, and the nights are glorious. But everything has its disadvantages and as I write I can hear the umph, umph of the Gothas going over with their loads of bombs for the back areas. We are working hard, because here as elsewhere, there is no possibly defensible system and one is at a loss to know what our predecessors spent their time at. Though really it is not their fault – they were merely ignorant. G.H.Q. has never laid down what a defensive system is to be, or the dimensions of a trench or anything else and the result is nothing is done on a system at all. However! Bn. H.Q. is very comfortable and we have a dugout in case of need! I am sitting in front of an excellent wood fire as I write.

I do wonder what the Russians are going to do, because if the Boche makes peace with them on their terms, he's rather done. But of course he can dictate what terms he likes if it comes to that. I wonder why a democracy always produces men like Trotsky and Lenin.

Your loving son
WILLIE

[DIARY] 24TH DECEMBER 1917 Awoken at 2.30 a.m. by the devil of a bombardo on the right and a minor one on the left. It sounded like the Boche attacking on the right – only its an odd time to do it. However it was not on our front, where all was more or less quiet. Fine day but very hazy. H.P.B. came up in the morning and we walked round the line. Took rather a toss and bruised my left knee, so am now a bit groggy in both legs. Working parties did very good work indeed last night.

25TH DECEMBER 1917 Christmas Morning – well it's thawing in spite of the date and the ground is getting very messy. 'Uncle' and H.P.B. came up about 11 o'clock. Asked them both to lunch later on and they went off to the right. Went up to the line after they left. The Boche was busy on the left coy. front with field guns, but did no damage to speak of. One man was killed this morning in one of the wretched shelters our predecessors erected in the front line. It makes one furious. The officers responsible for the construction of this front line ought to be tried for manslaughter.

26TH DECEMBER 1917 The world was a wonderful sight this morning, covered in its mantle of snow – the sunlight reflected off a million million tiny prisms. Seems a pity to sully its purity with shells and spatter it with blood. Had a moonlight walk last night to see a wiring party and don't know when I have enjoyed a walk more.

Spent a busy morning as the general decided to keep us in 8 days – which meant an inter-coy relief this evening. However got the orders out in good time.

After lunch walked up to the right sector, and had to do a bit of gingering up. Seton is not up to the mark and I fear there's only one thing for it. Came round by the left and so home. Heard that we have got 8 Military Crosses and 4 D.C.M.'s for the last show, but the fellow I wanted most to get a Military Cross has been left out – Mackay. It's very annoying. The inter-coy relief went off without incident and was completed about 7 p.m. Bright moon but thick mist this evening.

27TH DECEMBER 1917 Very bright clear day. The Boche opened operations by shelling about this H.Q. at 6 a.m. It is the result of a battery which came into position just behind us last night and opened fire. He shelled here all the morning and wounded 4 men. I was up in the line most of the time. The old Boche was pretty active with his guns everywhere today.

Went up again in the evening and wandered about seeing working and wiring parties. The night was very cold with a most brilliant moon, and the snow made it as light as day. Grand night for digging and wiring – there one's thoughts end these days. Bit of shelling when we started out but it quietened down later. Got back about midnight and turned in after a cup of cocoa. Very tired and sleepy.

28TH DECEMBER 1917 1 a.m. woken up by the Boche chucking shells at us – must really start a deep dugout which is habitable. Again at 4 a.m. Too sleepy to worry much. H.P.B. came to breakfast with MacDonald, after an early tour round the line. They had great appetites and ate a tin of sausages apiece.

30TH DECEMBER 1917 Went round the line in the morning instead of starting for Boulogne. However it matters not. *Je suis philosophe* which means 'What is, is best', and anyway a wire has come from Arthur saying he will be back tonight.

The 7th Argylls arrived to relieve us at 4 p.m. and we got away about 7 p.m. The coys marched out as they got relieved. I got a lift down in an ambulance. There was a tremendous bombardment on the right at 7 a.m. – the Boche was attacking at Ouzancourt and got a bit of our front and support lines. We counter-attacked in the afternoon, with what success I know not.

Have arranged a car for tomorrow to take me to Amiens, whence I train to Boulogne – if Arthur turns up. No sign of him at 12 midnight. So I turned in, having played a rubber of bridge with Uncle Harper.

31ST DECEMBER 1917 Very heavy gunning in the small hours – wonder if this is to be a great battle with the Boche attacking. Was called at 7 a.m. and at that moment Arthur arrived. He had missed the train at Charing X on the 28th and from that moment his troubles began. He crossed on the 29th, left Boulogne on the 30th. The train broke down and it was only by good luck that he arrived at the 11th hour so that I could get away. Dressed and breakfasted – pouring good advice into Arthur's somewhat tired ear – he had not been to sleep for 24 hours – between mouthfuls.

At 8.30 started off – Gray* with me. We got to Amiens at 10.15 and I found there was a train to Boulogne at 11.5. Went off and bought some fish for the mess and sent it back in the car. Met a very good fellow called Benson in the train – in the Oxford and Bucks. He is comdg. a London regt. and they hold the line near Poelcapelle. They have had a rotten time. We chatted away and told each other tales of war and of the good old days before the

*Private Gray, Gordon Highlanders, was Willie's soldier-servant.

war. An excellent lunch, too, helped to wile away the time, and in a very short 3½ hours we were at Boulogne. Found there was no boat until 10.15 tomorrow morning so booked a cabin and went off to Folkestone Hotel and engaged the best room I could get. After tea and a luxurious hot bath and behold me sitting in my room, writing the last page of my diary of 1917. An excellent dinner is next on the programme, made more enjoyable by the anticipation of England, Home, and Beauty tomorrow.

Goodbye 1917 – you have brought much sorrow to the world, but perhaps a little happiness mingled with it. Goodbye my diary – I have cursed you at times when I have been sleepy after a hard day's work – but in keeping you I have kept the resolution which I made on page 1, just a year ago. Therefore you have my thanks.

Welcome to 1918, only try to do a bit better than 1917 has done, old thing.

VII
The Last Crisis
1918

[DIARY] JAN 1ST 1918 The commencement of Vol II of this most interesting work, my diary. I awoke in Boulogne and Laurence Carr and I breakfasted together off a whiting and an excellent omelette. Food is of importance during the first day of one's leave, after which one takes it for granted. *The Boat* sailed at 11.15 and we reached Folkestone without incident, except such as was provided by a cold and choppy sea.

Thus Willie began 1918, as 1917, in England. His sister, Mary, was married on the second day of his leave and there was a large family wedding in London – with the sad aftermath of the loss of her husband, Commander Jack Codrington, Royal Navy, before the war's end. 'There is a lot of talk going on about peace,' Willie recorded on 3 January, but he didn't believe it. The Allies were at sixes and sevens to judge by their public statements. Lloyd George made a speech on war aims on 5 January which, Willie recorded, 'seems to form a basis on which peace might be made – but not yet.' Meanwhile President Wilson 'is saying that he will never make peace with the Hohenzollerns.' But – mistakenly – Willie wrote on the same day: 'A military defeat of Germany requires three more years of War – are we ready to suffer this and to pay the price? I know not.'

During his leave Willie heard from his brigade commander, Harry Pelham-Burn, that he had been selected by the XVIII Corps commander, Sir Ivor Maxse, to command the Corps School. Each corps in France ran its own training school; and Maxse, a great and gifted trainer, minded a great deal about it. It was a flattering appointment: Willie's battalion was no longer serving in XVIII Corps but Maxse had noted him well during the battles of the autumn 1917, Third Ypres. Willie was predictably sad to leave his battalion, but command in battle was a wearing

[207]

business and there can be little doubt that some relief from it was
timely – although as the dramatic events of early 1918 unfolded
he often recorded his feelings of guilt at being behind the front.
Away from home at the time Willie wrote to Bryanston Square.

Chartley Castle, Stafford
Jan 14th 1918

Dear Mother,

I have a bit of news for you which will please you and Father I
think, though my feelings are rather mixed. Anyway I have been
ordered to go and command the XVIII Corps training school.
Maxse who commands the Corps apparently asked for me, and
Uncle Harper said 'Right O.' It's a safe job and supposed to be a
leg up towards a Brigade, but I'm awfully sorry to leave the 6th
G.H. and I'm not at all sure I want to command a Brigade, having
always been rather against very young Brigadiers. However there
is no choice in the matter – it is an order and that finishes it – not
the Brigade I mean, but the training school.

It's awfully quiet and restful here – you know the sort of west-
country look in a place, not strenuous like the east coast. I shall be
up on Thursday. They have got a great concert on Wednesday in
aid of the French Red Cross, which they were very keen I should
stop for, so I said I would. It's going to be a very good concert too.

The machine gun course at Grantham was very interesting, and
I was awfully cold and the cold gave me awful gip where the
dentist had been at work. I came here by Notts. and Derby – I
hadn't been in Derby (where I had to wait an hour) since the days
when Master was down there. I wandered about, but it was dark
and I couldn't recognise any of his old haunts. With love to
Father.

Your loving son
WILLIE

During his leave, too, the family received news that the eldest son,
the Master of Saltoun, had been at last exchanged and allowed to
travel to Holland. He had been a prisoner of war for three years
and four months.

There were air raids on London most nights, and more often than not Willie recorded walking home to Bryanston Square after theatre or dining out amid the sound of deafening gunfire. 'These air raids are a nuisance,' he wrote on 29 January. 'They killed a lot of people, too, on Monday.'

[DIARY] FEB 4TH 1918 Said goodbye to Mother and Mary and Jack at the house after an early lunch. Father came with me to the station. The train left at 2.15 p.m. I hated going back as much as usual. Gen. MacNaghten C.R.A. 15th Div. was crossing too –this is third time consecutively we've travelled in the same boat. I made his acquaintance the first time through his lending me some money without being asked, and he has done me a good turn every time. Today I shared his cabin. Got to Boulogne without incident about 7 p.m., but the Folkestone Hotel was full up, so I had to take a room in the Hotel de Paris, which is rather dirty and smelly. Also I find that my train goes at 7.35 tomorrow morning which is too beastly early for words. By George, it's quite extraordinary what a different sort of place Boulogne is according as to whether one is going home or coming out again! But it's always sad too in a way – I always remember how happy we were, Billy and I, on May 28 – 1916 when he was going home to be married. We shared a room at the Folkestone Hotel – how I *hate* this war.

FEB 5TH 1918 Had to get up at 6 a.m. to catch the early train to Amiens at 7.35 a.m. – Benson (comdg. a bn. in the 58th Div.) was in the train too. Got to Amiens at 11.35 a.m. and after some difficulty managed to telephone to the XVIII Corps to arrange for some means of locomotion onward. They promised a car about 3.30 p.m. Lunched in Amiens at a funny little place called 'Les Huitres' which Benson translated 'The Lobsters', and where we had a very excellent lunch. Eventually left Amiens about 4 p.m. for Ham, about two hours run. However about ¾ of an hour out of Amiens we burst a tyre and had to put in a new tube which took some time, and when we started off again it was getting dark, and we had no lights. But in France, luckily, most of the main roads are straight. They are rather wonderful, these

French roads. Driving along in the gathering dusk, the trees on either side meeting overhead, it is rather like going along a giant passage and at the end there is a sort of pale light (the sky framed in a circle of branches). But you never reach the light.

Eventually we got to Ham and I found L. Carr. Found a billet at the main hotel which is a very dirty, grubby place. The Germans when they retired collected all the civilians from the surrounding country into Ham, and then proceeded to destroy all the villages. Ham itself they left intact after taking away everything worth having. There is no doubt that among the 10,000 civilians they left behind there is a good mixture of their spies. It appears that it is certain that the Boche is going to deliver a tremendous attack at this part of the line, and everyone is busy with preparations to meet it.

My school is at a place called Caix not far from Amiens, but I have to stop here for a day or two first. Turned in about 11.15 and slept like a log in spite of the small grubby room.

Ham is twelve miles south-west of the town of St Quentin, which was just behind the German lines. 'The Boche is going to deliver a tremendous attack at this part of the line.' He was indeed. This was the German offensive, the last – and greatest – 'Kaiser' schlacht', officially christened by the Germans 'Operation Michael' and informally referred to by their soldiers as the 'Hindenburg stakes'. Ludendorff had recorded in November: 'Our general situation requires that we should strike at the earliest possible moment, if possible at the end of February or beginning of March, before the Americans can throw strong forces into the scale. We must beat the British.' And there were no doubts whatever that the continuous flow of German reinforcements from the now non-existent Eastern Front towards the west meant that, at last, German power was virtually concentrated against the Allies in France and Flanders. That power had been gravely weakened by the previous four years' appalling struggle, but it was still formidable. In the west the Germans now had the numerical edge. The point of attack – the sector south of Arras, a frontage of forty miles just east of the old Somme battlefields – had been chosen. Three German armies, totalling sixty-three divisions, had been nominated. The blow would fall primarily on the British Fifth Army under Gough – four corps with twelve divisions. The second of these, numbered from Gough's right south of St Quentin, was Maxse's XVIII Corps.

[DIARY] 6TH FEBRUARY 1918 Had an interview with Maxse – the Corps Commander – in the morning. In the afternoon did nothing at all. It was a wonderful day from the point of view of the weather. In the evening read 'The Fortunate Youth'. Dined with the Corps Commander, and we had a talk about various things. Bed early.

8TH FEBRUARY 1918 CAIX Another rotten day as far as the weather goes. Left Ham at 10.15 with Carr and motored to Caix to take over the XVIII Corps school. It has only recently moved here (3 weeks ago) and Caix had been left in a most appalling mess by the French, whose ideas as far as concerns sanitary arrangements of every description are almost prehistoric. Three weeks hard work has made a great improvement, ovens and cookhouses, washing places, etc. etc. are springing up and in another month or so there will be a tremendous change. Lack of labour rather hampers things. There were 50 Boche prisoners detailed for work here, but after one day they complained that they had too far to walk to their work (4 miles each way) *and the authorities supported them.* So they no longer work. It is astounding.

Spent the day visiting the whole place. There are three subsidiary training establishments attached, ie Lewis Gun, Signalling and Gas schools. The place has been very well run as far as administrative arrangements go, one can see that – have not seen any of the training so far. But the Chief Instructor – Hill – seems an excellent chap. It seems his hobby is archaeology, and he has chanced upon some most interesting discoveries near here. Some reindeer bones and horns, which latter are very rare I believe, and flint instruments of various dates, some fashioned (he says) 400,000 years ago, between the two glacial periods. I never knew man existed 400,000 years ago.

[211]

It's not a very easy job taking on a school like this, and will need hard work to make it a real success. Especially when one has not much experience of this sort of thing. However it can be done all right.

9TH FEBRUARY 1918 CAIX My first whole day at the school. Spent the morning partly on parade and partly looking round the place. Did a lot of work inside in the afternoon, preparing an address for Monday, and reading a multitude of papers. Did some of the Pelman course in the evening, the first I've done for a long time.

There is one schoolmaster, O'Hanlon, among the instructors – he seems rather a good chap really. We had a talk at dinner about that book, 'The Loom of Youth', which was written about the school at which he is a master. He said it was very clever and very cruel – all the characters are recognisable at once and true to life. And perhaps the description of the house in which he (the author) was, is not too bad either. But apparently Waugh was a pretty vicious boy himself – it's a biography, the book, and surely all biographers have been lenient to their own vices?

Heard some more interesting geological facts this evening from Hill – in another 300,000 years another glacial period is coming for the earth due to variation of the angle of its axis. It's a nuisance of course, but I don't think I shall alter my mode of life. At any rate it will end the war.

HAM 15TH FEBRUARY 1918 Lectured on Training – Laurence Carr and Abbott turned up about midday and we walked round the school. After lunch the three of us went to Ham. Met Guy Campbell there, who is now Camp Commandant with the 36th Div. Went to the cinema in the evening where the secretary of the Navy League, Hannon, was lecturing on the Navy. It was very interesting for the men, who applauded vehemently. Made the acquaintance of Oliver Nugent commanding 36th Div. who was there. The Boche was over and dropped some bombs and broke a lot of windows and demolished one house. Fortunately there were no casualties. He gave the army a much worse time – the first day they have been in their new headquarters – which show that his information is pretty good. There were 15 killed and 30 wounded in their village.

HAM 16TH FEBRUARY 1918 Went and watched Levey doing some of the drill etc. demonstrations he is going to do for the Conference, and then went and examined the hole they made with a bomb last night close to Tom Holland's billet. Saw madame his hostess – a wonderful woman who is 63 and looks 40. Then he and I went off round some of defence organisations. It was a glorious day and we had a most pleasant walk for 3½ hours or so. He is a most pleasant and capable fellow but his legs are very long.

We shared a sandwich on Manchester Hill, and he explained his plan for winning the war. Which is a colossal raid to a limited depth with tanks – and come back.

We had a wonderful view of St. Quentin, as it did of us. The Cathedral overlooks the whole world behind our lines, and the town forms a comfortable residence for as many men as the Boche likes to put there. Because we are not allowed to shell it by the French. It is of course a beautiful town, beautifully situated, and at present almost in the Boche front line.

We saw some very good dugouts constructed by the French, they are very good at that sort of thing, though the trenches which they construct are laughable.

We walked through a lot of ruined villages, but the country has a less desolate appearance than in many other places. We got back about 4 p.m. with a great appetite for tea.

The Boche was over bombing again this evening, but did not drop anything on Ham. It is very cold.

17TH FEBRUARY 1918 Bright and cold. In the morning Laurence Carr and I walked down to the Corps Reinforcement Camp, and looked over it. It seems to be a well-run, going concern. It is commanded by a fellow called Bridcutt, now a lieut-colonel, once Sergt-Major of the Coldstream Guards. He is a fine type, and a real gentleman as so many of our old non-commissioned officers were. His H.Q. are now in a chateau once used as H.Q. by Prince Ruprecht of Bavaria, and he has never been so well-housed in his life, and appreciates it accordingly.

In the afternoon the Conference opened with an address by the Corps Commander. The Army Commander, Gough, was present and all the Divisional Commanders, Brigadiers & Commanding Officers in the Corps. The object of the Conference is to get – if not exactly uniformity of training – at any rate all training done on a really sensible and thorough system. It is almost extraordinary how few officers do understand how to train, or to organise for training. If one can judge by results, that is – to hear fellows talk one would think that every battalion in France was splendidly trained.

The Corps Commander's address was excellent in every way and very much to the point. If the result of this show is to wake fellows up and to promote discussion on these subjects of training, a very great deal will have been achieved.

18TH FEBRUARY 1918 The day commenced with a lecture by Lt. Col. Levey. He is rather a remarkable fellow in his way. His father was a Pole, who married a Scotswoman from Aberdeen. Levey enlisted originally in the Scots Guards where he made his mark in various ways as a non-commissioned officer, and was later made Sergt-Major of the Chelsea training school, where he was at the beginning of the war. Later he was at the Crystal Palace with the Naval Division, a battalion of which he afterwards commanded. He was my predecessor at the XVIII Corps School. Most certainly he does understand training, and is in addition a really brilliant lecturer. But this morning I think he did exaggerate the inefficiency in the matter of training which is prevalent in battalions, which rather put fellows backs up.

In the evening Laurence Carr explained the Corps defence policy. There seems to be little doubt, or at any rate it seems highly probable, that the Boche will attack here, and what we are aiming at is to get plenty of depth in the defence – to defend the tactically important points, and to provide as little cover for him in his advance, as possible. There was a short discussion on various subjects after Carr had finished.

Very heavy gunning this evening from about 7.30 onwards. It sounded away up north, but I believe affected the northern division of this corps too. Is this the commencement of the Boche offensive? *Je ne le crois pas.* I think that will be a bigger show and I don't think it will start at night.

19TH FEBRUARY 1918 Another glorious day, but very cold. I heard my servant, Gray, breaking the ice in my basin when he came in to call me this morning. We started off with another talk by Levey – he has got a most wonderful gift of the gab – followed by some more demonstrations of simple methods of training. After lunch he talked again, and then the Corps Commander spoke on the subject of the defensive battle, illustrated by some lessons from our reverse at Cambrai.

It is quite a mistake to imagine that Cambrai was a victory for the Bôche. It was on the contrary a decided success for us, diminished to a certain extent by a partial enemy success, the result of faulty training and a lack of appreciation on the part of commanders as to how to organise a defence in depth. But the balance remained very substantially in our favour. And what we have to do now is to train so that such a thing cannot occur again.

20TH FEBRUARY 1918 Dined with one of the syndicates of officers, and they had quite comfortable quarters and a very good dinner and presented me with the menu afterwards. We talked about their bns. and the things that came out were positively astounding. We have been holding a training conference of Brigadiers and Bn. Commanders and any amount of generals on the subject of training, and we made them enthusiastic. But it's no good – they are not organised, the battalions are not organised, and they CAN'T train. The state of affairs within battalions in this matter is incredible. I have never been so astonished in my life.

22ND FEBRUARY 1918 Two colonels of the 66th Division turned up this morning to see how we did things, and stopped all day. One was a fellow called Norton who was in my syndicate at Aldershot. Then in the afternoon came a training fellow from the Fifth Army H.Q. for the same purpose.

I tried an experiment this afternoon – we had a conference and got all the officers to air their grievances and hear what they thought about things. It was quite a success and some quite interesting facts came to light, as illustrating the extraordinary lack of organisation and method in some battalions.

23RD FEBRUARY 1918 Awoke to find the sun streaming in at my window. Today was really a spring day, and how it managed to follow yesterday is more than I can tell. Being Saturday it was a half-holiday and I seized the opportunity to go to Corbie. Drove most of the way in an ambulance, but walked the last mile and a half.

First of all I went to the church. It's an awfully nice church, and looking at one as one goes in is Billy's memorial tablet. As I was coming out I met Hutcheson. Then I went up to the cemetery. Now knowing the way I asked a little lady who was going along the road, and she looked so sad and white-faced as she told me where '*les pauvres anglais*' were buried, that I thought she was going to cry almost. Billy has got a happy place for his long rest, looking out across the valley and the river. Later on in the year it will be lovely. But his grave needed attention rather. I saw the lady who looks after the cemetery and she promised to dig and plant some new flowers. Madame Duboile, the lady who writes to Pam, had not been there for a long time – I think she has had a bad knee. I went to see her on my way back, but she was away from home.

There is a tremendous atmosphere of quiet and peace at Corbie, and I love the place where the cemetery is, away from the houses, looking right out into the distance, so quiet and close to God. I almost seemed to feel Billy's own self about the place for a moment. It was a happy day. I picked a leaf for Pam from each plant on his grave.

I can picture the procession as they carried him to where they laid him, the whole road lined with soldiers carrying wild-flowers, with which they covered his coffin. Death seems a little thing out here, but not his death – he never said a word to anyone without leaving him a little happier – the men loved him and trusted him as no-one else. I'm sure he likes the place where he is lying, he always liked high-up places and distant glorious views over flood and field to the far-away hills. Darling old Bill.

HAM 28TH FEBRUARY 1918 Started off with a lecture on training, followed by some demonstrations. In the afternoon more demonstrations on how to teach the soldiers to dig. In the evening a lecture from L. Carr on the Corps Defence scheme. The audience seem quite happy. Great wind up today – a few days ago they caught a German aviator who professed to have seen the Boche orders for a general attack between St. Quentin and the Scarpe – to take place on March 2nd. Today the R.F.C. reported big concentrations on this front. So everyone is standing to, ready for all eventualities, and the guns are moving up.

MARCH 1ST 1918 The conference continued. Delivered two more lectures on training and gave some demonstrations. In the afternoon the coy. commanders asked questions and L. Carr and I answered them to the best of our ability.

Last night the Boche raided all along the French front from Switzerland to the junction with us – mostly abortive according to the French report. Went to the show at the Corps theatre this evening, given by the 36th Div. troupe. Just before dinner a heavy bombardo started – on the front of the Corps on our right. The B. has been cutting wire at two points on our front during the day.

Tomorrow is *the* day if the aviator was right. There seems to be a strong idea that they will use tanks, and if they attack tomorrow, its probably true, as there can only be a hurricane bombardment lasting a short time.

Another aviator has been captured, who at first refused to give any information, but subsequently volunteered that the Boche troops covered the ground as far back as the Rhine – that in and round Laon they were so thick that you could not see the ground –that the attack was to start at once, with Paris and Calais as the objectives. So we shall see what we shall. Tomorrow possibly we shall be in the middle of the greatest battle of the war. I wonder if it's true – I can't say I have believed much in the Boche offensive since the happenings in Russia – he seems to have so little to gain and so much to lose.

The bombardment had ceased by the time I went to bed – midnight.

March 3rd 1918

Dear Mother,
I have been very busy lately with more training conferences,

but today is a holiday until the evening. We've gone back to winter after 6 weeks of spring, and the ground is white again. But the snow is wet and messy as it always is at this time of year.

I see they think the Boche is going to propose that both sides chuck bombing open towns, and I expect he thinks that the moral effect in Germany is greater than it is in England and France. But I would agree to it all the same – I think it's horrible dropping bombs on people who aren't in the war. I suppose the Boche is going to attack here, and I think it's the best thing that could happen from our point of view, because there is no doubt that we can hold him and a successful defensive battle is *the* way to kill Huns. These training conferences that we have are the best things going, because one discusses organisation as well as training and method of fighting and we get into direct touch with every officer in the Corps, so that everyone sings the same song. One really does feel that it's doing good. Most fellows are very keen but they get into ruts – very deep ones – and it's hard to get out of them when one is commanding one little unit in a wee bit of trench. And these conferences wake them up and promote discussion and *in time* action follows. All the same, one isn't always too happy sitting behind when one thinks there may be something doing up where the battalion is. It takes some getting used to.

I have been away from the school for some days now, but the work of getting the place into shape is getting on very well. Though occasional contretemps arrive – for instance I have just heard that the R.E. officers made a mistake with the drainage and the dirty water from the baths has been draining into the drinking supply. So the well has to be pumped dry and we have to start again.

I hope you and Father are both fit. Goodbye.

Your loving son

WILLIE

[DIARY] MARCH 7TH 1918 Hard frost early, but warm later on. We had rather an interesting fellow who came to lecture today, Dr Irvine. The son of a shoemaker in Co. Antrim, he left Ireland to try and find an education and wandered to Glasgow, where he found a job in a coal mine in place of an education. There he came across Professor Drummond who advised him to clear out. He went to Glasgow with intent to enlist in the Guards, but he had an accident there with a whisky bottle and when he woke up he found he was a marine. He enlisted in the army in order to learn to read. He learnt that and some other things too, for he knocked about the world, was mess waiter on a man-o'-war, where he learnt how to talk from studying the officers. After serving 7 years he came home and matriculated at Oxford – at eighteen the only book he had ever spelt through was *John Halifax, Gentlemen*. But he knew it was good and he memorised it, ten pages at a time, and when he could get away alone in the woods he spoke it aloud. Perhaps the trees and the birds understood the ideals and enthusiasms which came pouring out with the words. Well, Oxford proved too expensive, and after a year he left and went to America. It took him three years to get to Yale, but he got there and graduated there. And became a minister, – until he met Jack London, when he discovered that the religion he served was too narrow, and he was no longer a minister. He did some writing and later was professor of English literature at an American Military Academy. Then the war broke out and he came back after 28 years, to try and repay, as he said, some of the debt he owed to the British Army. I was rather attracted by him and we had a long talk.

CAIX MARCH 8TH 1918 The days are wonderful and full of spring, and the trees are budding and the earth looks so brown and clean. I watched an old French *cultivateur* digging this morning and I thought I could dig and dig and be happy all my life. With books and books to read. I finished 'The Beloved Vagabond' this evening and that is how Paragot finished his search. Got on to my old horse this morning and rode about looking at the work going on, and he thought it was a wonderful day too, and chucked his old heels in the air for sheer joy of life.

The 'Intelligence summary' today talks of an impending Boche attack on this front, with lots of tanks which sound like an improvement on ours. So perhaps he will attack and we shall have a great battle and we shall win.

CAIX MARCH 9TH 1918 Saturday – and a half-holiday. I rode over to see the VII Corps School in the afternoon, near a ruined village, Foncancourt. They are in the country from which the Boche retired, so there is no cultivation and they have all the world for a play-ground, but a bleak desolate world it is. However they have got a very good camp and arrangements, having been there for nearly a year.

Rode home across country and found quite a good track. Found an American general, Alexander, had turned up in my absence from the 51st Div. where he had spent a crowded and apparently happy ten days, and had come away full of praises of Uncle Harper. He was a nice fellow – they all seem to me very natural, these Americans, – they haven't got our self-repression or distrust of the world in general. He said, 'Well, I reckon this job seems bigger and bigger, the closer you get to it.' Which after all is a natural phenomenon – the closer you get to a mountain, the bigger it looks. But you've got to get close to it if you want to climb it. And when you start climbing you find that there is a way up even those precipices which looked unclimbable from the foot. Many of us out here have been close to the mountain for too long, and we are so busy trying to climb that we are unable to say if we are close to the top or not – we can only see the little piece of rock out of which we are trying to hew a foothold for another upward step. Even the guide can only plan a few steps ahead.

MARCH 16TH 1918 The course broke up and till Monday we keep holiday except for the clearing up which is always necessary. Went for a ride to the 50th Div. H.Q. at Harbonnieres in the morning, but all my friends are gone almost. Col. Cartwright is on some job at the base and Gen. Wilkinson home on 6 weeks leave. Then went via Guillancourt to Marcelcave, where my old Brigade is billeted. At Guillancourt I fell in with a small boy, and the two miles between Guillancourt and Marcelcave we journeyed together. He had come to see his brother off to the front, –who took the train from Guillancourt in order to pass by Viencourt on his road from Marcelcave; Viencourt where 'sa bonne amie' lived. The story of his short life (the boy's) unfolded itself as he trudged beside my horse – how he had had one brother killed on the 26th October last year, and how he (the brother) had expected to be killed on that date. On parting he had told his family, 'if you don't hear from me soon after Oct. 26th you will know something is wrong,' and on that date he was killed at 1 a.m. The old father was a musician, as were his father and grandfather before him – they have an old violin which belonged to the latter still. Now they all till the soil as '*ouvriers*'. Then there is the sister who marred a '*cultivateur*' and is no longer '*bonne pour eux*'. She has three cows, two horses, and four pigs, as well as some chickens. As her husband is at the war, her father and my small friend sometimes go and work for her, but she never gives them anything in return.

His mother is dead, he has another sister of sixteen, and a brother of five. In Marcelcave, a place of 1500 souls, there have been over 60 killed and many with limbs amputated. As we wandered on together along the dusty road, he seemed so small and so solemn, though every now and then he became a child again. I gave him a cigarette which he smoked with great gusto.

I found no one I knew at Bde. H.Q. – so cantered home across country. After lunch I sat in the sun in the garden and finished '*I will maintain*' – Marjorie Bowen. – I know why Pam liked it so. 'God has me by the hand' – that is what made William of Orange so wonderful.

Walked down later to see where Hill is digging for stone implements. I had a dig myself and found one or two quite good ones. When we got back we had some quite good games of badminton. Must really write some letters tomorrow. I think a table in the sun tomorrow morning.

The Boche attack is due to start tomorrow – the latest excitement is a very large number of funny looking dots on the aeroplane photographs of country behind his lines. They are thought to be tractors for getting ammunition forward for the guns in attack – there are now between 800 and 1000 opposite the Corps front.

MARCH 18TH 1918 Went for a ride in the morning. And in the afternoon the officers arrived for the first platoon Commanders' course. Dr Vaughan Cornish also arrived and lectured on the strategic geography of the world – very good lecture, but he's not a particularly attractive fellow. Laurence Carr also turned up and they are both stopping the night. He told me some astounding news – that the Boche has made a peace offer of Alsace-Lorraine to France in exchange for Madagascar and Cochin China (French), we to keep the colonies, and he to have a free hand in the East. And the French, backed by the Americans, are very keen to accept it. To me it's appalling – it's a complete Boche victory, and it means another war in the very near future, one would think. It sounds too awful to be true. They say that is the reason why the Boche has not attacked so far on this front, and indeed it's hard to think of any other reason. If it's true we may have peace by the end of the month. But there is not much elation in the thought of such a peace. Another piece of news – in a certain area recently, 2000 yards square, our high command with customary wisdom, had crowded 10,000 men. The Boche soon found this out and dropped 150,000 gas shells into the area and caused 4,100 casualties. Only 1 per cent was fatal, but the remainder were out of action for a time. Such events make one think of peace at any price.

They are sacking fellows right and left now, it seems, perhaps the man responsible has got the boot – one hopes so.

MARCH 19TH 1918 Got another lecture off my chest this morning. Then Hill carried on with demonstrations. The object of this 5 days course is to show the platoon commanders how to teach their men – a good system – preparation, explanation, demonstration, execution, interrogation, repetition. Those are the six words. Then, what to teach their men, in a simple way. Also to expound clearly the principle of depths in defence, and briefly to explain the Corps plan. So that in the end we hope to have comparative unity of thought and effort throughout the corps. It really is useful I think. L. Carr was to have gone on leave from here this morning but was recalled just as he was about to start. It seems they got some deserters last night who stated positively that the Boche intended to attack tomorrow morning, so perhaps he does. We shall know tomorrow morning. It looks as if the rumoured peace *pour parlers* had broken down.

Had rather an interesting talk with Vaughan Cornish after lunch today. His view is that if the French got Alsace-Lorraine and we keep the German colonies, we could almost afford to give him a free hand in the east, were it not for breaking faith with Serbia and Rumania. That it would be an armed peace, which would bind France, America and ourselves together and would possibly be better medicine for our national soul than a really victorious peace which would enable us to disarm. Perhaps!!

Anywat, I'm sure of one thing, that we shall have to stop economising on Imperial Defence after the war if we are to continue a great power. But these days one not only has to show how to defend the Empire, but *why* it should be defended, a point which it never occurred to us to raise before. And of course it can be shown, and conclusively, but it needs time and careful thought. And again Education must play a large part in our national defence scheme, – if we continue to economise in that we shall go down. As the Church refuses to teach patriotism we must teach in the schools.

The weather has broken, and rain rather interfered with our programme this afternoon – if it's wet tomorrow I don't know what we shall do. All the same the Boche attacking troops won't like it either – they won't all be under cover probably and there is nothing like a few hours in wet clothes to damp the ardour of mind and body.

Orders for the great German offensive had been issued on 10 March. In the southern sector of the front, where Willie was, Von Hutier's Eighteenth Army had the initial task of breaking through and reaching the line of the Somme, before further deep advances directed on Amiens and Montdidier. It was planned to be – and it in fact became – that phenomenon which had eluded both sides for three and a half years – final end to stalemate, the forcing of the enemy's trench system, restoration of open warfare.

The technique and tactics were brilliant. Despite Willie's prognostications tanks were not used. Fog helped the attackers. The assault was led by specially picked and trained 'storm troops', supported by gas; and was preceded by a very short, concentrated bombardment of great intensity, aimed at paralysing Allied communications, especially artillery communications. There was no attempt by the attacking infantry at keeping formation or 'lining' up after a stage of the advance – instead the orders and the training were for the infiltration of small groups, armed with a very high scale of automatic weapons, which would be reinforced instantly were they successful in penetrating the British wire and defences. Only success would be reinforced.

The day was fixed – 21 March. At 4.30 a.m. on that morning the British artillery positions and headquarters of Fifth Army – and the southern part of Third Army to their north – were subject to the fiercest hurricane bombardment most of them had ever experienced. Two hours later it was the turn of the front-line trenches. And three hours after that the German storm troops began moving forward. Their success was uneven: many parts of the line held firm, and it had in any case been recognised that the 'outpost line' would probably need to be given up in whole or part – the British defence was in considerable depth. In certain sectors, however, German penetration started to erode the fabric of the British position. There were, increasingly, withdrawals 'to conform'. What followed was nightmare. Willie's school at Caix was about twenty-five miles behind the initial front line; news –and rumour – was uneven in quality.

[DIARY] MARCH 21ST 1918 The Boche attacked this morning but the news that we have even yet is very scanty. Everyone is so busy that one cannot bother for news. As far as we know he launched 40 divisions over the bogs, on the fronts of the 3rd and 5th Armies. In most places he has been held up in the forward zone, but in places he has broken the battle zone. On this corps front he has everywhere been held up in the forward zone which is good. I don't know what the frontage is, but it must be about 50 miles in all. It is very hard to concentrate on work back here, when the greatest battle of the world is being fought on our front. All day the air has been full of the rumble of guns – since ten o'clock last night it has been continuous, though it died away at dusk this evening. One feels it more almost than one hears it, it is in one's mind all the time, even when one is asleep. Tomorrow this intensive course ends and the other two are postponed – indefinitely I should think.

Went for a ride with Hill this evening to get some exercise and shake off one's anxiety.

Have just had a message (telephone) from Carr – the reinforcement camp will probably move here tomorrow. The news is not so good now – Apparently the Boche used about 50 divisions, and he has taken the forward zone on the whole front of both armies, and in many places has penetrated the battle zone. We still hold the battle zone on most of our front, but he has got to Grand Serencourt which is behind our battle zone, on the front of the right division. Also he is shelling Albert, which looks as if he had made a big advance there, for it was 25 miles behind the line. Of course he may just be using a long naval gun. Anyway, to sum up, the position is very serious, I don't think the day can be called a reverse for the Boche. There is a lot of shelling going on still, and if he manages to launch another very big attack tomorrow – and I think he will – things may get very serious indeed. All these ammunition tractors will enable him to feed his guns.

MARCH 22ND 1918 The battle continues. As far as one knows the net result of yesterday was that the Boche captured the forward zone on the whole front of the Third and Fifth Armies, except part of the northern front of the Third Army which was not attacked. But almost everywhere he was held up at the battle zone, i.e. the Corps line, – although he penetrated it on the III Corps front on our right and on the front of our right division, which necessitated a withdrawal across the St. Quentin Canal. The line last night was very much as shown on the map.[*] This morning was comparatively quiet, but a thick fog enabled the Boche to prepare unseen for another attack. Luckily a deserter gave us warning. Unfortunately for the moment we are outgunned, as many of ours were captured yesterday. At 12 noon he attacked again with 10 divisions (making a total of sixty used since yesterday morning), but on our front at any rate made no progress. His objective was Ham. He has managed to push forward north and south of Honlon Wood, and tonight we shall withdraw from it voluntarily. The 61st Div., who were holding the Honlon Wood sector, the centre of the Corps front, never budged from their battle zone throughout the attack, so they must have put up a very stout fight. Apparently G.H.Q. are very

[*]Willie drew small maps on the pages of his diary.

cheerful – they say that the Boche attacked everywhere in masses and that the gunners had a magnificent target and the slaughter was great. Also that they have captured a map showing the Boche objective for 2 p.m. today 15 miles in advance of where he is now. So if that is all true it is satisfactory, but the battle is not over yet and it does not do to be too optimistic when one knows very little. It is hard to keep an even mind, and to remain unswayed by rumour.

Some of the staff of the Corps Reinforcement Camp, which has been moved here from Ham, have arrived and are firmly convinced the war is lost, mainly because they were gas-shelled and are tired out. It was a glorious day, when the fog lifted – went for a ride in the evening with Hill. We visited a village near by and found the H.Q. of a G.H.Q. Flying Wing, who told us that the R.F.C. were doing very well in this battle and had downed a lot of Huns. A ride is good for the liver, and keeps one's mental equilibrium in order. There is still very heavy gunning going on. The Boche came over here and dropped two bombs at the edge of the village while we were at dinner. It's a brilliant night, almost full moon and there is a lot of bombing going on.

23RD MARCH 1918 The third day of the battle. It is most glorious weather. It's quite impossible to say what is happening. This morning the Boche got through Ham and advanced towards Nesle, apparently from the south. It seems as if the Corps on our right had given way completely. Apparently in the afternoon we counter-attacked and drove the Boche back to the neighbourhood of Ham. They have pushed up some more troops, apparently the French are ready to assist us too. Nesle has been badly shelled and the Corps has moved to Roye. The country is full of refugees from Nesle and Ham, also from Rosieres which has been cleared to make room for troops. They are a most pitiable sight, with the few possessions they have been able to take with them in wheelbarrows and ramshackle carriages.

The air is full of rumours – as an example a despatch-rider sent from Army to Corps H.Q. came in here this afternoon and said he had been to Nesle which he had found deserted and where he had seen Boche Cavalry – thence to Roye* where he found the Signal

---

*Caix is about ten miles north-east of Roye.

Office packed up and the Corps gone. On enquiry it all turned out to be false and I sent him to Roye again. Another rumour is that we have attacked at Paschendaele and have advanced 8 miles on a nine mile front. I hope this is true, the only thing that lends colour to it is that this front seems to have been kept very short of troops. We have used divisions very sparingly, the 20th (only the 4th division used by the corps up to date against some 15 Boche ones) was not engaged until this afternoon, and until then we had not counter-attacked at all. It would put a different complexion on things. However its probably as untrue as the average rumour. We have also heard that the Boche has captured Peronne. So one does not know in the least what to think. I am unable to think that we are unable to deal with affairs here without French assistance, so prefer to believe that there is something doing in the north. One is very helpless – my command at the moment consists of about 180 men, the majority of whom are unfit for general service – and a vast quantity (about 80 lorry loads) of stores. So if we have to move we shall have to lock up most of the stores and leave them. We shall make a funny spectacle marching down the road. It will be marching in the wrong direction too. However I fear very much that we shall have to move. Had a long letter from Mr Wallop today, which had been opened by the censor.

LATER – The Boche have got Peronne,* that means our line runs behind the Canal and not far east of Nesle probably. Things are moving fast, but everyone appears content except the poor French refugees. I prophesy that we shall have to move from here tomorrow which will be a nuisance.

24TH MARCH 1918 It's an impossibly beautiful day and really hot. Everything is growing so fast, the trees are hurrying all they can to catch up with the butterflies. The air is full of these and the busy humming of the bees. And it is still March really. The battle is still raging furiously, but the situation appears to be in hand. The Boche attacked this morning – the results we don't know yet. Here we spent it organising the permanent staff so far as is possible in order to fit them for eventualities. And in packing up everything possible and generally preparing to move so far as we

*About twelve miles away.

can. At least that is how everyone was employed except myself who, having given the orders, retired to the garden and read 'The Pastor's Wife' in the sun and listened to bees and the trees growing. And the distant sounds and shoutings of people on the roads, and aeroplanes and the rumbling of the guns. One cannot be in the battle, so it is no good thinking about it – but this morning I read in the paper that the 51st Division had put up a magnificent show and I'm sure the 6th Gordon Highdrs. had a finger in the pie. One longs to be back with them. This is such a helpless job in a battle.

LATER – The pie is getting more mixed. Persistent rumours in the evening that the Boche was at Chaulnes. 19th Corps H.Q. having come to Harbonnieres I went up there to find out the situation. The Boche was not at Chaulnes, but the news such as it was decided me to send the school off at once. Got them on the march about ten p.m. with the fields beyond Moreuil as their destination, Hill in command. We have 80 lorry loads of material (every sort of thing from a lamp to a Lewis Gun) spread all over the village, and only two lorries to move it. Sent off some of the important stuff at once – the lorries to return for more. Just as they were moving off there was a sort of panic alarm – Boche cavalry on the road from Rosieres.* Went up to see what was happening – naturally there was no truth in the rumour, but could not find out who started it.

The Boche has dropped a lot of agents from aeroplanes, dressed as British officers, whose job is to spread alarm and despondency. We then picketted the roads with men from reinforcement camp and examined everyone coming in.

March 24th 1918
Dear Father,
    I am sure the London air is full of rumours, so just a line to give you a rough idea of how things are. The Boche as you know attacked on the 21st on a big front. He got on a bit in places and by the afternoon of the 23rd at one place he had got rather further than elsewhere. That was rectified the same evening, and by that

* About 1½ miles away.

time the position was good, as the Boche had calculated on being about 50 miles into our lines by then. So he must be a somewhat disappointed man. He attacked again this morning and I don't know with what result but I think the position is quite sound now and he probably achieved nothing. There seems to be quite good ground to suppose that he has had pretty considerable casualties. Everyone has got their tails up and feel that whoever is winning the battle – it certainly isn't the Boche. However it's not finished yet by any means.

One is very much out of it here, I wish I was back with the 51st Div. I hear it has done magnificently. I have had little to do – one takes all the precautions one can and prepares for eventualities and then sits still. This morning I spent in the garden with a book – the weather is really glorious. So you see my share is not a very exciting one so far.

The most astounding rumours abound here – so what they must be like when they get to London I can't imagine. We have just got some official news in and it is decidedly good. And really more than that I cannot tell you for the moment, – the situation really is satisfactory, and there may be even better news in the near future.

Love to Mother.

Your affectionate son
WILLIE

This letter was more comforting – and probably intended so to be – than accurate. Gough had ordered that the line of the Somme (between Peronne and Ham) must be held at all costs, but the Germans forced a bridgehead across the river that day, and the general situation was not far from desperate.

[DIARY] 25TH MARCH 1918 In the morning I got orders from the XIX Corps to get all our corps reinforcements organised into battalions so that they would be available for use as such. Got in touch with Bridcutt, who commands them, and he put the job in hand. All this time we are out of touch with our corps. I was certain however that they would disapprove, as these reinforcements form the nucleus on which the divisions will have to be reformed. Bridcutt did his job with celerity and efficiency – he was sergt. major of one bn. of Guards and has learnt in a good school. Helped him as far as I could with Lewis Gun and small arm ammunition.

In the afternoon managed to get in touch with XVIII Corps H.Q. and told them what was happening. They were very perturbed and – as I learnt afterwards – protested to Army, who at first sided with them, but later decided the other way. Meanwhile Bridcutt had moved to my H.Q. so that we were in close touch. About 4 p.m. Landon and Thorburn turned up from the Corps and while they were with us orders came from XIX Corps for Bridcutt to send up the two bns. he had formed to assist the 24th Div. They were rushed up in lorries.

All my arrangements were complete and the lorries and loading party moved off at 7.30 p.m. Lebell and a few men were left as guard over the stores left behind, with bicycles and orders to remain as long as possible. Just as I was preparing to leave, Daly (Comdg. 24t Div.) turned up – he told me that his division mustered about 1500 rifles all told. A liaison officer from G.H.Q. happened along at the same time. The heaviest fighting is west of Bapaume, where they are back on the old battlefield of the opening days of the Somme, and names like High Wood and Marincourt again figure in present history.

Rode to Corps H.Q. with Law, who took my horses on to Rouvrel,* where the school has found billets. Had dinner there. The Corps is normally to be withdrawn now, the French having taken over, but one never knows what may happen. Much of our difficulty is the result of forced reliance on the French, who, although very good when they start, are notoriously unreliable. Reliability is a great virtue.

Corps H.Q. is in an enormous chateau at Moreuil† and the staff all look somewhat tired. They have moved three times in as many days. Rejoined the school by car, and found a comfortable billet, where I slept like a log.

MOREUIL MARCH 26TH 1918 Went over to Corps H.Q. in the

*About four miles west of Caix.
†South-east of Amiens.

morning. Wished to move the school back further as their present position is very unsuitable. Corps agreed, so returned to Rouvrel and got them packed and started off by 2.30 p.m.

Corps H.Q. remained at Moreuil. The situation in front was more or less in a state of flux all day. The Boche did not make any big attack, but he tested the line in various places and kept pushing on up the valleys. Our men are all very tired and they have lost a lot of officers – the result is that they are rather inclined to walk back even when not attacked. The French too, who have troops intermingled with ours, are not very inclined to fight the Boche – one suspects that they have orders to support us morally, but on no account to become seriously involved. So the general trend is a slow advance on the part of the Boche.

We got a few prisoners yesterday including a battalion commander, who was in possession of some very interesting documents – the original orders issued to him for the attack on March 21st and the accompanying map. It appears that up to four hours previous to the attack he did not know it was coming off. He had been told that we were expected to attack and that extra troops, guns etc. were being brought up to resist it. This story sounds improbable though, especially in view of two Alsation deserters who came over and told us all about it.

Four hours before zero hour (according to this bn. commander's story) he was handed sealed orders, and a map marked with lines of advance down to companies, all worked out by the General Staff. He had to follow his lines with the aid of a compass and go as far as he could. It requires a high standard of training – we could not do it. Throughout the battle the Boche has proved himself very well trained, – he is an expert at dribbling forward in small parties and getting round our flanks. When a gap is found light signals are put up to show the place, and he starts working up from all over the place to the weak point. When enough men are collected the attack is launched. What helps him, too, is the fatal idea in our army that you must retire if your flank is turned – so he keeps trickling forward and we keep trickling back.

Got a billet, but just as I was about to turn in at 1 a.m. the old housekeeper turned up and asked who had given me permission to sleep there. I told her, but she remained unpacified, because – she said – the lady of the house had forbidden that anyone should ever sleep in the room again. It belonged to her son who had been killed. However I had nowhere to go to and was very tired so we came to an agreement and I turned in. Personally I had no scruples – had I been killed, I should be only too pleased for my bed to furnish rest for any weary soldier, so long as he was not a Boche.

They have been evacuating the people from the country east of the river Avre today – it is a most piteous sight to see the people trekking off – the few poor possessions they have been able to save pushed before them in wheel-barrows or perambulators or any sort of dilapidated box on wheels. Often you will see a child's toy tied on among the rest. I met two old ladies from Caix on the road. 'Ah,' they cried, 'c'est Monsieur le Commandant qui était à Caix.' I asked them how far they were going. 'Ah, nous ne savons pas. Les Boches avancent, nous avançons aussi.' They were following their blue line without a map or any training save the pitiless stress of war. They take their fate very differently these people – some weep, others are quite cheerful – true philosophers. 'C'est la guerre' they say, and shrug their shoulders with a smile.

MOREUIL MARCH 27TH 1918 It appears that the morning is always the time when disquieting reports come in most frequently, and this morning was no exception to the rule. The Boche has apparently pushed up the banks of the river on our southern flank and into some large woods in that neighbourhood – two battalions are reported to be concentrating in that direction. We informed the French, who have now taken over command of the front (General Mesple, a dear ineffectual old gentleman with long white moustachios). 'Oh,' said the Staff Officer, 'we are just about to counter-attack – in two hours we shall be here'; and he pointed to a line on the map well to the east of the reported Boche concentration. 'The two battalions – bfff!!' and he waved his hand in an airy way.

However the counter-attack did not materialise, for the reason that the division he had said was to carry it out was twelve kilometres away. They are extraordinary fellows the French! Later we heard that the French 22nd Division had run away and uncovered the southern flank of the division on our right and they had had to swing their right back, and were heavily engaged. Later the Boche developed strong attacks against the XIX Corps on our left and the French on our right. He progressed a bit, mostly to the south, where he pushed the French across the Avre and captured Montdidier.

ST SAUFLIEU[*] MARCH 28TH 1918 Spent the morning in the office. The 61st Division (Colin McKenzie) which has been sent up to the XIX Corps, counter-attacked the village of Lamotte this morning and captured it, – a pretty creditable performance for troops who have been fighting hard for eight days and had 60% casualties. They were however obliged to evacuate it later in the day. The Boche also made some progress west of Montdidier, although the French regained some of the lost ground later on.

Went over to Quevanvillers with Monty in the afternoon to see the school. Of course they are not functioning as a school at present. They had found quite comfortable quarters. The whole country in rear is a mass of refugees from Amiens and the district east of it, and Hill and Rochfort had organised all their forces to feed them and convey them to Poix where they can entrain for safer regions.

Visited Bridcutt on the way back. It was dusk and pouring with rain when we got home, terrible weather for these poor refugees, who many of them fail to find shelter at all. After dinner there were rumours of a debacle on the XIX Corps front, but they proved to be quite untrue. The other excitement was a spy who had been telephoning about the country asking for locations of troops – but on investigation he proved to be not a spy at all.

Then we got orders to move the school and reinforcement camp to Abbeville tomorrow – so we had to send off Special D.R.'s and generally get a move on. Rumour has it that Gough has been *dégommé* and Rawlinson has taken command of the Army. The latter part is true, but I don't think G. is *dégommé*. Foch is C-in-C of the whole front and probably likes R. better than G.

Turned in about 1 a.m.

It was not, in fact, until 3 April that Haig told Gough he was to give

---

[*]To which Corps HQ had withdrawn the previous evening.

up command and go home. There was demand at home for a scapegoat. The scapegoat was Gough. An inquiry was demanded into the reasons for the 'setback' on the Somme – in effect into the conduct of Gough's Fifth Army.

MARCH 29TH 1918 Good Friday – it was raining hard early but cleared later into a bright sunny day. Got into a car at 8.45 a.m. and started off to Abbeville, picking up Felix and Law to do the billeting for the Reinforcement Camp and School respectively, en route. Called at Prouzel, where entrainment takes place and found Hill there with his merry men.

Of the battle – the French are apparently walking slowly back without fighting much – the worst of it is that they don't tell us when they are going to do it. They must have orders not to get involved. If only they would warn* our gunners! Today they retired through the line of guns, who took on the Boche over open sights at 1100 yards range, and fought a rear-guard action, withdrawing the guns one at a time. All were got away safely too. Our gunners are covering the French, as theirs have not yet arrived. Report has it that the Boche has now got Moreuil, but it requires confirmation. One supposes that the battle is going well!!

As soon as we can get our divisions extricated, we go to the Abbeville area to train and refit.

MOLLIENS-VIDAME MARCH 30TH 1918 Left St. Sauflieu at 9 a.m. and came to Molliens-Vidame.* Thence Monty and I got into a car and went to search for training areas near the coast. It poured with rain the whole day without stopping and to make matters worse the clutch was slipping badly and the car would not go at all. However we persevered and managed to see a good deal of the country – we visited one chateau inhabited by a very nice lady and her small daughter, who fed us on chocolates and offered us lunch, which we had to refuse as we had a long way to go. Eventually we lunched at St. Vary and then went on by the Point d'Hourdel. Soon after passing there we stuck in the sand which had blown over the road and had to be pulled out by some

*West of Amiens.

[234]

stray fishermen. At Ault, another place on the coast, the car almost struck work altogether and it seemed as if we were destined to spend the remainder of our days there – however we got out in the end.

Returned by Abbeville to Molliens-Vidame.

APRIL 1ST 1918 Another long day in the car – we went north to try and find a more central place for the school. Found what we wanted at Crécy (scene of the battle) and had got things more or less in train, when we met a staff officer of the Fifth Army H.Q. It seemed that they were coming into Crécy, so we had to clear out. However we found what we wanted at Nouvion, the other side of the Forêt de Crécy. Went on and saw Rochfort at Huchenville and made all arangements for the school to move to Nouvion tomorrow. Thence back to Abbeville and from there out to a place called Sailly-le-sec, which we had been told might do for the Reinforcement Camp, but that fell through, as it belonged to the gunners. So we had to return to Pont Remy with that part of our business unsettled. Then at 11 p.m., just as we were turning in, Tom Holland returned from G.H.Q. and the whole plan is changed and everything is to stand fast for the moment. So we had to send a D.R. to Huchenville to cancel the move – and our work of the last three days would appear to be wasted. It's really rather difficult to compete when orders change every two hours. Wonder what the authorities are playing at – we are in truth an amateur lot of soldiers!

We have here over 100 men of the 16th Div. (South of Ireland) awaiting trial by F.G.C.M.[*] They threw down their arms and refused to fight. Rumour has it now that they are bringing in conscription for Ireland from May 1st. One hopes it is true. Gen. Fasseu was up the line today and brought us news of a very good counter-attack by the Second Cav. Division on a wood N.E. of Moreuil, which was held by two Boche battalions. They got the wood and about 60 prisoners and 13 machine guns – and the wood was reported full of Boche dead. There are bright spots in the story of this battle – one is the charge of one Cavalry Squadron on some Boche infantry. They got 150 prisoners and

[*] Field general court martial.

[235]

killed 74, their own casualties were 60, owing to going on too far and getting into machine-gun fire.

APRIL 3RD 1918 Still at Pont Remy.[*] There are still no definite orders as to how exactly the corps is to function in the future, so it is impossible to get busy at anything.

In the afternoon Laurence Carr, Monty and I took a trip over to Fourth Army rear H.Q. to try and find out what was going on. They did not seem to know much, but apparently we got a move on to them somehow, because when we got back, Montgomery[†] (the M.G.G.S.) rang up, and it seems possible that we may get Pont Remy for the Corps Reinforcement Camp and Nouvion for the Corps School. Things seem to be gradually shaping themselves into some sort of order. Our tired divisions are being sent north to relieve fresh divisions for the battle front, so it seems they think the Boche has put all his eggs into this basket. There is nothing much doing on this front – the chief news is that the French troops are looting all the chateaux and houses deserted by refugees, they are very bad at that. A territorial regiment sent to defend Moreuil spent most of its time in looting the cellars and getting drunk. However they are getting up some good troops now and their artillery is appearing on the scene. Apparently what upset them was our failure to hold the line of the Somme, though how we could be expected to do it without any fresh troops isn't very clear. There is no doubt that the Boche has been very fortunate in the weather.

First of all this wonderful dry spell enabled him to great extent to dispense with roads – secondly, the thick fog on the first two mornings of the battle enabled him to penetrate our battle zone. But for that I believe we should have been fighting there yet. At the same time its only fair to say that he knew how to use those advantages – if we had had to attack in a fog we should probably have made a mess of it. In any case it may turn out to have been all for the best, in the end we may kill more Boches this way than the other. He claims 75,000 prisoners this morning, but of course one must remember that nearly all our wounded were captured. Two days ago G.H.Q. estimated our total casualties at 100,000, which

[*]Now the site of Corps HQ.
[†]Sir Archibald: later to be CIGS.

[236]

really isn't excessive in a battle of this size. I should think the Boche had lost more than that.

A gunner called Jeff was dining with us tonight, he had been over all the same ground in the retreat in 1914 – St Quentin, Ham etc. He told us the true version of a story I had heard before. He was with Tom Bridges' squadron who were the last British troops into St Quentin. When they got there they heard that two British battalions were there who had surrendered to the Maire. Then Bridges got a message from Sir John French saying that these two bns. must be got away at all costs – also an extraordinary document which the C.O.'s of these two Battalions (E and M) had concocted and handed to the Maire in token of their surrender. There had been a lot of casualties and apparently these two fellows were partly gagga from worry and fatigue. They had shown the document to their officers and said that anyone who did not agree with it might clear out and all had left except one subaltern. By the time Bridges appeared upon the scene E. had disappeared and M. seemed unable to speak or to understand what was said to him. The men too were partially drunk and wholly out of control, and at the same time so worn out that they could hardly move. Bridges assembled them all near the station and posted his squadron so that it appeared far more numerous than it was, and then proceeded to make a speech. He told the men of these battalions that they could either march on out of St Quentin and continue to serve their King and country or they could be shot down by his cavalry where they were, and he gave them five minutes to make their choice. In five minutes the whole lot had fallen in in fours and he marched them up to the square headed by two French musicians playing popular airs, who had been raked out from somewhere. Meanwhile eight or ten huge sorts of pantechicon vans had been collected and the men – they were only about 400 strong and very tired – were put into them and driven off. The next question was how to get the document out of the maire, who proved obdurate, thinking probably that its production would pacify the Germans when they arrived. Bridges argued with him for an hour and a half and eventually it had to be taken from him almost by force. He then got all the women in the town to make cheese sandwiches for his men. The whole of this time the only troops between him and the advancing Boche were two picquets which he had posted on the roads leading in to the town. He eventually left St. Quentin at 2 a.m. – the Boche marched into the square at 2.30 a.m. So it was a pretty fine performance.

Tom Bridges recently lost one leg when commanding the 19th Div. – I remember well stopping with him when he was head of the British mission at La Panne (Belgian Army) in the summer of 1915. He is a fine fellow.

I hear Seely has done well in this last battle – it was his brigade of Canadian dismounted cavalry which carried out such a successful counter-attack two or three days ago.

April 4th 1918

Dear Mother,

Have only just got your letter of 20th March. The mails have been rather upside down with all this moving. The school had to move as you will probably have guessed and has not been functioning for some time now. I have been at Corps H.Q. during the battle. We had cruel luck – both the first days of the battle were thick fog all the morning which enabled the Boche to break through unseen – otherwise I don't think he would have got through at all. But it may be all for the best – we may kill more this way in the end. Our losses are not unduly heavy – you must remember that all the wounded, nearly, got taken prisoner. There is a lull now before another storm.

I think in many ways this battle has done good – it must have given many people at home a jar – it stopped the engineers strike anyway and it does provide another opportunity to enact conscription for Ireland – I wonder if they will use it or not. I think really the situation out here is all right, everyone has got his tail up over his head – and perhaps we are nearer beating the Boche than before if it brings us all together. I don't know what his casualties are and it does no good to guess. It's funny weather, alternate rain and fine and quite warm. The country is looking glorious – I grudge the Boche the small village where the school was and all the work we put into it.

A school is a very rotten command in days like these and at Corps H.Q. one is odd man out and unable to do much good. I'm awfully glad you have had some letters from Master. These last days have

[238]

been a little like the early ones in that the country has been covered with refugees – poor people who have left their homes and all their possessions, except for the few things they can carry in a wheelbarrow or some ramshackle box on wheels.

I see in the papers that at home they think Gough has got the sack and that his army did not do well. This is quite untrue – there are reasons for many things which cannot be given to the press, although they shout and clammer twice as loud – which would be difficult. The battle isn't ended but it will be all right in the end, so don't worry over much about it. The Boche intended to beat our army in two days and he failed and will continue to fail. I shall be awfully interested to see the account of the capture of the 1st battalion.*

Your loving son
WILLIE

[DIARY] APRIL 5TH 1918 The papers say that Gen. Foch has guaranteed Amiens against capture, but the Boche will get it all the same at this rate. Eight fresh divisions were identified yesterday which had not so far been employed in the attack. But I think the Boche is probably making up his tired divisions quicker than we are. We are in a wholesale muddle behind here and no one knows what he is commanding or for how long.

APRIL 6TH 1918 The Army has sanctioned Nouvion as the location of the Corps school, so I got into a car in the morning and went over to Huchenville to start the move. They got on the road by 2 p.m. and should have arrived by 7 p.m. Went on to Nouvion to see that everything was all right that end. It's good to think one is going to get to work again, but I'm not sure now I can stick the school with this battle going on. I want something more on the spot. After all this is the greatest battle of the war, and to be more or less out of it!! The question really is how far the school is going to be of value under present circumstances and how long circumstances are going to remain as they are. One does feel one ought to be doing a job of work in the battle. It looks now as if the

*Gordon Highlanders – In 1914.

[239]

Hun was going on hammering away – if he does I don't think he will get much good of it. I wonder if he can put in the devil of a push elsewhere now – it might make things awkward if he could. Anyway, it's pouring with rain tonight which may damp his ardour a bit.

APRIL 7TH 1918 Have rejoined the school at Nouvion – a delightful village and suitable for us, and we have to get to work at once and prepare for Lewis Gun and signal courses, which gives one something to do. The country is too wonderful for words – I sit writing at an open window looking out on to a little wood – intersected with overgrown paths, and carpeted with primroses and cowslips and violets, and the feel of spring and growing things is in the air. It is quite cold too, to remind one that April is but beginning. And the birds are singing their nesting songs. But how can one remain here peaceful, when the greatest battle is being fought?

I have talked about getting back to a battalion, but there seems little hope of it. Pam said in one of her letters that she was sure Billy was out here, but it is up in front that he will be, not back here in the peaceful places.

APRIL 8TH 1918 No news of the war at all – one is rather cut off here and dependent to a certain extent on the French communiqué on the door of the village post office. But there was very heavy gunning this morning. Went for a ride to have a look at the country in the morning and wandered into the Forêt de Crécy, which is the abode of a good many deserters from the British army, according to local report. They are said to live on wild boar – of which there are any amount – and what they can steal from farms. After a month or two of that sort of life a man ought to be able to take care of himself and make a good soldier. However I didn't come across any of them.

It rained very heavily during the middle part of the day, but cleared in the evening. Went for a walk then down towards the sea, which is only about 6 miles away, and came to a stream meandering along through marshy reed-beds, the abode of duck, snipe and curlew. A grand place to come with a gun in the autumn, but I'm not sure I don't like it better in the spring without a gun.

April 9th 1918

Dear Mother,

My letters have been rolling up in budgets the last day or two to compensate for the fortnight without any. I am still out of battle and there seems small chance of being anywhere else at the moment. I am back again with the school now and we are preparing to re-open.

The Greatest Battle continues and will do I suppose for months. I don't know quite what is happening now, but I suppose the Boche is preparing for another colossal attack. I daresay I shall have a dart before the end.

It's wonderful weather you can see all the things growing and the woods are carpeted with flowers. One thing about this battle – it's bound to bring the end of the war nearer, one can't keep on at this rate indefinitely and it had to come before the end. This is our hardest year – if we can hold out successfully till the winter, we shall be in a very favourable position.

I haven't any news as one is rather cut off here and the communications are not very good. Goodbye and love to Father.

Your loving son
WILLIE

[DIARY] 10TH APRIL 1918 Rather a depressing day. It was dull and wet. Took Rochfort for a ride in the morning – feel its rather a duty to make him do things with his one arm and he had not been for a ride before. We went to the Forêt de Creçy – there are some glorious rides through the wood. Had hardly got back when Monty turned up with Nevile. Everything is changed again and we are to have no courses here – at any rate at present, and all instructors are to go to the two divisions we have now got in the corps – which leaves me without a job. The point is we shall probably only have the divisions for so short a time, that even 7 day Lewis Gun courses cannot be fitted in. It's a bad business all the same if we can't give divisions long enough out of the line to get re-organised and properly absorb their drafts. Wired for the officers who have gone on leave – I'm afraid they will be disappointed.

The Boche has attacked again between Armentieres and La Bassée,* where he was partially successful and mopped up the Portuguese, – also between Ploegsteert and Wytshaete, where he was also partially successful and got Ploegsteert Wood. It would appear that his game is to outflank Armentieres on the north and south and capture it. He has outflanked it, but his penetration has only succeeded on a narrow front in both cases and if we have got sufficient troops to counter-attack we should be able to push him back. That at any rate is how it looks from the map and one's knowledge of the ground.

We are all wondering when the French are going to counter-attack, they were to have done a show yesterday, but it turned out to be only a 'project'. They are funny devils, they tell you they are going to do a magnificent show, and then – nothing happens! 'Oh,' they say, 'that – that was only a "project".' The difficulty is to know when they really mean it.

APRIL 11TH 1918 Rode over in the morning to St Valéry† to see the 24th Division, to explain how they would get the best value out of the instructors I am sending them. It was rather a pleasant ride. Lunched with them and saw Gen. Daly who commands them. Had met him before at Château d'Eperlecques with the d'Hespels, and again the other day at Caix. His division had fought hard but had not fared too badly and had only lost two C.O.'s. Saw many of the men about and they looked very well and well turned-out. He is very depressed though about things in general. They all seem a bit down in the mouth.

Heard while there that the 55th Div. had counter-attacked yesterday evening near Givenchy and taken 750 prisoners. The Boche is concentrating against us and means to knock us out and we have got to fight every inch, tooth and nail, and refuse to be knocked out – that is all. We have got to make up our minds to it. The sun came out in the afternoon and I had a very pleasant ride back to Nouvion. Craster and Chambers turned up from the

---

*Far to the north, near the France-Belgium border.
†At the Somme mouth, not the St Valéry-en-Caux famous in a later war.

Corps soon after I got in, to see if we wanted anything, but of course with all these changes going on we don't. There is nothing like the sun to increase one's morale. The mess is very small now, most of the instructors who were not on leave have gone off to the 24th Div. today.

Heard quite a good story today, which I believe is true. Some American R.E. were holding a bit of line and on their left was a tunnelling coy of ours which had been put in to the fight. The Boche attacked and the Americans thought discretion the better part of valour. The tunnellers drove off the Boche and then proceeded to go through the Americans' packs which they had left behind them. Presently the latter returned somewhat ashamed of themselves (they fought quite well later) to find their patent razors etc. in the possession of the tunnellers. They took it in good part, and said that if our men had the guts to drive the Boche back and then go through their packs, they deserved the razors. Which was true enough.

April 11th 1918

Dear Father,

Many thanks for your letter. As you say this battle is only just beginning – at present the Boche is concentrating everything he has got including the guns he captured in Russia against us and he means to knock us out and we have got to set our teeth and refuse to be knocked out. That is what it comes to. And we are going to set our teeth. It's a pity though we have not got a few more divisions. You will see that he has attacked again on a big front in the north and again only been partially successful and attacks that don't succeed cost a lot of men, as we have learnt with bitter experience in the past. Things are changing so from day to day out here that one does not know where one is – at present I am more or less out of a job but I don't think that will last very long somehow, and one may find oneself well in it at any time now I think.

It is just like the people at home to start talking again the minute the Boche receives a temporary check, but I think they are really sound in spite of the wretched pacifists in Parliament. If Lloyd George can carry through his new programme that will be a step in the right direction. I'm very glad to see about conscription for Ireland. Our greatest difficulty, I need not tell you, is discipline, and this sort of battle tests it far more than an attack. That and the training of commanders which is also defective, but after all when you have made an army like ours in the middle of a war, it is bound to have many weaknesses, and one must do the best one can with what one has got. I don't think your story of the Corps Commander is true – it certainly did not happen on the right flank. This inquiry as to the conduct of the Fifth Army is all rot too – the men fought quite well, and after all it was taking on at least 3½ times as many Boche divisions as it had at its disposal. Of course there were errors made – there always are.

Your affectionate son
WILLIE

It was on this day that Haig's Order of the Day to all ranks of the Army was issued. 'With our backs to the wall,' one sentence ran, 'and believing in the justice of our cause, each one of us must fight to the end. The safety of our homes and the freedom of mankind alike depend upon the conduct of each one of us at this critical moment.'

The German advance had been dramatic; the German Army was already threatening Amiens. But in fact – although German attacks continued to make considerable headway for the next three months – the worst crisis was past, although it did not seem so. The German tactical success had not been able to be exploited by equivalent operational successes – by the deep penetration and advance of reserve formations. The Allied line shifted, sagged – but was never completely broken. A front held.

[DIARY] APRIL 13TH 1918 The Boche is pushing on on the northern front of attack, and has now occupied Merville which is not very far from Hazebrouck, which as a railway junction is a most important place for us. I must say I think that his object up north is to draw off troops, and that he intends to push again on this front for all he is worth. However, one can't tell with so little to go upon, and I daresay the C-in-C would be rather glad of an answer to that question.

There seems to be a good deal of opposition to the new Government bill on the man-power question (the raising of the age limit and Conscription for Ireland) – that is in the House of Commons. They are a set of dirty dogs, not a spark of patriotism in many of them.

This evening I cut out of the paper a long list, apart from the Irish Nationalists, of members of Parliament who at this greatest crisis of the war voted against the government on a bill which was carefully framed to enable us to prosecute the war with greater efficiency – and it seemed to me that the names of such unpatriotic swine ought not to be forgotten, so the list is here.

Rode over to see the old battlefield of Creçy in the afternoon. It is about ten miles from here – there is a cross which commemorates John, the blind kind of Bohemia, who fought there on the side of the French, and did jolly well according to Froissart, as is recorded on the stone. The cross itself looks very old, but the base is new. Then we went up to the site of the old windmill from which Edward III watched the battle. The mound on which it was built still exists, and it must have served as an excellent O.P. in 1346. War has changed somewhat since then.

The extract from the report on Parliament to which Willie referred was cut out and stuck in the diary. The names listed as voting against the Government, apart from the Irish Nationalist members were:

LIBERALS

Alden, P.
Arnold, S.
Baker, J.A.
Barlow, Sir J.E.
Burns, John
Buxton, Noel
Chancellor, H.G.
Clough, W.
Davies, E.W.
Gelder, Sir W.A.

Hogge, J.M.
Holt, R.D.
Jones, Leif
King, J.
Lambert, R.
Mason, D.M.
Morrel, P.
Ogden, F.
Outhwaite, R.L.
Peel, Hon. G.
Ponsonby, A.W.
Pringle, W.R.
Rowntree, A.
Smith, H.B. Lees
Whitehouse, J.H.
Williams, L.L.

LABOUR

Jowett, F.W.
Macdonald, J.R.
Richardson, T.
Sutton, J.E.
Taylor, J.W.
Thomas, J.H.

[DIARY] APRIL 16TH 1918 Went for a long ride in the Forêt this morning, mostly along the little paths where one is absolutely alone with the trees and flowers. They will be a mass of honeysuckle in a few weeks time. Cannot help being a bit depressed at present, the war doesn't seem to be going well, and all the stories one hears of the battle on the Fifth Army front only deepen ones gloom. There is a most absolute and entire lack of leadership and they are all impressed with the superiority of the Boche. And there is lack of faith in their divisional commanders on the part of battalions.

All my instructors came back today from the 20th and 24th Divisions and it is the same story everywhere – the men are good and keen, although very young, but the officers are hopeless and there are no N.C.O.'s. The officers say that their men are rotten because they don't know how to handle them, and if the men are to be sent into battle under that leadership, it is like sending sheep to the slaughter. It is bound to end in disaster. And the commanding officers have no idea of organisation or training. One could sit down and weep. How is it all to end – if many other divisions are that way, there is only one possible end. But I can't, won't believe it. And one feels so useless doing nothing here.

APRIL 17TH 1918 Heard that Parish in the 60th who was with me at Aldershot is commanding the battalion which has come to Forêt l'Abbaye – a village about a mile and a half away. He has been in the battle and thinking he would be short of officers and N.C.O.'s I rode over to see him this morning to see if we could be of any assistance. Found him just as I thought, all his good officers and N.C.O.'s gone, – with a draft of 600 men from England and no one to deal with them. So have arranged to take on his battalion with the whole staff of the school, Lewis Gunners, signallers and all, for as long as we are here. It's great to find a really useful job of work again for a change. He was delighted and I brought him back to lunch and we got the whole thing fixed up. It only remains to hope that we shall now be here for a few days longer, to really be able to get some sort of results. I saw the battalion on parade this morning – they are in much the same state that the 20th and 24th Divisions are in – everything had been thrown into the battle and no nucleus remained on which to reform the battalion. It really is awful. How can one turn that into a fighting unit fit to meet the Boche, under three months at least?

The news is bad this evening – Bailleul has gone, and they are fighting in Meteren – Wytschaete and Messines have gone and the Boche is into St Eloi. That has widened out his salient so much that it is no longer a salient. And I'm afraid he will get Ypres, which we have defended with so much blood and misery, and it looks as if we might have to withdraw from the Passchandaele Ridge which it cost us so many lives to win. But still I know nothing about it after all – except that most of our divisions are tired and untrained and lacking in good officers – that is what depresses one far more than the loss of ground. What have we got to hold him up with? The men are good individually, brave enough that is – they are only a quarter trained – but a collection of brave individuals does not make a good army. And of course all this time the Boche is improving in morale. Yes it is depressing, the only thing is to carry on doing ones job and leave the rest to G.H.Q.

I have arrived at the stage of a blind faith in the C-in-C because any other course would mean absolute dismay. And in God, but of course He doesn't work that way – He uses men to carry out His designs, and it is by the strength of our own efficiency and courage that we shall win, if we do win. And we shall win in the end, because after all we are fighting His battle – He is sending us dark days for our own good, because without them the war would have failed in its effect, its purifying effect, on us. All these fresh lives have to go still to wipe out the stains of our self-indulgence and materialism. That must be it.

ROELLECOURT APRIL 18TH 1918 Fixed everything up to start work with Parish's battalion this afternoon, and was just having lunch when a letter arrived from Monty by car – the car was to take me to Corps H.Q. and my instructors are to go to the 20 and 24 Divisions tomorrow. So it's again a case of the best laid plans of mice and men etc. Got into the car at 2.30 and after a very cold drive of 40 miles arrived at Corps H.Q. It's wonderfully cold. This is near St Pol – we drove along the St Pol – Arras road, which I have not seen since we marched up from Fouflin-Ricametz to St. Omer after the Arras battle last year. Hear that Dick Cunyngham is wounded and a prisoner. He was temporarily in command of a Bde of the 51st when that happened.

The Boche attacked with about 5 divisions on our army front today (we are now the First Army) and got repulsed everywhere more or less, and suffered heavy casualties. The situation is not so bad really, I suppose – report has it that he is considerably disorganised.

APRIL 22ND 1918 Started off with Grassett in the morning and we went to see Duncan's Brigade training. They seemed to be trying hard but to know very little about it. However they have got their battalions organised.

Came back to lunch and went down to see the two demonstration platoons which the Sergt. Major is training, afterwards. He and Hill had also had a few old men of the Corps H.Q. troops on parade. The latter told me they were very bad and at the end he had given them a short address to encourage them. Asked what he had said, it transpired that he had told them he was jolly glad we had got a good navy.

Monty and I then went on to Bryas to see the XIII Corps. We rode over and then back to our H.Q. It served as a bit of exercise. Too much of this work is done in a car.

There is a terrific bombardo going on tonight.

APRIL 24TH 1918 Went over to the 73rd Bde and Dugan took us (Grassett and self) round one of his battalions. We saw the best training going on that I have seen in France – the whole bn. was really organised with the result that the section commanders really commanded their men. The platoon commanders were all really teaching their platoons something useful, and Dugan taught everyone he met something. I learnt a lot – it was really a useful morning.

Dined with Gen. Congreve in the evening at Hauteclocque Chateau.

The Boche attacked today with tanks on the Fourth Army front at Villers Brettoneux* – he has captured that place which is rather serious. It looks as if he may get Corbie. Report says that his losses are heavy – but they always say that.

APRIL 25TH 1918 Went to Duncan's Brigade, and saw one battalion. The training struck me as being poor, the men were listless and uninterested. I attached myself to one company – and a few questions to section commanders revealed the fact that it was not organised at all. A really poor show. I should like Duncan to go and see Dugan at work. Corps H.Q. took over Bryas Chateau from the XIII Corps today and we moved across in the afternoon. It's a very much nicer place in every way. Grassett is leaving us and going back to the IX Corps, I'm sorry to say, because he is a very nice fellow as well as a very capable one.

CHAU DE BRYAS APRIL 26TH 1918 A long day in a car with Monty hunting for another place for the Reinforcement Camp

---

*Immediately east of Amiens, in the Somme sector.

and the School, which has got to move from Nouvion. Partial success, we found a place for the Reinforcement Camp, but not for the School. We lunched at Montreuil. Had never been there before, it is rather a nice old town with ramparts round it.

The news is none too good today – we have recaptured Villers-Brettoneux, but the French have lost Kemmel, the key of all our positions to the north. That means that we shall lose Ypres and the Pilkem Ridge and probably Poperinghe, unless they retake the place, and I don't think they will. They were to have counterattacked this morning but the troops weren't for it and were non-starters. It may be rather difficult to extricate some of our people to the north I should think.

CHAU DE BRYAS APRIL 28TH 1918 Went to the 59th Brigade and showed them a few things with a demonstration platoon. It was rather damp and cold. Got a letter from Pelham today telling me of Donald Clark's death. He commanded B. Coy most of the time I had the 6th G.H. and was a splendid fellow, always cheery and full of joie-de-vivre, and very young – and now he has died of wounds. I am sorry for his father, who is a banker at Alford. He (Pelham) also told me something of the 6th G.H. 'A' Coy had orders to hold a bridgehead at all costs. They interpreted the order literally – they were still fighting 3 days after they were surrounded, and no officer or man came back, and I think there were not many prisoners. Perhaps that will be accepted as a sacrifice to wipe away many of our country's sins by the Judge of all.

CHAU DE BRYAS APRIL 29TH 1918 The news on the whole was good today from the northern battle front. The Boche attacked on a wide front and was practically repulsed all along except in one small place. So it looks as if we shall relieve the Canadians. The concentration of artillery by the Boche in Flanders now exceeds anything in past battles, so the fighting must be very unpleasant.

At the Doullens Conference on 26 March, held at the height of the battle's emergency, the British and French High Commands had

*met, with Clemenceau, the French Premier, also present.
Hitherto British and French operations had been coordinated 'by
agreement' – agreement which pressure of events often nullified.
At Doullens it was agreed that General Foch should have power
to 'coordinate the action of all the Allied Armies on the Western
Front'. This, in effect, had made Foch Supreme Commander. He
was a man of indomitable fighting spirit.*

May 1st 1918

Dear Father,

I am still with the same Corps and my job is still the same, only
the school has not been functioning lately so I have been doing a
job of work at Corps H.Q. – that is all. The papers aren't quite
correct in saying that the Hun has only gained a little ground at
enormous cost – he has got some very important ground,
including Kemmel Hill, which makes the ground to the north
untenable really. I should think that we shall have to give up a lot
more ground in the north yet. He made a big attack on that front
the day before yesterday and was repulsed everywhere – that
possibly meant a heavy casualty roll. But it's no good pretending
that we are winning the battle at the moment. I don't think that
the northern front is the main show – he had an unexpected
success in the initial stages of his attack there and is exploiting it –
that's all. We may lose Dunkirk, but I don't think Calais at the
moment.

The artillery concentration by the Hun is beyond anything yet
seen, and he is making very extensive use of gas shell. But I expect
his main attack will come on the original front opposite Amiens.
As to what his losses are I don't think we have much to go upon,
they are probably pretty heavy, but he must have allowed for that
before he started. I think we are bound to rely now to a certain
extent upon the Americans. One advantage we have got now
which we never had before, we have got one supreme command,
and I think we ought to have confidence in Foch. He is a fellow
who refuses to get rattled or to allow his plans to be interfered
with. I heard the other day that many people in England are

saying that he is sacrificing us for the benefit of France, but of course that is nonsense. It happens to be our role at the moment to set our teeth and fight it out and kill as many Huns as possible, in order to let the French play theirs later on. It's true that things don't always work out well when we are fighting alongside the French in the same battle, because their methods are different, and they very seldom carry out what they plan, and if you have started to co-operate and they don't start at all, you are apt to get it in the neck. Of course there has been an awful lot of nonsense written, about the French saving Amiens and gallant generals riding about (French ones I mean). That's all newspaper gup – as was also all that rot about Carey's force. The true story of Carey's force is somewhat different and better not written. You see that Dick-Cunyngham and all his staff are missing – he had taken over Pelham-Burn's Bde. The Division had been sent up to try and restore the line or part of it, abandoned by the Portuguese, and the Hun got in behind them. The P-E ran like rabbits, the few who waited for the Hun held up their hands. A cyclist bn. was sent up to help them and left their bicycles on the road when they got near the front. The flying -guese pinched them in order to get away quicker. Unfortunately for them a machine gun detachment saw blue uniforms coming down the road on bicycles and thought they were Huns and opened fire and scuppered the lot. Good job too – only I'm not quite sure the story is true. I don't pretend that the débacle – it was almost that – was entirely due to the Portuguese, but it very largely was. You see their failure exposed the flanks of our men, and our men don't fight well with an open flank. It's defective training of course, but it's hard to create an army of millions during war. Especially when we have very few men who have ever really studied war as a profession. Our training at home is very indifferent.

That was a very good show of the navy at Zeebrugge and Ostend. I'm sorry their casualties were so heavy. About Ireland, I believe that if they carry out their plans firmly there will be little trouble; what one rather fears is wavering by our government, and then the Irishman will get bobbery at once.

It's turned very cold again and the sky is always grey – we haven't seen the sun for a week past.

[252]

I'm awfully glad George has had a bit of leave, it's sure to have done him a lot of good. It's bad news to hear you have not been so fit lately, I expect you've been worrying a bit about this old battle. I shouldn't – it had to come and it's bringing the end closer – and in the end we shall win it. Not in a sensational way I think, but the Hun will fail, and things will settle down again and we shall go on getting stronger until we can crush him. I don't look for any very sudden ending though.

The trees were coming out beautifully, but this cold grey spell has delayed them, and there is little difference to notice in the last fortnight. Pelham-Burn is home sick and has got a training Bde. which he will command well. But I hear he is talking too much about inefficiency out here and saying everyone ought to be sacked. And of course much of what he says is true, but even that is better left unsaid at dinner parties, etc. You see we are an amateur army and many things are rotten and inefficiently run and our organisation is bad – but you have got to fight your battle with what you have got, and we are lacking in great soldiers. And destructive criticism of superiors in public by comparatively junior fellows is very harmful really. I'm afraid his career as a soldier will suffer and he may do harm. It would be no good telling him though – he's an obstinate devil. Goodbye and love to Mother.

Your affectionate son
WILLIE

[DIARY] CHAU DE LA HAYE MAY 2ND 1918 We moved our H.Q. today as the divisions (20 and 24) take over the line from the Canadians tonight and we assume command tomorrow morning. It is the northern part of the Canadian line in front of Lens. It seems probably that the next big attack by the Hun may come on this front, probably from the north of Lens with the intention of turning the Vimy Ridge from the north. But it will probably extend a long way south as well.

Fressin* has been fixed up for the school, and I shall probably go down there tomorrow and get started with the work as soon as possible.

*Near Hesdin on the River Canche.

FRESSIN MAY 4TH 1918 Paper work and various arrangements for coming courses occupied the morning. In the afternoon went for a ride and got to the Foret de Hesdin. It is one of the most beautiful woods I have ever seen. It is all beeches, the most graceful of all trees. They are so clean-cut and delicate, almost ethereal, and the black stems standing out against the mist of green – and what a wonderful green – made a picture of peace and beauty which will live long in my memory. We came back through the Bois de Fressin, looking for a Lewis Gun range – we found one that would do (*faute de mieux*). It (*the Bois de Fressin*) is a paradise of wild flowers, and is full of rabbits of which one does not see many in France (of the wild variety that is – all the people keep tame ones).

This is rather a pleasant village – Fressin – there is an old castle, which was destroyed by the English after the battle of Agincourt (1415). The battle-field is close by here. After tea went for a walk with Rochfort to find a better L.G. range and I think we succeeded. It is close to another village, and it may be necessary to billet the L.G. School there.

Heavy bombardment can be heard tonight and I believe that they are expecting another attack in the north tomorrow. If it comes, may it share the fate of the last one.

May 4th 1918

Dear Mother,

I am back at the school again now and normally we shall reopen shortly. Our present location is quite a nice village not far from the ancient battlefield of Agincourt, so we rather go in for old *champs-de-bataille*. It's not a very good place from our point of view as the accommodation is very limited – however these days one has to do with what one can get. The weather has brightened up considerably the last few days and is much warmer and more pleasant.

We think the Boche may have another boost in the north tomorrow morning – in any case I think he will attack again there and try to improve his position before he goes on in the south. I should think that we have just about reached the half-way house in this battle, he cannot go on for ever on account of man-power, though of course if he gets his prisoners back from Russia it would help an awful lot. Meanwhile we have all got our tails up and feel convinced we shall worry through. Don't really know why we should, because the Boche has got more men, better trained and better led and more guns. However we shall. Did you hear the story of old Clemenceau after a conference of the 'Allies'. He said, 'My admiration for Napolean is constantly diminishing – throughout his career he fought only against "Allies".'

I do remember Bradford – his soldier brother was one of the infant prodigies of the war – VC and a Brigadier General at 25. He was a fine fellow – was killed at Cambrai.

I haven't much news really. The Boche has over-run many of my old haunts in Flanders – what I grudge him most is the Mont Noir and the Mont des Cats. He hasn't got them yet but is very near them. I spent many happy days there when Billy and I were out of the line at the same time, and it was from there he came home to get married. And of course he has got back the spot where I buried poor old Sim. I'm afraid it will be very hard to find that place – the country is so changed.

Spring is further on here than in any other part of the country I have been to and the country is perfectly beautiful. It's a wonderful place for mistletoe, on almost every tree you see a great mass of it. We have got rather a good house for a headquarters, but the owner is a horrid old woman. She married a boy of 20 and beat him and knocked him about for three years after which he committed suicide, and now she is engaged to another of the same age. And an awful old hag she is too, but very brawny and muscular.

The American Press have got a house here – one of them came to see me this evening about something – and seemed a very good fellow indeed.

Your loving son

WILLIE

[DIARY] FRESSIN MAY 7TH 1918 It started wet, but cleared up later into a topping afternoon. Had nothing much to do after lunch, so rode over with Rogers to the next valley where there is quite a nice trout-stream. Although we caught nothing we spent a very pleasant two hours by the water. Got back just in time for dinner. Had a letter from Mother in the morning – in it the story of Master and the file he had made to saw his bars through in his prison in Germany. He had sent it home to her. It's rather a wonderful story – he was awful miserable because he could not get a file anywhere, and he wandering about his prison-yard, kicking at stones on the ground as he walked, and suddenly his foot struck a small piece of metal, and lo and behold it was a file. He tempered it himself so that it would cut iron or soft steel. It's rather wonderful really.

All day the air has been full of the sound of guns – it seems to me to be up north, but where they expect the next attack is on our corps front.

MAY 9TH 1918 We got our parade ground fixed up today, and work started on the Lewis Gun School. Things are getting a move on slowly. We also got our telephone through to the Corps which is a comfort. In the afternoon I went over to a place called Hesmond and fished. One of the inhabitants of this village drove me over there in his car – he is really a charming fellow. Had no luck, got only a few small trout which I returned to their watery home. They were not on the feed at all.

When I got back I found that all the officers who had been attached to the 24th Division had been sent back. It seems the Boche is expected to attack tonight with 22 divisions, from Lens northwards as far as Robecque – he is to use gas and tanks. The bombardment is to start at 10.30 p.m. (It is just after that now, but I do not hear it) – perhaps they have postponed it. God grant they get it properly in the neck.

FRESSIN MAY 10TH 1918 The Boche never attacked after all. Everyone was lined up to receive him and he never came. I suppose he has put it off for some reason. Started off all the instructors in two bodies in the morning to do tactical schemes, which will keep them occupied for a day or two. In the evening I got hold of my American friend, who produced a motor and he and Rogers and I went over to Hesmond to try and catch a trout. It was a bad day and they weren't rising at all, – I got one about

¾lb and that was the total bag. Just happened to see him rise in some very still water and he took my fly a minute or two later.

FRESSIN MAY 12TH 1918 Went to kirk in the morning – it being the Sabbath. About 10 o'clock we received an invitation from the *Maire* of a neighbouring village to attend a Boar shoot. He also asked for some men to assist in the battue. As I had never seen one of these performances I decided to ride over. The wood (The *Bois des Sains*) which they were going to beat belongs to the director of the Bruay mines and he was very much averse to the Shoot taking place. However the boars have done untold damage to the crops, (it is wicked to keep them in an agricultural country like this), and the *Maire* ordained that it was to take place. So all the farmers turned out armed with guns of every description – I saw two old muzzle-loaders. And the farm servants and a posse of soldiers acted as beaters. Just as the show was about to commence the agent of the proprietor turned up and made all sorts of difficulties, but beyond threatening to brain him, no one took any notice. Everyone talked at once at the top of their voices, and they all cocked their guns and kept them cocked from that time on. All the guns are lined up on a 'ride' through the wood, while the beaters drive the pig towards them. No one is supposed to shoot in front of him for fear of shooting the beaters, but they pay little attention to that rule and blaze off indiscriminately whenever they see a pig. To add to the danger there were a number of officers from the R.F.C. armed with service rifles and revolvers. However fortunately they were recalled to their aerodrome soon after the operations commenced. There was one casualty, a sergeant in the Flying Corps who was mistaken for a '*sanglier*' by an excited Gaul – who discharged two barrels at him and got him with both. Fortunately he wasn't killed. The only pig killed while I was there was shot by a rubicund old boy to whom I had attached myself. He took no notice of the rule that it must go past before you shoot and shot it straight in front of him. He was hugely delighted – 'Ah comme c'est beau, un coup de fusil!' and he shook my hands and those of everyone else within reach, and invited me warmly to visit him at Freyes in order to drink a glass of champagne.

I departed soon after this, not wishing to tempt Providence

beyond a certain limit. On the whole I think fishing is a more attractive and less dangerous way of passing one's leisure moments.

MAY 14TH 1918 Laurence Carr turned up in the evening and we had a talk about things – apparently the Boche is now expected to attack tomorrow morning. It was a rather glorious evening, very light and warm.

MAY 16TH 1918 All quiet on the Western front.[*] We had rather a pleasant walk in the morning doing tactical schemes. Started at 9 and got in about 1.30.

After tea I went with Hill to a pool in the small stream which runs through our village and we fished. We got several little trout about 1/4lb weight, and I hooked a much bigger one, but lost him. I had to be very firm with him to prevent him running under the shill-gate and the hold gave.

It was a real summer evening, delightfully soft and cool when the sun had gone down. The sun begins to get quite hot.

May 19th 1918

Dear Mother,

I sent the cheque (£6.18.0) to you on April 17th, so I suppose it has not arrived. If this is so could you write a line to Child's and ask them if it has been cashed? If not I suppose payment had better be stopped. The number of the cheque is 44537. Then I will send you another cheque.

I was awfully glad to see an article in the Observer of May 12th on that fellow Repington. I've thought for a long time that the Morning Post and Repington in particular ought to be suppressed. They always claim to write for the soldier out here, which is of course a fable. I don't think it's too much to say, that the reason why we look forward to the future with confidence is because we have at last got a united command, and in particular because

---

[*] A prophetic turn of phrase. Remarque's great novel *Im Westen nichts neves* would not be published, let alone translated into English under this title, for another eleven years.

Foch is the commander. I think we are on the verge of the next phase in this battle.

As I have absolutely no information beyond the ordinary I will give you my forecast for what it's worth. The Boche will attack on May 21st in the north with the object of forcing us back to the line St Omer – due north to the sea. At the same time he will push in on the southern flank of his present salient from Lens to Merville and try to get the Bruay coalfields and incidentally turn the Vimy Ridge from the north. This will be followed up by his main attack a day or two later in the south, with Abbeville and the mouth of the Somme as his objectives. He may accompany the first attack with a show at Arras with the idea of turning the Vimy Ridge from the south. So we may expect to be pretty busy for the next two months. I think of course that he will get on a bit at first, but that we shall hold him up in the end. All the same we haven't got too much ground to spare.

Willie had been mistaken in his prognosis of the next enemy move. On 27 May the Germans launched a great attack southward with twenty divisions between Soissons and Reims, across the Aisne and soon reaching the Marne. It seemed to be September 1914 again; and the German artillery concentration and bombardment was the heaviest of the war.

[DIARY] MAY 27TH 1918 The news is that the Boche attacked this morning or yesterday in the south, the Chemin des Dames, and has driven back the French and two of our tired divisions which had gone down there for a rest. He also attacked our Second Army and drove them back a bit on part of their front. Later in the evening we heard that the French had recaptured most of the ground lost in the south, and that we had repulsed the attack in the north on most of the front. But the news is very sketchy at present.

Our padre's brother was passing with a transport convoy and I managed to do a bit of a deal in the horse-flesh line, getting rid of a dud in exchange for quite a good horse. Which is not a thing which falls in one's way every day of the week.

MAY 29TH 1918 No news of the Boche attack in the south except from his wireless, which claims 25,000 prisoners including one British and one French general, also that he has crossed the Vesle River. Spent the morning on parade and did some writing later on. Wednesday being a half-holiday we played the sergeants at football, and defeated them. I don't think I have played for five years and was absolutely done when we had finished.

In the evening Hill and I walked down to the pool, we had no luck with the fly, but Hill got one in the landing net – it was lying close in to the side. I must say he used great cunning but we returned him to the water as it was not a very sporting way to catch him. The people in the mill thought we were mad.

The camp is progressing well and our officers' course is due to arrive on June 5th.

Got rather an amusing complaint the other day – a letter signed by '*plusieurs mères de Fressin*', to the effect that delighted as they were to lodge officers and sorry as they were that the accommodation they had to offer was so poor, yet they had a small grievance which they were sure I would put right. It seemed that some of these officers (students at the Gas School) had been disrobing themselves with their windows open, and '*croyez-vous, mon colonel, des petites filles les ont vu*' in a costume '*plus que negligée*'. So I had to insert a para in the Gas School orders that officers must not undress in front of open windows.

FRESSIN MAY 30TH 1918 A glorious day – The Boche is continuing his advance in the south – the report this morning put his maximum penetration at 20 miles and the attack is on a very wide front. I think he will get Soissons and Rheims. Probably has the first by now.

FRESSIN JUNE 1ST 1918 June 1st again. Two long years since Pam and Billy were married. This afternoon two years ago I saw them off to Pam's garden. Who could wish to foresee the future who has seen the past? Wrote to Pam – she will be at Chartley – alone.

Am still depressed somehow – the Boche has reached the Marne, which we thought he had seen for the last time in 1914, four dreary years ago.

Dear Mother,

Very many thanks for the notepaper which has arrived as you see. I like these big sheets, which gives one's pen a chance to wander without feeling cramped. The last two or three days I haven't been frightfully well and that combined with the Boche attack made me rather short-tempered at times. It is ridiculous that outside things should have power to make one irritable. However today I am much better and the Boche took a knock east of Reims, so I am once more equable. Have been doing a certain amount of writing trying to get all the lectures I have to give down to essay form, and its not really very easy, but it does help to straighten out one's ideas and get them into a logical sequence. But the summer is in the air and the birds are singing the most impossibly happy songs and often an entirely wrong set of ideas will come into one's head, and things like discipline and defence in depth fade into a sort of hazy impossibility. Or else one has no ideas at all but simply sits and looks at a little white cloud far up in a sky of pale blue, and exists without thinking at all.

However I'm making some progress, though I confess to having 'skimped' in places, and shall probably have to re-write. Isn't it horrible to think of the Boche back on the Marne again in 1918, when we all thought he had seen it for the last time in 1914, four dreary years ago? There is no doubt that his attack there was a complete surprise – he was very clever in making us think that it was coming elsewhere. I think it will come elsewhere too. But the Marne is not very far from Paris and the Boche any nearer Paris would be a bad egg.

I have been reading Stevenson's 'Travels with a donkey' – it's quite short and I suppose you have read it, if not I believe you would like it. I have read a good many books at odd times in the last four months – they provide the best distraction from other things, and there is no need ever to read a rotten book – there are so many good ones.

The roses are just beginning to come – we are going to have a wonderful show of little red rambler roses here a little later on – there are masses of them. Also we've got a wonderful ash tree in our garden. I'm not over-fond of the ash as a rule, but this is one of the most beautiful trees I have ever seen – it does one good only to look at it. The leaves are like a delicate green lace.

Dead Turks haven't rolled up yet, but I expect they are on their way – the post has been a trifle uncertain lately in arriving. Goodbye and love to Father.

Your loving son
WILLIE

[DIARY] FRESSIN JUNE 4TH 1918 Oh! but the weather is wonderful. I should love this country if there was no war. I should like to buy a donkey – like R.L.S. – only unlike him I should add a fishing-rod to my impediments, and I think that the last four years have taught me how to travel 'light'. And I should know how to load my donkey. There are woods in this country to provide ideal resting-places, and the most happy little streams in which to angle one's breakfast. Perhaps one day the dream may come true! Who knows! One does so long to be a private individual again – its awfully hard to carry on being a lieut-colonel when one is barely 28. Hard, hard work! pretending to the knowledge and acquirements of 40. However so it is ordained, but sometimes one is tired. And tonight I am tired.

The breeze is sighing in the trees and it feels like rain.

JUNE 5TH 1918 But it didn't rain after all. We have been sent a platoon of the 52nd Division to train as a demonstration platoon in a week, and they are so bad that its quite impossible. They have only one merit – keeness. Our camp is getting on apace, there is a tremendous joy in construction and in seeing things grow under one's eye. The S.M.T.O. (I always forget his name, but he is the head of all the lorries in the Corps) turned up in the afternoon. I received him with suspicion because I thought he had come to try and pinch some of our lorries. However he protested that he had come to see if we wanted any more. This I didn't believe but pretended to.

It is a wonderful night, all peace and quiet. Went for a little walk before bed. Stevenson remarks in one of his books how at about 2 a.m. all nature out-of-doors seems to be still for a moment, and a sleeping man wakes an instant to full consciousness. And it is quite true. In the jungle the animals stop feeding for an instant and prick their ears. At this time too, man's vitality is lowest, and I think that just for the moment we get nearer to spiritual things, that it is the spirit hour, and that all nature pauses for an instant in its business, and turns to its Creator. I hear a dog barking in the distance – there is something very melancholy in the barking of a dog at night. Oh! I found a mulberry tree today, covered with silk-worms.

FRESSIN JUNE 6TH 1918 The officers' course arrived at 8.30 p.m. so at last we shall be going at full speed again. At more than full speed, because we are taking on an extra platoon for the 52nd Division. Holdich, the G.S.O.1. of the 52nd came over in the afternoon and we had a long talk about things. He is a most charming fellow and awfully keen to improve his division – and they can stand it, by George! But they are excellent material. The thing is that a few days ago, being very annoyed at the really appalling turn-out and frightful ill-discipline of the men they were sending here on courses, I wrote a real stinker on the subject. Tom Holland put it in his pocket the next time he went to the 52nd Division. And now it has been issued to the division as a circular letter – the signature taken out I'm glad to say.

Holdich brought his G.S.O.2 with him and who should it be but Squeaker Curtis in the 60th. Laurence Carr turned up a little later in the evening, so we had plenty of brass hats about. After dinner, which we had a bit early, Hill and I went down to the Pool, and I picked out half-a-dozen trout, two being quite nice ones, though I failed to land any of the real monsters which still inhabit its green depths. How many peaceful evenings we have spent by that same pool, I shall have very happy memories of it in days to come. Close by the road though it is, one would never dream of its existence but for the music of the falling water.

June 7th 1918

Dear Mother,

I like your visit to the famous author – you know I have to write a certain amount now and then. And after I have written anything I always make a point of going through it and cutting out all the flowery periods. I don't believe you had many all the same. As for punctuation, it's a natural gift and one has it or not – like spelling – the only way to make it better is to read what one has written aloud to oneself. I think R.L. Stevenson's books are a lesson in writing, if one reads one or two, especially his essays, one sees how simply he puts everything down in its right place. I'm glad Alice Meynell is a dear old lady – I thought she probably was.

Oh! You know I didn't give the cross to any of the men, because I don't know them nearly so well as I did the battalion and I don't feel to them personally in the same way, so I didn't want to. You see one's staff here is only a means to an end in a way, the end being the people who come for instruction – one looks after them, so as to make them happy and to get plenty of work out of them, but they are mostly old P.B. men, who go round and clean up the place and they live in safety and comfort (comparative), so its rather different. You've no idea what a hard-hearted job soldiering is, one gradually finds oneself looking only for efficiency, and that forces out the personal feelings to an enormous extent. Only it is hard to explain what I mean.

I had a terribly sad letter yesterday from one of the little d'Hespel girls – you remember how my bn. H.Q. was with them at the château d'Eperlecques about a year ago. Their brother-in-law Gaston de Colnet (and he was really a splendid fellow) has been killed. And his poor little wife has lost her home as well as her husband in the German advance. Also the d'Hespel's house in Amiens is almost certain to be destroyed and their château at Eperlecques is getting very near the war. They ought not to be there any more really. It is terrible, everything together like that. Does it not make you realise what France has suffered?

In my spare time I am reading the history of the 19th century – how easy to be wise after the event, one can see one event upon another leading up to the exact culmination which has come about.

Your loving son
WILLIE

[DIARY] FRESSIN JUNE 11TH 1918 More lectures – Haskard (G.S.O.1 of 20th Div.) and Laurence Carr came down about 11 a.m. and we went off to work out some tactical schemes. Had a very pleasant and instructive morning. Haskard is a first-rate fellow. After lunch we started off again and did a few more, finishing up on the Lewis Gun Range where they were working the Madison gun. That is the weapon about which there is so much excitement in Parliament, to know whether the Government is going to buy it or leave it for the Boche to do so. Those which we had were captured from the Boche in 1916 – the gun was discarded by him shortly afterwards as being an inferior weapon, as indeed it is. Comment seems unnecessary – the ignorance of politicians of the subjects they talk about is colossal.

By the way the tree in the garden is not a mulberry and the worms are not silk.

Boche is still attacking in the south, but not making much headway.

June 12th 1918

Dear Father,

Bright sunny weather again and the Boche attacking in the south, and not doing much good. Attack on a front of 22 miles which only penetrates to a depth of a mile or two in three days is bound to be a costly affair for the aggressor. All courses in full swing keep me pretty busy. I am getting a few Americans now, they are fine fellows and full of keenness and energy. Of course they have a lot to learn, but think of it – they come into the fight today animated by the spirit which possessed us in 1914, longing to be in it, fighting for an ideal, and all the rest of it. And that will last them for a year or two. And there are ten millions of them. And they *mean* to go to Berlin. If we can hold the Boche and give them time and I think we can now, aren't they going to be irresistible! I think so. And when they get lined up we shall get a chance to train, which we have never had yet.

You see, this year the Boche has had the advantage of having been able to get, shall we say, seventy divisions right out of it, and to train them for several months. And his training was first-class, his junior commanders did brilliantly as a result. I suppose we may expect another big attack up here at any time now. We shall get no rest till the winter comes.

I was pretty amused to see all this talk in the House of Commons about the Madison Gun, and the efforts to make the Government buy it to prevent the Boche getting it. It might interest the speakers to know that I have got here at the school some of these guns which were captured from the Boche in 1916. He discarded it shortly afterwards as being an inferior weapon. This is the identical gun about which they are making all the fuss. And just imagine altering the type of light machine gun in the middle of a war! Quite apart from the alterations required in your plant, and the scrapping of all the kind which you were using before, just think of having to re-train all your personnel (millions) in an army this size. Either the speakers were absolute fools, or else it was a put-up job by someone interested in the gun from a pecuniary point of view, or paid by the Boche. It is rather hard on a government to be attacked on a subject like that.

Your affectionate son

WILLIE

[DIARY] FRESSIN JUNE 20TH 1918 Carey was here in the morning and told me that the Corps Commander[*] was going, and mighty sorry I am to hear it. He's a good little man to serve and does not let you down – besides, he knows his job. They are making him Director of Training, a new appointment and a very important one, and he is certainly the man for the job. But it's a great loss to the Corps. And his successor is – Hunter-Weston![†] There's a great tale about him which describes his character to a nicety (plays to the gallery and strikes the wrong note).

He was going round the trenches once, and there was a man in a certain platoon hopelessly drunk – a very awful offence in the trenches. The platoon commander didn't know what to do with him, and H.W. was drawing nearer every moment, so he put him on to a stretcher and covered him with a water-proof sheet. Presently the general appeared and seeing a stretcher with what he supposed to be a corpse lying on it, he drew himself up

[*] Maxse.
[†] Lieutenant-General Sir A. Hunter-Weston. Familiarly known to all as 'Hunter-Bunter'.

and raising his hand in a salute gave forth 'General Hunter-Weston salutes the noble dead'.

At this moment a very tipsy voice came from beneath the water-proof sheet, 'What the 'ell's the ole buster saying?' – and the tableau was rapidly dissolved. The comment is: Pompous ass, it served him right!

June 20th 1918

Dear Mother,

My circular invitations to commanding officers to come down and see the place met with a really hearty response, and I have been flooded with them. They look at the training and spend a day away from shells and noise, and are fed really well, and they all go off quite anxious to come again. So the liaison is excellent and I think the results to the school ought to be excellent too. It means a lot of work though because one has to walk them round in addition to one's ordinary work – result letters etc. have got a bit behind hand.

I think it quite possible that I may not be here much longer, because my Corps Com. has got another appointment and his successor is a man who has his own protegés, and one whom I think I might not hit it off with. But I'm no carin', it doesn't concern me what work I am told to do, and I find that point of view most conducive to a quiet mind.

We have got a grand garden, you can almost see it growing while you wait – peas planted a month ago are over three feet high. And we have got a first-rate strawberry patch, which combined with porridge and cream in the morning helps to make the school popular with battalion commanders. I don't see any prospect of leave much before October, but one never knows.

The farm is going well, pigs are likely to prove most profitable, and I need a bit of money. Also it's a pleasure to make it out of the French civilians – they make enough out of us in all conscience.

Your loving son
WILLIE

[DIARY] FRESSIN JUNE 23RD 1918 Sunday – and I got through a certain amount of work one way and another. Gen. Maxse came here in the afternoon to say goodbye on his way to G.H.Q. He told me I was third on the Corps list for a Brigade, but I'm in no hurry for it. He walked round the place and had some strawberries and cream for tea, and left about 6 p.m. Monty and Guillaume were with him.

We had a concert from a party from Hesdin, and it was a good show and everyone enjoyed it. Didn't attend myself, went for a walk in the Bois de Fressin instead.

FRESSIN JUNE 29TH 1918 Spent the morning with Gen. Hill comdg. the 52nd Div and Forbes-Robertson, one of his brigadiers. Hill is a fat, rather swash-buckling type and did not impress one v. much. Forbes-Robertson, though, is a bit of a character from his appearance. Terrific temper I should say – and very strong fellow physically, and very capable and practical though not very brainy. But ideas and a will of his own, also a V.C., D.S.O. and Bar and a M.C.

When they had left, about 2.15 p.m. I did a bit of work and then went off to play cricket. The first cricket match I have played since 1914 – the officer students played the officers of the staff. The staff won pretty easily. It was a glorious day for it. We had a pitch of matting on dust which worked fairly well.

Was dead tired at the end, so had dinner in my room and went to bed.

June 30th 1918

Dear Mother,

My time has been the Government's from dawn till dark for the last few days and I simply haven't had time to put pen to paper. Even today – Sunday, until just now 7.30 p.m. I have been hard at it, so forgive me for not writing.

This morning I was out preparing a tactical scheme – this afternoon the new Corps. Commander turned up – a truly wonderful man. He was here about 4 hours. On arrival he said he had a bad throat and could not talk much – I was to take him round and he would nod his head as a sign of comprehension while I talked. Having said that, he started off and never stopped talking once. He looked at everything, and gave learned dissertations on every blooming thing – he teaches the cooks to cook, the engineers to do their work, everyone else his work, including the doctor how to use a lancet and treat the influenza. And he expects all he says to be noted and a typed extract of it all to be sent to him later. Some document, my word!! I told you he was here 4 hours, and my wretched adjutant will have to take it all down.

Since he has been with the corps – just a week – he has done a lot of these inspections, and so far I believe I'm the only fellow who has got a good mark. Touch wood! Though I wonder if I should have minded much if it had been a bad mark.

I shall be awfully interested to hear about the house and whether you take it. It seems probable that I may get a bit of leave about the end of July now, but by no means certain. For one thing I think the Boche will very likely make his great effort before then, and so plans are never very safe. It's got warmer again now which makes me feel much fitter.

[DIARY] FRESSIN JULY 2ND 1918 Tactical schemes – it was topping hot day. L. Carr came down about 11.30 a.m. and stopped till the evening. He told me that the Corps Commander, the day before he came down here, sent for Abbott and ordered him to wire for Levey to come and run the school. This, too, before he had even seen the school and without consulting anyone who had. It tickled me enormously because it wouldn't worry me at all to be sacked by Hunter-Bunter. Then he came down and saw the place and immediately ordered a wire to be sent cancelling the other one.

I was sitting in the garden this evening when a baby swallow came fluttering up to me. I picked it up and it sat in my hand quite happy and unfrightened. But it's become rather a responsibility, I can't leave it in the garden because some of these horrible cats will get it, and one doesn't want to shut it up in a cage. So I have sent for a ladder and we will put it back in a nest. The question is whether the inmates will keep it if it's the wrong nest.

LATER – The wee swallow was successfully returned to his nest – poor wee chap.

FRESSIN JULY 6TH 1918 We had some sports in the afternoon,

but I was unable to get up to them. Then in the evening L. Carr and Thomson turned up from the Corps, and I heard all about the Corps Commander's projected visit for Monday. He wants a special parade, and goodness knows what. He likes to walk on in the full lime-light and declaim: 'I am Sir Aylmer Hunter-Weston, your Corps Commander – look at me.' However he has a lot of good points, and we will try to give him a good show. Have just remembered that yesterday was my birthday – 28 years have I lived in the world.

FRESSIN JULY 8TH 1918 A very hot morning. The Corps Commander arrived at 10.15 a.m., and the fun started. He inspected everyone and everybody most minutely and nothing escaped him. We got off parade about 1.15 and came down to lunch. There were two divisional commanders and nine staff officers with him, – such a mass of red hats has seldom been seen in Fressin I should think.

After lunch the C.C. delivered an oration to all officers on the premises and then proceeded to inspect cook-houses and billets. He seemed fairly satisfied with the whole show – but it was something of an eye-wash day. My brain is in a state of torpor after it anyway.

FRESSIN JULY 11TH 1918 The news of the war is that the Boche attack is expected on the 16th of this month – or perhaps 'rumour' would be a better word than news.

In this instance Willie's information was well based. The last attack in the series of blows which the Germans had delivered since 21 March was to be mounted on 15 July.

July 11th 1918

Dear Father,

Many thanks for your letter. Your evening on the Chess sounds delightful, and when one knows the river and surrounding one knows it must have been so. I haven't thrown a fly for a long time now, except for a few minutes one evening about three days ago, when I got one something under ½lb.

I don't think the Boche can put off his attack much longer – he has got a good many divisions to play with now and it is pretty sure to come before the end of the month, and quite possibly in a few days now.

The school is having rather a *succés* in the interior economy line just now, and everyone is asking if they can send doctors to look at the sanitation, quartermasters to look at the Q.M.'s stores, cook-houses, etc. Don't know how long the enthusiasm will last – it has its disadvantages from our point of view, but provides a pleasant joy-ride for the people who come down. I'm afraid our present Corps Com. takes more interest in the way in which an officer's belt is polished than tactical schemes. The first is very important of course, but the second shouldn't be neglected. He's a man with a wonderful eye for detail though, and he never praises without meaning it, so one learns a lot going round with him. In fact I think one learns more in many ways than one does comdg. a battalion. At any rate one learns more easily what a very little one knows.

Love to Mother – your letter bucked me up no end, because a day on the Chess and a 12 handicap at golf sounds something nearer your old form again.

Your affectionate son

WILLIE

[DIARY] FRESSIN JULY 15TH 1918 The student officers asked us all to dinner in the evening and afterwards various people sang a song and altogether we had quite a pleasant evening. They are quite a good lot.

The Boche attacked the French on both sides of Reims this morning on a front of 90 kilometres.

FRESSIN JULY 16TH 1918 More gas, and more damp heat. A very ordinary day. It finished as far as work was concerned with an inspiring farewell address by the commandant, and a photograph of all the officers by the local expert. He – the expert – insisted on waiting for a cloud to come and cover the sun after he had posed us. To our sceptical eyes the sky appeared cloudless, but after ten minutes or so a cloud arrived and the deed was done.

We had a little cricket after tea, which is quite a common occurrence.

The news we have from the battle front is splendid at present. Except in one or two small places the French seem to be holding this battle zone everywhere. The Americans have done very well indeed. Is this going to be a tremendous defeat for the Boche?

The German attack made very little headway. It was the turn of a tide which was soon to ebb at a furious rate. On 18 July Foch launched a great counter-attack to drive the Germans back from the Marne.

[DIARY] FRESSIN JULY 19TH 1918 Yesterday the French counter-attacked west of Reims and apparently with success. Present reports say about 17,000 prisoners and 200 guns. Which is a biff in the eye for Mr Boche.

This morning Hill and I went off to do a tactical scheme, but we discarded it after studying it for a bit.

In the afternoon I found myself idle, so I went off and had an hour or two by the river and very pleasant it was too, especially in the evening when it got cooler, and we had two very refreshing showers. Got three not bad trout.

FRESSIN JULY 20TH 1918 Inspected the LG. School. Better turnout than I expected. Then rode over to Agincourt and looked first at the church, which is a small gem, and then at the battlefield which is marked by a '*Calvaire*'. L. Carr and Monty came to lunch and we discussed a bit of business.

In the evening Lowrie drove me down to Boulogne in his enormous auto-de-luxe – we did the journey in 1½ hour. We dined together with Lochbuie as third – we found him at the Folkestone Hotel. He had brought down the 24th Div. troupe and had been performing at the hospitals. Lowrie went off after dinner and Lochbuie and I went down to the Quay to see if I could get over on an unofficial boat as the leave boat does not leave till 2.15, but there was nothing going.

Between 21 July and 4 August Willie was on leave in London and at Nonsuch Park, a house the Saltouns had taken in Surrey. The days were filled with golf at Walton Heath, theatre, dances, clubs and seeing friends. Although he didn't know it, he was only to have another four weeks at the Corps School.

During the last weeks of July and at the beginning of August preparations were made for what turned out to be the decisive battle of the war on the Western Front. The Fourth British Army and the First French Army were placed (by Foch) under Haig's command for the first stage of a new Allied offensive. The area chosen was the Somme. Eighteen divisions from Britain, Canada and Australia formed the Fourth Army, with a further four divisions as subsequent reinforcements. By the day Willie returned to France the artillery was already concentrated; a complex deception plan – foreshadowing the practice of later wars and using, extensively, simulated radio traffic – was executed; and the troops (including 400 tanks) formed up for a great attack east of Amiens. The operations of the preceding weeks had led the Germans to abandon most of the ground won in the March and April pushes. The stage seemed to be set for a triumph – but triumphs had promised before and proved mirages. The conditions for this one had arrived with perplexing speed. The day was fixed: 8 August. Ludendorff was to describe that day as 'the black day of the German Army'.

[DIARY] FRESSIN AUG 8TH 1918 Fine day on the whole. Had nothing much to do in the morning so rode over to look at the château at Framecourt. When I got there I found that the King was staying there so I beat a retreat. It was a very pleasant ride, but the fly was rather bad. Got home to find Bailey and de Scheer paying a visit to the school. They said the attack was going well as far as could be ascertained, but the news was very uncertain. It's too early for definite news yet, and even now we have had no reliable information on how things have gone.

FRESSIN AUG 9TH 1918 Did a certain amount of French in the evening. The sergeant students for the next Infantry Course turned up today, so tomorrow one will be properly in harness again, and I shall have to start giving lectures, which is a most astoundingly unpleasant performance – at any rate for the lectured. What a boon it would be to like getting up on one's hind-legs, as does for instance our famous (or notorious) Corps Commander, Hunter-Bunter. He is coming all the way down here on Sunday for the purpose.

The news continues to be good from the battle-front and the latest is that our patrols are outside Chaulnes – that the prisoners number 20,000 and we have captured nearly 300 guns and much booty including a Corps Commander and a railway train. (*Sotto voce* be it said – I should like to offer the Corps Commander back to the Boche on condition they took Hunter-Bunter as well.)

So Caix, the scene of our quondam activities, is once more in our hands – though much delapidated I fear, by all accounts. They say among other things that the church is destroyed, and it was rather a beautiful church.

FRESSIN AUGUST 10TH 1918 Started the day by getting rid of an opening address to the Infantry Course. So there it is – launched. We then went up to the parade ground, and had a demonstration for the benefit of the students – of how a company or battalion should fall in on parade, followed by other demonstrations. The padre was up doing a bit of work on the cricket pitch, which is a great change. He is certainly one of the laziest of men.

In the afternoon we had a great cricket match – it really was rather fun. The married men on the staff had challenged the celibates, and had been swanking a bit as we have got a new Q.M.S. at the Lewis Gun School, who is a professional from Lord's and a married man. However we won the toss and went in first, made 150 for 9 wickets and declared – the captain[*] made an inglorious duck *en parenthèse*. After tea the married men had a knock and we trundled them out for 47 – the captain taking 6 wickets for 19 runs. It was a truly glorious day with a light cool breeze which kept it from being too hot.

[*]WF.

The news is good – progress north of the Somme where we had been held up, and south of it the advance continued almost to Roye. A great new attack by the French which has resulted in a complete success, and among other things the envelopment and capture of the salient about Montdidier.

It was one of the most glorious star-lit evenings I have ever seen – and the sky was alive with shooting stars.

And on the following day, unbeknown to any in the Allied armies, the Kaiser told his own General Headquarters, 'The war must be ended.'

VIII
Victory
1918

[DIARY] FRESSIN AUGUST 11TH 1918 Sunday – another glorious day, but hardly one of absolute rest. We had a church parade in the morning, followed by an inspection of the sergeant's course. The turn-out was far from perfect. The Corps Commander descended upon us at 11.30 to lecture to the Infantry Course, and he did it too – for a solid hour – *très solide*.

Then he inspected them, and after that the officer instructors, and managed to pick a lot of holes. Then he looked at a few billets, and professed himself pleased. All this occupied over two hours. I then provided him with a good lunch, after which I told him what I wanted for the school, and if words count we would be amply provided. He then left – I'm glad it's a long way to Corps H.Q.

FRESSIN AUGUST 12TH 1918 Glorious day. Started off soon after 8.30 for Corps H.Q. to attend a demonstration and lecture by the I.G. Training, Gen. Maxse. It was work I knew fairly well, having run an exactly similar show with M. at Ham. However I expected to see a lot of people there, and did. Hunter-Bunter was answering for the Army Commander as president. Proceedings opened with a short address by him, followed by a lengthy and very able discourse by Maxse, explaining 'the doctrine'. He was in very good form. Then we had a long and very hot day of unadulterated Levy – very boring to me as I had seen it all before. Had lunch with Wallie Green, who told me all about the exploits of the 51st Division on the Marne. After lunch more Levy, followed by a discussion of the day's work. The fellow I pitied the whole day was Hunter Bunter, who was compelled to adopt the unaccustomed role of listener, and unable to get a word in at all. However he managed to get a bit of his own back after the conference in a somewhat lengthy finishing oration.

Left Corps H.Q. at 5.30 p.m. and went to see the 6th G.H. who were in the vicinity, and spent a happy hour among old friends – and they all appeared glad to see one. I like Thom who is now commanding the battalion. He impresses one as a man.

I finished up by carrying off two young sergeants to attend the present course at the school (sub rosa) and Risk, who is now adjutant, for a day's holiday. We got home about 8.45 p.m.

Champagne for dinner to commemorate the 4th anniversary of Hill's landing in France. Also the new port which was very good. After dinner Wallace sang, and Craster and I sat in the garden and listened.

It was a most wonderful evening, quite still – the stars overhead and the young moon, in the distance the flashes of the guns, but so far off that no report reached our ears.

I often wonder how many, even of those who have suffered most, could they put back the hand of time four years and so arrange it that there should be no war, would do so? Not I certainly, – I think I have seen more real happiness here in France during the agony of these days than ever I saw before.

Our evening ended with the hum of Boche aeroplanes over-head, the sky lit up with the questing search-lights, and the flash of the bursting shells from the 'archies'. So we put the lights out.

CAMBLAIN L'ABBÉ AUGUST 21ST 1918 We started off (Carey and I) at 8.30, and after calling at 24th Div. HQ went on up to the line. We left the car at Maroc and walked on up to Loos. I had never seen this part of the line before, and Loos Towers and the Double Crassier had been names to me. Loos was full of gas, and wild-flowers and garden flowers run wild. Then we turned up by Hart's Crater, and away southwards, calling on battalions as we went, but without any luck in the way of finding people at home. We met the car again later on, and then went to see Cochrane at his H.Q. To find he was away on leave, – a fellow, Compton-Smith, who originally commanded a battalion in the 76th Bde. was answering for him. From him we took a drink. Then we drove off to Thelus at the far end of the Vimy Ridge, where we left the car and walked to the crest. And there – with a wonderful view of Lens and the country to the south – we sat and ate our lunch. And watched our gunners getting busy on Lens and sending up clouds of red dust. Our dessert consisted of blackberries picked on the spot. Then back to the car, in which we picked up Compton-Smith and returned to Chateau de la Haie where the Corps Commander was to deliver a lecture at 3 p.m. which we had to attend. The day was very hot, and the glare of the chalk had been very trying.

And that lecture, which lasted 2 hours and ten minutes in a tin roofed hut, very nearly finished me. The subject was the defence by the French Fourth Army between Reims and Verdun, and very well-delivered, though somewhat egotistic and too much interspersed with exhortations to the audience to go and do likewise.

FRESSIN AUGUST 24TH 1918 The Corps Commander has asked Father to come out and stop with him which is splendid.

The news is really excellent – The Third and Fourth Armies have both made a great advance and taken thousands of prisoners. Probably we have got Bapaume again.

FRESSIN AUGUST 25TH 1918 The news is splendid again to-night and I don't think we have heard all of it. The Third Army have made another big advance with very few casualties, and their total prisoners come to fifteen thousand. The Fourth Army also advanced, and the French, but we have no news about them. It would be something if one was up there doing a job of work instead of sitting comfortably back here. However the time is coming for that I expect.

There was now a general eastward advance along the entire front of the British Expeditionary Force. Fourth Army had begun it. Third Army, next to their left, took it up. By 29 August the positions of the old Somme battlefield had been reached – ground insignificant in itself but profoundly significant in the celerity of German withdrawal it implied. This, once again, was open warfare rather than the siege-battering of the trenches.

[DIARY] FRESSIN AUGUST 27TH 1918 News from the front good – the First Army attacked today with the Canadians and the 51st Div. which means my old 6th G.H. are in it again, I suppose.

FRESSIN SEPT. 2ND 1918 Wet and cold. Two commanding officers came down from the 24th Division this morning to stop till tomorrow.

Had a bit of a surprise this morning, was rung up from the Corps by Stirling and told that I was being sent to command our first battalion. I can't deny that I was a bit disappointed at first, because after all I was promised a Brigade when I was given this job, and Maxse told me two months ago when he gave up command of the corps that I was third on the list. At which rate I am now top of it because two fellows have been promoted since then.

Went over to Creçy in the afternoon and saw Gen. Maxse and Monty and Tom Hollond and heard a lot about training. The general told me that they had a rule now at G.H.Q. that no one under 30 could get a brigade, which finishes me as far as promotion is concerned. But what does it matter after all – one is meant to do just what comes along as best one can and have faith that it's all for the best.

Willie's father had been invited to stay by General Hunter-Weston, an eagerly awaited visit.

Sept. 3rd 1918

Dear Father,

I hardly know how to tell you, but I'm afraid the visit must be off. I have been ordered to go at once to command the 1st Bn. of my Regiment and shall be away in two days. And they are in the battle, so you see I can't put you up. It's all been so sudden. I only knew for certain this evening about it. And now this Corps will be engaged and everyone at Corps H.Q. will be awfully busy and all the cars will be engaged, and it won't be any catch stopping here, because you see I shall be away. So you see I'm afraid we shall have to cancel the whole thing. I can't tell you how sorry I am about it all, I'm afraid you've had a lot of trouble making all arrangements, and it will be a bit of a disappointment not to come out, because I know you would have loved it. But later on when things quiet down a bit I daresay I might be able to fix it up again.

About myself, I was a bit disappointed at being sent back to a battalion at first, but I think they have got a rule now that one may not get a brigade until one is 30, and that being so I couldn't wish for anything better than to command the 1st battalion. Also they are in the battle, which is much better than holding trenches. And I'm still on the list for a brigade, so I hope you won't be disappointed about that too. I think it's a good thing – I have been here quite long enough. It's a bit strange though to think of being back with a battalion after living in comfort so long. It's jolly good for one. My address will be: 1st Gordon Highlanders, B.E.F.

I'm in an awful hurry, there is so much to settle up. I have a good deal of surplus kit which I shall send to 1 Bryanston Square. Love to Mother, will you thank her for her letter.

Your affectionate son

WILLIE

[DIARY] FRESSIN SEPT 3RD 1918 Fine day. Spent part of the morning on parade with Hodson and Hepden, battalion commanders from 24th Division. Then Gen. Bonham-Carter came down and I had a talk to him about my successor. The Corps Commander wants to have a fellow called Corrall and I know he's quite the wrong type of fellow for the job. And said so, and B-C agreed with me. And I daresay it won't come off. It won't be happy if it does.

Also I put in the recommendations for four of my fellows who are probably going away. It seems I have got to go at once – so Father's visit will have to be put off and I'm afraid he will be very disappointed about that. It is bad luck. It seems I am about 3 months off a brigade now, that's not long, and it's a jolly good thing to have fresh experience of a battalion before that comes off – if it does – so it does seem as if everything was working out for the best already. And what can one want better than to command one's own battalion? Gen. Bonham-Carter is an awful good fellow, and found out all about it for me. I must say I am looking forward to it, to getting up to the front again, it's so jolly good for one when all's said and done. One sheds the little material things that creep about one when one is back behind. And I'm sure Billy has got a hand in it and will be there to help, – it's odd how I felt him close the other night and spoke to him about this very thing. And now I'm going back to his old brigade.[*]

The sad part about the whole thing is Father's disappointment. I must say I've been very happy here with these fellows, and many a happy hour I've spent reading and fishing this summer which fellows in the line have missed.

FRESSIN SEPT 4TH 1918 My last day at the school. Spent the morning making various arrangements and sorting and tearing up old letters, sending off my surplus kit and generally preparing for an upheaval. Then I had to go and say goodbye to the curé and give him back a book he had lent me. He told me that the Rosary plan was going like wild-fire and had spread to the villages round about. So that's good news for Mother. Then I had to say goodbye to the Desmons family. Law and I had a last look at the camp and other work which is at last really progressing now we have got some labour – I should have liked to see the camp finished.

In the afternoon I had to go to Corps H.Q. to see the Corps Commander and fix up one or two things, and say *au revoir* to my friends there. Got back rather late for dinner to find champagne on the table, and Hill full-primed for a farewell speech – to which I replied somewhat lamely.

Then I played a last game of chess with the doctor and defeated him once more. And so I suppose farewell to another chapter, and rather a happy one.

1st Battalion Gordon Highlanders, in which Willie had commanded a company in 1915, had been committed to the Battle of the Somme on 18 July 1916 at Longuessel with a loss of over 300 officers and men. After hard fighting in the rest of that July and August the battalion had lost almost as many men again in a

[*]76th.

[284]

further major attack at Guillemont on 18 August – only a short distance from their July attack. And in the last stages of the Somme battle, the fighting known as the Battle of the Ancre, the battalion had lost a further 140 men in conditions of frightful November mud. They had taken part in the Battles of Arras in 1917, not far from Willie's 6th Gordons although in a different division and Corps, and had suffered 260 casualties there. And in September 1917 1st Gordons had been committed to the appalling later stages of 'Third Ypres', attacking in the shattered area known as Polygon wood – with a further 260 casualties.

In 1918 the 1st Gordons had been caught up in the German March offensive. They had then carried out a limited objective attack with success in June. On 21 August the battalion had been committed to the second phase of the great British offensive which had started on 8 August. They had undertaken some comparatively small-scale operations in 'open warfare', the principal assault tasks having been allocated to other battalions of the 76th Brigade (3rd Division) in which the battalion was still serving. There had been a constant dribble of casualties throughout these operations. When Willie assumed command they were in rest billets near Moyenville – bleak, battle-devastated country; a battalion tried in many fires.

[DIARY] SEPT 5 1918 IN THE MIDDLE OF MILES OF NOTHING. Left Fressin at 11 a.m. after saying goodbye all round.

Started off in a car to find Corps H.Q. but they had moved from the location which I had been given. Found the rear echelon after touring the country until 1.30 p.m. and cadged some lunch from them. They told me where the Division (i.e. my new one – the 3rd) was supposed to be, but I went there and could not find them. (They were there all the time as a matter of fact, but rather well camouflaged.) Eventually I found Corps H.Q. and the old A.B.[*] taking a rest. He was very pleasant and got me the location of my new Brigade – the 76th. Also told me where Jim Burnett was – quite close by, so I went on and saw him. Found Porter – my new brigadier – with him, and we had a cup of tea together. Called on

---

[*]The Corps Commander VI Corps was Lieutenant-General Sir Aylmer Haldane, formerly Gordon Highlanders.

the A.B. again on my way back and had another cup of tea, and then on to H.Q. of the 76th Bde. Porter walked with me over to where the battalion was lying. The men are in trenches, and we have got 3 tents for all the officers, so the quarters are less comfortable than Fressin. Luckily the weather is fine. We are in the middle of miles of absolute nothing, not a tree nor a house. It is where the front line was before our recent attack and in the middle of the destroyed area. Looking out towards the sunset one saw miles of rolling, shell-torn country covered with rank brown grass, and far away on the skyline one broken ruined tree stood up against the sun.

The battalion has had pretty heavy casualties and is pretty disorganised, and so far no drafts. But everyone is cheery, which is good. I see a lot of difficult work ahead.

GANDIEMPRE* SEPT 6TH 1918 We got orders early in the morning that we were to move from the land of nothing by march route, back to an area where there are still some houses. At 11 a.m. we moved off, – rather hot and dusty. So I got a chance to see the battalion on the road – the march discipline is not good at present. At 2 p.m. we had a two hours halt for dinners, and moved off again at 4. Porter, our brigadier, came to lunch with us.

At 6 o'clock we got to Gandiempre, a village of dilapidated barns and houses, and containing dirt and flies beyond any village I have ever seen, I think. Even today the streets are muddy, so they will be 'orrid if it rains. However a roof is always preferable to open trenches, so the change is for the better.

Our billetting officer had fixed up a meal for everyone on arrival, and I had sent on the cookers, so that tea was ready for the men. At 8 p.m. we had a conference of company commanders, and I explained what I wanted in the way of organisation, and what was to be done the next day. Then early to bed.

GANDIEMPRE SEPT 7TH 1918 Spent the morning walking round billets and trying to arrange tables and feeding places for the men. But I fear it's impossible. Washing places we shall be able to fix up. But nothing has ever been done to improve the place, though dirt has been scattered everywhere most lavishly. It

* A village between Arras and Doullens.

is a disgrace – the way in which the men have to pig it in these villages, for want of forethought and organisation on the part of the authorities. And still they are expected to be disciplined and clean and smart.

Inspected some of the cookers and the cooks, and both need cleaning up considerably.

Rode up to brigade H.Q. for tea as I wanted to see the general, and while there heard that Jim Burnett was on his way over to the battalion [*] so I went back. We saw the pipes and drums, and then had a talk and he told me a lot about the battalion. We then went over to the Brigade for dinner. Got home about 10.30 after quite a cheery evening. Maxim in good form throughout as usual.

GANDIEMPRE SEPT 8TH 1918 Sunday, but church parade, which I did not attend, was brought to an end by heavy rain. Yesterday afternoon was wet, but today is perfectly miserable, and the streets in our village resemble ditches more than roads.

Have been busy all day one way and another. Definitely decided yesterday to appoint one Pirie adjutant. He is very young but a nice cheery boy and quite capable. There is no one else suitable in any case. He arrived today from Brigade H.Q. where he has been attached.

GANDIEMPRE SEPT 10TH 1918 Started the day with an effort at a battalion parade, but we had hardly got started when the rain came down in a deluge. It cleared up later but showered at intervals all day. The Brigadier came over in the morning and stopped to lunch.

In the afternoon had some demonstrations of musketry exercises. It appears that this is our last day in billets and tomorrow we move forward and live in the open. It will be devilish wet and cold unless the weather changes. No drafts as yet, and lately no whisky – don't know which is worse. This evening someone insulted us by sending us a case of Irish whisky and it's more like castor oil than anything else!

IN THE WILDS NEAR DOUCHY SEPT 11TH 1918 Very wet in the morning. Orders had come during the night for us to move up to

[*] Which Burnett – later Major-General Sir James Burnett of Leys, generally known as 'Maxim' – had himself commanded earlier.

the Douchy[*] area today. It cleared up about 11 a.m. and we moved off about 2 p.m. under a bright sun. The march was about 9 miles and a good day for marching, so the men made nothing of it. The accommodation in our new area consisted of trenches with a few shelters in them – but the men are old at this game and before dark all were under cover comfortably enough, and as long as it is fine we shall be as right as rain. We move again tomorrow.

Rumour has it that the 62nd division is going to do an attack and that we are to be behind it, but whether this is true I know not.

IN THE DESERT SEPT. 12TH 1918 An awful wet morning – fine wetting rain and a high wind. It had cleared a bit by 10.15 at which time we got on the road, but the mud was horrid. However we pushed on well and got to our destination soon after 1 p.m. At first sight it was a bit of waste ground with a few trenches in it, but a little investigation (technically termed 'scrounging round') disclosed comfortable quarters for the whole battalion – made by the industry of the Boche, and which the rapidity of our advance had not given him time to destroy completely.

By the time we had got everyone settled in and dinners over, it was after four o'clock, so the rest of the day was spent in cleaning up which was badly needed.

I walked over to Brigade H.Q. in the evening. The 62nd division has apparently done a fairly successful show, and it seems probable that we may be here for a day or two.

SAME BIT OF NOTHING SEPT 13TH 1918 And not such a bad place now the weather has cleared up. We spent the day training, and I should say at least half the time was wasted completely owing to the inefficiency and lack of thoughtfulness shown by all platoon and most company commanders. Odd how many fellows do splendid work in the line, and how few know how to teach their men anything out of it.

In the afternoon we did an 'attack with tanks,' but as the show had not been prepared or properly worked out – it was rather a

[*] All this was in the sector between Arras and Bapaume.

fiasco. The trouble with tanks is that they always want the infantry to conform to their manoeuvres and forget that the infantry too have their limitations, and that they (the tanks) must conform too – to a certain extent.

I saw Brand today, whom I had not seen for a long time. After dinner the Doctor and I were reading the Open Road. He is a well-read fellow and appreciates what he reads.

Sept. 13th 1918

Dear Mother,

Many thanks for your letter. Here I am, and there is plenty of work to do, but at present no results visible. It's very uphill work, because one is working against time always. I daresay we shall be in again before many days are over.

The French and Americans seems to have done a good show south of Verdun, but news is scanty with us. I'm v. happy in the battalion, but I don't think it's a v. happy division, and one doesn't get much help from those above as far as I have seen so far. We are rather fortunate here because we have got quite good quarters constructed by the Boche and are away from mud to a great extent.

Will you tell Father that he is looking too far north if he wants to follow our doings. Do you remember the last battle I was in last year?[*] With a battalion one really hasn't very much to write about, because one can say so little. My great difficulty at present is that none of the officers or NCO's have been taught to regard themselves as teachers, and it doesn't worry them a bit if all their men look thoroughly bored the whole time they are on parade and learn absolutely nothing. And they don't realise that it's their fault, and think you can curse a man into taking interest in what's going on. And as I say one has no time to get down to things from the beginning and all the time we are stumbling along at a run before we have learnt to walk. It's extraordinary how few fellows there are in the army who have any conception of what training means. What a long grouse!! So the result is one is always fighting battles with half-trained men, no not half nor yet a quarter-

[*]Cambrai.

trained men. But they have mostly got experience of fighting which carries them through as a rule, though with double the casualties one would have if they were trained.

And now I must stop. Love to Father.

Your loving son
WILLIE

[DIARY] SAME PLACE SEPT. 14TH 1918 Another day of training. I think the training is improving too. Lunched at Bde. H.Q. to meet a tank fellow who did not turn up. Rode over to Corps H.Q. in the evening and saw the A.B. and Gen. Pereira, who happened to be there.

I asked the A.B. if he could not help us in the way of getting more Sandhurst boys for the battalion, and he promised to write to the A.G.* – Macdonogh. So perhaps something will come of it.

The French and Americans in the south seem to have done pretty well so far. Sad to say we move from here tomorrow, 5½ miles nearer the line, and although I don't know, I foreshadow that we shall go into the line the day after.

We got a draft of 114 boys of 18½ years this evening – they are too young and it is a pity to send them out here. The battalion is still much below strength and it will be a pity if we have to do a show at present.

FREMICOURT SEPT. 15TH 1918 Sunday and a glorious day. We had a voluntary church parade in the morning in the open air, and the attendance was phenomenal. The battalion moved in the afternoon from comfortable quarters in the desert, to the remnants of a village about 3 miles away. The march afforded no untoward incidents – one of our observation balloons was brought down in flames just as we were starting.

Our new billets compare very unfavourably with those we have left and most of the men have made themselves bivouacs with the remnants of Nissen huts. It is a glorious moonlight night and the Boche was over while we were having dinner and dropped a few bombs – one or two rather close for comfort, and I make no

*Adjutant-General.

doubt that he will be over again shortly. Report has it that he also shells this village, and popped 26 into the vicinity of our billets last night.

The doc. and I have decided to share a tent for the night, though I'm not sure a deep dugout wouldn't be wiser – if less pleasant.

10.30 P.M. We have just seen the Gotha which has been bombing us brought down in flames by one of our aeroplanes. It was a great sight. The Hun was caught in the searchlights, so that he looked like a great silver bird. Then our fellow shot him with tracer bullets, and the silver was changed to a golden flaming mass, which lit up the whole sky as it fell about half-a-mile away. The cheering which greeted his fall could have been heard for miles.

SEPT. 16TH – NEARER THE LINE (NEAR MORCHIES)* We are in Divisional Reserve and live in a sunken road to which we moved this morning, leaving Fremicourt about 8.30 a.m. It was a march of about 4 miles. The accommodation is very indifferent and so far we have not been able to get sufficient material to make proper cover for all the men. In the evening Pirie and I went forward a bit to have a look at the country in front and a view of the promised land, i.e. that which is still behind the Boche lines. It was a very hot oppressive day and I had a head-ache the whole of it. Bicycled down to Bde H.Q. for dinner and sat talking to the general till nearly 11 p.m. after it. The doc. and I were sharing a tent which was part dug into the ground. It was very pleasant when I turned in, though developments happened later.

SEPT. 17TH – SAME PLACE The day started about 3 a.m. when I was awoken by the 60 pounder battery located about 100 yards behind the tent. The noisiest guns of the whole armament of all the participators in the Greatest War – they nearly burst my ear-drums at every shot. However their activity was brought to a sudden end about 20 minutes later by one of the most over-whelming thunder-storms I have ever seen. The night had become so stifling that one could not sleep, but lay and sweated. And then

*Between Bapaume and Cambrai.

the storm broke. The night grew pitch-black, and the thunder was able to laugh the loudest bombardment to scorn, and the sky was a continuous blaze of lightning. And between the flashes the darkness was so oppressive that it almost hurt. The rain came down in torrents and flooded the floor of our tent and dripped through the roof on to my head. It lasted about 20 minutes, then all grew quiet again, but only for a moment – the 60 pounders started again to try and rival the thunder. So one way and another it was a disturbed night, and I have foresworn a tent for the future.

Many of the men had got soaked to the skin owing to insufficiency of cover for all, and had to spend the day drying their clothes. The remainder carried on with training.

At 2.30 p.m. I had a lecture for officers and NCO's and had hardly begun to speak, when the 60 pounders started again and I had to give in and wait until they had finished. It went well enough when we got going – a demonstration followed which was quite instructive and interesting. Anyway we did not finish until 4.35, and the men who did the show told me they had thoroughly enjoyed themselves. After tea we went out shooting partridges and got a brace which I handed over to the general. Rum issue tonight, so I must now make the rum punch.

SEPT 18TH 1918 SAME PLACE Training in the morning. In the afternoon there was a very heavy bombardment from Moeuvres down to Havrincourt Wood[*] and I thought we should have to go forward. No definite orders came in for a long time, though we got orders to be ready to move at short notice. About 6.30 p.m. I rode over to Bde H.Q. and the situation then – as far as could be ascertained – was that the Hun had attacked our divisional front and to the south of us. Most of the attack was repulsed, but he got in on the front of one of our battalions and the situation was not clear. Things quieted down towards evening, but now they are warming up again, though apparently further to the south.

However, I shall be very surprised if we are still here tomorrow at this time, and it is quite probable that we shall move tonight. So the thing is to go and get a bit of sleep now.

[*]South-west of Cambrai.

SEPT. 19TH 1918 SAME PLACE Wrong again, we did not have to move after all. The Brigades in the line dealt with Boche and captured about a hundred.

Training in the morning. Had a lecture for company and platoon commanders in the afternoon. Tea at Brigade H.Q. and the general and I discussed the Brigade's next battle, which would appear to be a difficult show.

Old Boche put a few shells near our dwelling place today – dirty dog. All quiet on our front and good news from the south where the Fourth Army have taken 5000 prisoners. Rum issue, so rum punch made a good ending to the day. I never expected to be here tonight.

SEPT. 20TH 1918 SAME PLACE Training in the morning. Practised companies in attacking under a barrage. In the afternoon we ran through a battalion attack as a tactical exercise.

Called at Bde H.Q. on the way home – the part that we have to play in forthcoming operations is somewhat changed and become more difficult perhaps.

We have a nasty nut to crack – the place[*] which caused us some trouble in November of last year. The battalion is still very weak.

SEPT. 22ND 1918 SAME PLACE All Company commanders went up to have a look at the line in the morning. Walked over with the general to see de Crespigny who commands the 1st Guards Brigade in the morning – also the C.O. of the 1st Irish Guards, Baggaly. They attack on our left. The weather has changed to wet this evening and the ground is getting greasy. Pray God it clears before long.

SEPT. 23RD 1918 SAME PLACE We did a battalion attack[†] in the morning, rather cramped at first by masses of artillery horse lines. However it went pretty well on the whole. Lunched at Bde H.Q. to discuss the battle again – de Crespigny was there too. After tea was summoned to go to Div. H.Q. to discuss a change in plan, as I

[*] Willie was referring to the Cambrai battle. Fontaine-notre-Dame, Bourlon Wood and the Flesquières ridge.
[†] Practice.

[293]

know the ground. Wish we could get definite orders, all these changes make it very difficult for the battalion commander who has to train his men and do the actual show. And so much depends on everyone knowing what they have to do.

Got back a bit late for dinner and wrote a few letters after it. Glorious night, quite warm and a wonderful moonrise. There is a very good tale of two 18 year old boys in this battalion under shell-fire for the first time. Three big shells landed close to them; two exploded, one was a dud. One boy turning to the other remarked in his slow sing-song northern voice – 'Twa brak, yin didna.'

Sept. 23rd 1918

Dear Mother,

Very many thanks for two letters. The move I told you of in my last did not come off, because the people in the line biffed the Boche and we were not required to lend a hand. So we are still in the same place, training to a certain extent. I'm afraid I've been rather bad at writing for the last few days, but to tell the truth I have been very busy indeed. And still am for that matter.

I see we have had rather a good show in Palestine and snaffled the whole Turkish force except old Liman von Sanders, who will probably get a warm welcome when he returns minus his soldiers. However that's his business.

You are quite right when you say we want all the luck we can get, and I should be awfully grateful if you would help the battalion all you can when you get this. I don't forget to do my best in that way. But this is a very special time. Everyone is in good form out here, but the nearer one gets to the front, the more one realises that there is no question of the Boche being beaten yet – he has plenty of fight left. But not so much as we have, and there is no question about it – his infantry is not what it was. What we suffer from is lack of training – we get men of three months training sent straight to battalions and the front line, which happens in no other army. Bad organisation etc. somewhere. But they are good fellows and their hearts are in the right place even if their military knowledge is nil. I have seen twice recently a sight I have never seen before in the war, a Boche bombing 'Plane brought down in flames – a glorious sight though one cannot help being sorry for the poor devils inside. But it must be instant death. You see a great white bird, all silver in the searchlights – then suddenly it transforms into a molten mass of flaming gold which lights up the whole sky as it falls. Like the fall of Lucifer from Heaven perhaps – he was the bloke that took the toss, wasn't he!

Your loving son

WILLIE

[DIARY] SEPT. 25TH 1918 SAME PLACE Got up at 5 a.m. to go and reconnoitre the line. It was a dark drizzling morning. The Brigadier and Pirie and Hutchings and I started off together, and we saw what we wanted. Things were very quiet indeed – hope they will be equally so for the assembly. Got back about 9.30.

Still no orders from Brigade, so I wrote out the battalion orders without them. Eventually they came at about 2 p.m. but with certain important details unmentioned.

We had a conference of company commanders at 6 p.m. and went through the orders, issued maps, etc. I think all preparations are as good as they can be in the time and under the circumstances. Wrote letters after dinner, and eventually went to bed very tired at 11 p.m.

Sept 25th 1918

Dear Mother,

The ball begins to roll again, and before you get this you will have heard of great doings. And we shall be in the midst of them. So you see we need the luck. I think everything is going to be all right, and I think all the preparations one could have made are made. And the men are in good form and certain of success, and Field Service Regulations puts it 'the moral is to the physical as 4 is to 1'. I think one might change the 4 into an 8. Our moral is high and I think the Boche is a bit nervous and possibly shaky. The only things that we have to fear at all are artillery and machine guns and wet weather. And I think we shall overcome the first two and that Providence will arrange the third. So I am full of confidence.

[295]

Today has been a very long day as I was up very early doing a bit of reconnaisance in the front line, and there was much to do when I got back. I don't find our Brigade too helpful, not from lack of will but lack of knowledge. If I was Brigadier I should get a new staff. However one always grouses at those above one, it's the habit of the British Army.

So you are back in Bryanston Square and I can imagine you sitting in your room and feeling rather pleased and comfortable to be back. I daresay Father is sitting reading now 9.45 p.m. and you are probably writing letters which will have to be posted before bed-time. I would do it with pleasure were I there.

I am sitting in a sort of shelter writing letters, rather a grubby shelter under a bank in a country of barrenness and barbed wire and shell holes. A shelter though that is not so uncomfortable after all and has some of the feeling of home about it, because we have been here some days and are soon like to exchange it for a worse. I shall sleep well tonight anyway. It's rather exciting just before a battle, you know! Help us all you can, what I call 'back prayers' are all right. From time to time one hears a shell whining through the night air overhead – destined for someone further back perhaps.

Your loving son
WILLIE

Sept. 25th 1918

Dear Father,

Very many thanks indeed for the flask which arrived today with your letter. It is very nice and just what I wanted. Also for seeing about the brandy. The flask has arrived at the psychological moment for we are on the eve of great things, and we shall be in at the doing. By the time this reaches you all will be well I hope – anyway you will know from the papers. The great thing to remember is that by the time this gets to you I shall either be all right or you will have heard to the contrary. In all human probability that is.

The battalion was not in the show the other day, we were all ready and I thought we should move, but in the end we were not needed. The news from Palestine and Salonika is splendid, isn't it

– I hope it will be from the western front before long. I think so, the men have all got their tails up, and I doubt whether the Boche has. I've had a very long day and still have a lot of writing to do one way and another, so you must forgive a very short letter. I have written to Mother too by this post.

This letter is dated 25th but I shall not send it off till the 26th, because one must not write anything of future operations. I have every faith in things going well, and if we give the Boche a real knock now it may hasten the end of the war.

Your loving son
WILLIE

The Allies were now about to undertake a mighty offensive right along the front, with the object of breaking the Hindenburg Line and driving the German Army from their main position in France. The Americans and French were to attack northward towards Mezières, on the extreme right of the Allied Line. On the left the Belgians were to attack in Flanders towards Ypres. And in the centre the British were to attack between Cambrai and St Quentin, the battlefields of the preceding March. The offensive constituted one vast convergent operation.

The Hindenburg Line was immensely strong. The German Army, advancing successfully from it, had now been thrown back into it; but that was certainly no particular indication that the Allied attacks would carry it. It might be another Somme.

1st Gordons, in 76th Brigade, were to attack towards Cambrai and take the Flesquières Ridge – once again. Their parent division, 3rd Division, were part of VI Corps, the second northernmost of the four corps of the British Third Army under General Byng. After the opening paragraphs of his entry for 26 September, it is clear that Willie wrote up the ensuing days immediately the first phase of the battle was over, on the evening of 27 September.

[DIARY] SEPT. 26TH 1918 SAME PLACE The day before the battle, for it starts tomorrow. I believe it started in the south today. Delivered a short oration to each company in the morning after inspecting them. I hope one has left nothing undone which might make for success. We are due to start this evening at 7.30 p.m. for our assembly positions, and 4 hours ought to see us into them. Arrangements have been made for hot tea and sausages for the men before they attack, as well as an issue of rum. Before they leave here they are to have a good solid supper.

The assembly and the preliminary stages of the attack are what cause me anxiety – once we are formed up under the barrage I think all will go well. However this time tomorrow we shall know more about it; if all has gone well I hope once more to have had a look at Cambrai from the Flesquières ridge.

We have just heard that the French and Americans have attacked between Reims and Verdun and that all is going splendidly. Pray God it's true. I have a feeling that if we do well tomorrow, the end is not far off.

We moved off from our billets at 7.30 p.m. marching by companies at intervals of ¼ hour. The track to our assembly positions had been well marked by Hutton and the assembly was completed without casualty by 11.15 p.m. I had asked to be allowed to assemble later, but it had not been permitted, and I was very glad in the end because the Hun started shelling the canal crossings with extreme accuracy about midnight. Battalion H.Q. were located in the support line and in advance of the battalion.

SEPT. 27TH 1918 The forward march to the Red Line, on which we were to pass through the 8th Brigade had promised some difficulties on account of a change in direction. These were enhanced by large quantities of wire behind our own trenches, which we had to cross. The 8th Bde had promised to cut frequent gaps prior to the attack, but this was not done. This made an advance from our assembly positions in artillery formation, in the dark, quite impossible. Rain during the night had made the trenches, which were not boarded, so slippery as to be almost impassable for troops. Eventually we decided to cut one good gap in the wire and to pass the whole battalion through it by platoons. The move forward from the assembly positions to take place not at zero as arranged, but at 5.45 a.m. when it would be comparatively light. Zero hour was 5.20 a.m.

It was an extraordinarily dark night and the rain made it rather depressing. At 5.20 a.m. the barrage opened and one heaved a sigh of relief. It is always a strain waiting for the hour. At 5.50 a.m. I met companies as they crossed our old line. The two support companies had advanced too soon and as a result had bcome intermingled with the two front companies. Lack of training and lack of experienced officers and NCO's made themselves felt and it was a work of considerable difficulty to re-organise the companies. However we got them sorted out fairly well and the advance proceeded. Everyone was excited, but the men were full of fight. The only officer who really kept his head and displayed power of command was Lee.

I accompanied the battalion up the ridge almost to the Red Line, and then returned to H.Q. It's no good being too far away from them – one can do nothing. As soon as I got to H.Q. we moved forward again after the battalion. Having found a suitable place for them, Perry (comdg. the King's Own, who were attacking on our right) and I went on again after our battalions. All the news coming back was to the effect that Flesquières had been captured, but that companies were mixed and disorganised. On my way forward I met Gillespie (comdg. A Coy) with only a few men. He told me that the 8th Bde. had failed to get their objective on our front and that we had been obliged to take it before forming up under the barrage for our own task. At the time I thought that we had probably arrived too early and had got mixed up in the 8th Bde. attack, but later accounts showed that Gillespie's version was true. At any rate many casualties had occurred and much disorganisation had been caused before we ever started for the attack on our own objective.

In result A & C Corps. captured their own objective all right, but were too disorganised after it to follow the other two companies through the village and go on to the final objective according to plan. When I arrived in the sunken road east of Flesquières I found it crowded with men of the battalion mixed up with many other units. Unfortunately nearly all the NCO's were casualties and although there were several officers about they were mostly without experience. The whole was really a mob of men – disorganised. I found no trace of B. Coy or Lee and it afterwards turned out that he had kept direction and gone forward towards the final objective, but was finally held up by machine gun fire. The remainder of the battalion had got a bit too far to the south.

We made efforts at reorganisation and continued the advance but the barrage had been lost and machine gun fire was very hot, also that of field guns which were shooting over open sights from the left flank. In fact the left flank was responsible for all our difficulties and Graincourt – a village on the left which should have been captured about 9 a.m. – did not fall until 3 p.m. This night we spent in the captured positions – the 62nd Division had gone through us, and for the moment we were behind the war. The battalion had carried out its task, but had suffered heavily especially in NCO's.

SEPT. 28TH 1918 EAST OF FLESQUIÈRES Rather a cold wet morning. Battalion H.Q. moved to a position just in rear of companies. Coy. Sergt. Major Rollo was killed this morning by a stray shell. He came up to the battle of his own free will, because it was his turn to be left out. And he was a magnificent fellow, covered with decorations which he had far more than earned. I think he was the most absolute type of Gordon Highlander I have ever seen. Not very tall but tremendously broad, talking the careful and accurate English of a man whose native tongue is Gaelic, he was the embodiment of the spirit of the regiment. There was no one we could so ill afford to lose at this time. His men trusted him implicitly, he was always cheerful, he always knew what to do – and to be killed today by a stray shell after surviving yesterday.

About midday we got orders to move back about 2 miles to the vicinity of Havrincourt, starting at 3 p.m. Just as we were moving off a mule trod on a bomb in the road and exploded it and three men were wounded. Two of them lance corporals – it seems a sort of fatality that we must lose NCO's in this show.

The men were in trenches in the new area, but a good many managed to make bivouacs out of corrugated iron before dark. Bn. H.Q. was a spot on the map, except for a small, dirty and very cold dugout. Don't think I've ever been colder than I was this night – it was almost impossible to sleep, although one needed it. And the Brigade who had ordered greatcoats to be sent up for the men, entirely forgot the needs of the officers.

SEPT. 29TH 1918 HAVRINCOURT WOOD Spent the day improving the accommodation. There is no water so that it's impossible to get the men clean. Reorganised the battalion as well as possible with hardly any NCO's at all. It's making bricks without straw with a vengeance. In the afternoon, orders came that we might move at any time.

SEPT. 30TH 1918 IN THE DESERT EAST OF RIBECOURT We remained at Havrincourt to start with, prepared to move at short notice. Then it seemed probable we should not move, so C.S.M. Rollo's funeral was arranged for the afternoon. Orders to move came just as the battalion was parading for it, so the pipers went on alone. I'm glad we were able to give him a good funeral, I think it would have pleased him. He was a grand fellow.

We moved at 5.30 p.m. to an area east of Ribecourt where we understood we were to be for the night. There was no accommodation and we arrived in the dark, but we got the men finally settled in trenches, rations issued etc. by 11 p.m. – I had ordered companies to be ready to move at short notice and it was just as well, because I had hardly arrived at bn. H.Q. about 11 p.m. when the Brigadier appeared and informed me that we had to attack at dawn. So I wolfed a meal while he talked. Then we went to the H.Q. of another battalion for a conference and to fix up about guides, and I finally got back to my H.Q. at 12.45 a.m. where company commanders were waiting for me. We had a rapid conference and orders were issued verbally. The coys. moved off soon after 1.30 a.m. Oct. 1st.

OCT 1ST 1918 – MASNIÈRES It was the darkest night I have ever seen and raining hard, and I must confess I was doubtful if we should get the assembly done in time. The guides (found by another division) were very bad indeed. But somehow we got there – my companies by 5.40 a.m. – zero hour was at 6 a.m. And still no sign of the King's Own who were to attack in front of us. It was a very anxious time. Then they appeared, just in time to walk up and deploy under the barrage. The weather had cleared and it was a lovely morning. And the account of the battle is here, as it was sent in to Brigade HQ.

The Account

REPORT ON OPERATIONS CARRIED OUT

BY

1ST BN. THE GORDON HIGHLANDERS

OCT. 1ST 1918

At about 11 p.m. on Sept. 30th orders were received that the 76th Bde would attack Rumilly[*] and the enemy positions to the south and east of it at 6 a.m. on Oct 1st. A Brigade conference was held at the HQ of the 4th York and Lancs. Regt. 62nd Division where details were settled about guides to assembly positions. The plan of attack was explained. This conference ended about 12.30 a.m. Oct. 1st. Company commanders were assembled at Bn. HQ at 12.45 a.m. where orders were issued verbally and the battalion moved off soon after 1.30 a.m.

Plan of Attack The 76th Inf. Bde was to attack and capture a line from G 11 b.1.0 to G 23 d.1.3 including the village of RUMILLY.

The 2nd Bn. The Suffolk Regt. was to attack on the left and capturing the village to advance beyond it to the line aforesaid. The 8th K.O.R.L. were to attack on the right in a N.E. direction as far as the grid line joining G.16 central and G.22 central – thence in an easterly direction to the line aforesaid.

The 1st Bn. The Gordon Highlanders were to be in support – two companies supporting the left of the Suffolk with orders to advance round the west side of the village, should the former be held up – two companies supporting the right of the King's Own, with orders to fill a gap which was liable, on account of the direction of the advance, to occur between them and a New Zealand battalion which was to attack on the right. The Commanding Officer was ordered to go with the right two companies and make his H.Q. with the CO of the K.O.R.L.

The two left companies were placed under command of Capt. Lee M.C. who was to make his H.Q. with OC 2nd Suffolk Regt.

The Assembly The arrangements for guides were as follows:
Right Companies. Two guides were provided by the 4th York and Lancs to guide them up to the Lock Bridge[†] (K24 6.) where 4

[*]Three miles south of Cambrai.
[†]The objectives were east of the Canal de St Quentin.

guides per coy were to meet them and lead them into their assembly positions in G 27 a. The guides of the 4th York and Lancs. led coys by a very difficult route and Lewis Guns had to be carried by the men from the time of leaving the battalion area. The companies moved off at 1.30 a.m. – they did not arrive at the Lock Bridge until 4.35 a.m. and eventually reached the assembly positions at 5.40 a.m.

Left Companies. Guides were provided from Bde H.Q. to lead these coys to H.Q. 185th Bde. 62nd Division where guides from the 5th Duke of Wellington's Regt. were to meet them and take them to their assembly positions. These latter guides were uncertain of the position and the coys were eventually formed up immediately behind the wire west of Rumilly Trench. in G.20.a. They reached this position about 5 a.m.

The Barrage The barrage opened at 6 a.m. Throughout the operation it was extremely ragged and many casualties were thus caused to our own area.

The Attack *Right Companies* (A & C). These companies advanced in rear of the King's Own, who had only arrived on the scene of battle in sufficient time to get into artillery formation and go forward under the barrage. The right company of the King's Own maintained touch with the New Zealanders throughout the advance, with the result that a gap appeared between this company and that on its left. This was filled by the two coys. of this battalion. Heavy machine gun fire from the left flank, as well as from posts in G.22.a., b & c & G.25.a. & b hampered the operation. A post in the sunken road near the Crucifix G.29 also caused casualties. This was dealt with by a platoon of A Coy detached for the purpose.

The objective was eventually gained about 9 a.m. with light casualties. About 150 prisoners were taken by the battalion.

Left Companies The 2nd Bn. The Suffolk Regt. assembled just in rear of Rumilly Trench. As soon as the assembly was complete about 5 a.m. units of the 62nd division proceeded to withdraw from the trench itself, which was left empty as the Suffolks did not occupy it. It appears that before zero hour the enemy infiltrated machine guns into this trench. These guns were naturally unaffected by the barrage and opened immediately our advance commenced. The two left companies of the Suffolk were held up not far in advance of their assembly positions in G.14.c & d. The two companies of this battalion (B & D) also suffered casualties from this fire (the commander of B Coy was severely wounded). They succeeded however in pushing forward in spite of it, and eventually reached a line facing N.E. in G.14.b with their left on the railway about G.8.d.5.0. The whole of this advance was carried out in the face of very strong machine gun opposition and there were many cases of individual gallantry in dealing with these guns. At the above line they were held up by very intense machine gun fire from a quarry close in front of them, and from the railway sidings in G.9.c.

Subsequent Events *Right Companies*. About two hours after the objective had been gained the enemy commenced to advance from the direction of SERANVILLERS, apparently intending to counter-attack. He was engaged at long range with rifle and artillery fire and retired towards the village. About the same time very heavy shell-fire was directed on our positions from the right flank. Machine gun fire from the left was also very accurate.

As men were very crowded in these positions it was decided to withdraw the two coys of this battalion about 500 yards in order to introduce the principle of depth into the consolidation and to save casualties. At the same time it became certain that much of Rumilly was still in the hands of the enemy. One company was therefore withdrawn behind the ridge in G.22.d., the other was ordered to form a defensive flank towards Rumilly in G.22.a. Heavy casualties were incurred in these positions from hostile artillery fire, which enfiladed them from the right flank, especially by A. Coy. This company numbered at this time about 20 rifles.

Left Companies No touch was gained with these coys. during the whole day. Captain Lee made repeated attempts to get forward to the position which they had reached, but was as often driven back by machine gun fire. They were eventually withdrawn after dark.

The Attack on Rumilly At about 4 p.m. it became almost certain that the whole of Rumilly was held by the enemy, and a personal reconnaisance disclosed German machine gunners in the southern end of the village. They were very alert and ready to take advantage of any target offered them. This fact was reported to 76th Bde H.Q.

About 4.30 p.m. orders were received to attack Rumilly from the South at 6.30 p.m. with A & C Corps of this battalion. They were to be supported by a body of the 2nd Suffolk and two sections of the 76th T.M. battery.

The two companies were accordingly withdrawn from their position in support of the 8th King's Own to Bn H.Q. They were both very weak, A Coy numbering about 20 including company H.Q. It was decided therefore to organise them into 5 squads (this was the number of capable leaders available) and to arm them with bombs. The whole were placed under command of Captain Preston (C. Coy).

The operation was to be supported by as many men of the Suffolk as were available and the adjutant of that battalion reported to me at 5 p.m. and arranged to collect what he could in this way at the assembly position. A runner from the 76th Bde T.M. Battery reported to me at 5.30 p.m. and was ordered to bring the two sections of the battery, which were to support the operation, to the assembly position at 6.20 p.m.

A & C Coys reached the assembly position at 6.20 a.m. The two sections of the T.M. battery reported to me there at that time and were attached to Company H.Q.

The adjutant of the Suffolks reported to me at the same time and told me that he had been unable to find any men of his battalion to support the operation.

The attack had been carefully prepared as far as time permitted. The village had been divided into sections and a squad detailed to deal with each section. It had been shelled with heavy guns between 6 and 6.30 p.m. At 6.30 p.m. the Field Gun barrage opened. It was very ragged and many shells were falling as much as 300 yards behind the barrage line. At zero plus 5 minutes A & C Corps advanced from their assembly positions and closed up under the barrage. At zero + 10 they commenced the advance. Each squad proceeded to mop up the section of the village allotted to it. As soon as the companies had started I returned to my H.Q. and en route discovered about 100 men of the Suffolk. These were sent up to the village under guidance of Sergt. Christie of this battalion. They presently caught up the barrage and assisted in mopping up.

Trench mortars were not used in the operation. The attack was completely successful and about 80 prisoners were captured including a battalion commander. A large number of machine guns were later discovered in and about the village. Elements of the enemy still remained, but they were captured or escaped during the night. A body of about 20 attacked A Coy H.Q. during the night. They were driven off and escaped in the darkness. A position was consolidated north of the village immediately after its capture and placed under command of Capt. Gillespie, (Captain Preston having been wounded).

Casualties suffered in this operation were:- one officer killed, one wounded. One sergeant killed, two wounded, one of whom afterwards died of wounds. Sergt. Christie was one of the wounded. These casualties were the result of our own shells falling short.

The battalion had suffered heavily on 27 September, the attack on Flesquières; and less heavily, as Willie's account makes clear, in the subsequent attack on Rumilly, although it was carried out by small groups, using whatever leaders survived, and amid considerable disorganisation. It was, however, completely successful. And a week later another attack, ordered at particularly short notice, was also successful.

[DIARY] OCT 2ND – MASNIÈRES Battalion H.Q. had moved into Masnières[*] after the attack on Rumilly and remained there. The dispositions of the battalion as follows:-Two companies in posts north of Rumilly, the other two companies in trenches south of the village. My impression is that the battle has done the battalion a world of good and that the men are in better form now than they were after Flesquières. Although we are tired and disorganised and almost entirely without N.C.O.s – there is only 1 C.S.M. and 2 sergeants left in the battalion. But I was talking to some of the 18 year old boys this morning and they were full of fight and felt they had done well. As indeed they had.

*Just south-west of Rumilly.

In the evening we were relieved north of Rumilly by the King's Own, and withdrew to trenches in front of Masnières.

H.Q. in the same cellar in Masnières and the flies are perfectly awful.

OCT. 3RD – MASNIÈRES Insisted on all the men washing and shaving, as we can get water. Very little movement is possible by day so that reorganisation is difficult. There is a draft of 160 private soldiers waiting for the battalion and no N.C.O.s among them. The Brigade ordered them forward, – I refused to take them – on the principle that uncontrolled men are worse than no men and that it is merely waste of life to put them into a fight. Eventually we compromised and I had up any men who had served in France before – about 80.

OCT. 4TH – RUMILLY In the evening we relieved the Suffolks in posts north and east of Rumilly. The posts are small rifle pits and quite close behind the front line, so that the men have to keep quite still by day and improve their positions at night. It is very trying work for tired men.

Battalion H.Q. moved to Rumilly.

OCT. 5TH – RUMILLY The Boche shells the village and the vicinity of our posts pretty freely. Our Brigadier, Porter, went off today for a six months tour of duty at home, and a new bloke (Metcalf in the Lincolns) has taken over from him. Seems a queer sort of bird – he came up to see me this afternoon. Anyway he appeared energetic!

OCT. 6TH – RUMILLY Brigade conference in Masnières this afternoon at which it was disclosed that we are again going to tackle the Boche. The 9th Brigade are to do the show and we are to be in support to them. Except the Suffolks who are lent to them for the attack. I hope that we don't have to do a show, because of the lack of N.C.O.s and experienced officers. We lost two coy. commanders in the last show and one has gone on leave, which leaves only one officer of any experience with companies. Have now sent Hutchings, the signalling officer, to command one company. Anyway it seems quite a straightforward attack and we ought not to be needed.

OCT. 7TH — MASNIÈRES Got the orders for the show and wrote ours. Got hold of coy. commanders in the afternoon and went through the orders and did a short reconnaissance of assembly positions and our probable line of advance if we have to move forward. The battalion moved back to cellars in Masnières as soon as it was dark and H.Q. returned to the cellar which we had previously shared with the King's Own, who were still there. Perry who commands them is a very good chap, and we all get on well, so it's rather cheery being together, as well as tactically sound.

It appears that the Fourth Army attack tomorrow on a large scale with very ambitious objectives, striking northwards towards Le Cateau. So that ought to ease things here.

A further short conference after dinner, — also all the various gadgets which have to be carried in an attack now-a-days were issued to the men. The attack comes off tomorrow at 4.30 a.m. So to bed at 10 to get some sleep before the noise begins.

OCT. 8TH — MASNIÈRES & SERANVILLERS We arose about 4 a.m. and had a wash and a shave, and breakfast appeared as the barrage opened at 4.30 a.m.

The Boche retaliation as far as Masnières was concerned was very feeble and all went down towards the canal. News from the front was very slow coming in, but when it did come it was to the effect that all was going well, and a large number of prisoners were coming down. Then came the news that both objectives had been taken. And later that the Boche was counter-attacking with tanks, mainly against the 2nd division on our left. What actually happened in the light of after-knowledge was that the Boche sent over two or three of our captured tanks, which began cruising around, and everyone ran away. No infantry followed the tanks. Eventually they were knocked out, but the infantry did not go forward again.

About 1 p.m. the King's Own — Perry and I were sharing a H.Q. as usual — were ordered forward in support of the 9th Brigade and shortly afterwards we came under the orders of the 9th Brigade —

unfortunately. But the Guards, who were to go through us, had gone forward and I thought that we had a good chance of not being used. However at 3.45 we got orders to go up and replace the King's Own, who were to attack the 2nd objective which had apparently been lost again. The battalion moved at 4 p.m. and I went to see Potter, comdg 9th Bde. He immediately told me I should probably have to attack on the right of the King's Own, but it was all indefinite and I couldn't get a definite order of any sort out of him. I sent Pirie up to stop the battalion relieving the King's Own, and to concentrate them north of Crèvecoeur.[*] Then rushed off to Perry's H.Q. to see what he was going to do. Found him also without definite orders. I then decided to attack without them and rushed off back to the battalion meeting Taldo en route. Got there about 5.15, explained the plan to company commanders and they moved off at 5.30. Quick work but we had to attack at 6.30 and a long way to go. Left Taldo where he could get a wire through to Brigade and went forward with the battalion. It was very dark and one had a very hazy idea of the show, the orders had been so indefinite. We established a H.Q. in the Reda'me just south of SERANVILLERS.[†] Having seen B & D companies who were to attack go on all right from there, I went to look for the 3rd Coy. behind. We only had three coys, being very weak. It was very dark and I couldn't find them anywhere, which was worrying, because it turned out about this time that there were Boche in Seranvillers, and that would be behind our people on their objective. Went back to rear H.Q. and told Bde they must send someone to clear the village. Got rather badly gassed en route and sick as a dog and very unhappy.

Got back to forward H.Q. as soon as possible, and found A. Coy had turned up all right. Bn. H.Q. was a very cold place in an open trench so the doc. and I walked up and down and discussed philosophy to get warm. Doc suggested we should go and round up a machine gunner who had been worrying us from the village but I met the proposal rather coldly. Soon after I got the information I wanted from Bde. H.Q. and went forward to see the companies. They were all at La Targette. Got things straightened out up there, and returned to Bn. H.Q. They had

[*]Small village south of Cambrai.
[†]South-east of Cambrai.

found a much warmer place in a Seranvillers cellar while I had been away.

OCT. 9TH 1918 About 2 a.m. Taldo appeared with orders for a withdrawal at 4 a.m. when the Guards were to go on. So we cleared off back to Masnières at the appointed time, the men occupying trenches just outside the town. At 12 noon we left again and marched back to Havrincourt. The men marched very well considering they had had no sleep to speak of since 4.30 a.m. on the 8th and had done an attack into the bargain.

Arrived at Havrincourt about 3 p.m. where we found our accommodation consisted of bare field with no shelter whatever against the elements. However we got something rigged up before night. I think I will put in the official account of the show of yesterday, here.

REPORT ON OPERATIONS
BY
1ST BN. THE GORDON HIGHLANDERS
OCT. 8TH 1918

Preliminary Events The battalion had been standing by since zero hour, 4.30 a.m. ready to move at ¼ hour's notice. It came under direct orders of G.O.C. 9th Inf. Bde about 2 p.m. At 3.45 p.m. an order was received to the effect that the King's Own would carry out an attack on the Green Line in conjunction with the 2nd Division, who were to attack Fosenville. The Bn. was to replace the King's Own in the old British front line with two companies, one company was to be disposed behind this line. (The battalion consisted of only 3 companies at the time.) Orders were issued and the battalion moved off at 4 p.m.

Orders for Attack At 4 p.m. an order was received for the O.C. 1st G.H. to report to G.O.C. 9th Inf. Bde. He did so at 4.5 p.m. and was informed that the battalion would probably have to attack LA TARGETTE and the Cambrai – Esnes road north of it at 6.30 p.m. The attack was to depend on whether the attack of the 2nd Division on Fosenville was successful. The King's Own were to attack on the left of the battalion and the boundary between battalions was pointed out on the map. Orders were immediately sent to the battalion, which was proceeding to the positions originally ordered, to concentrate on either side of the Crucifix G.29. b, and the Comdg. Officer proceeded to H.Q. The King's Own to learn their plan of attack. He eventually reached his own battalion in G.29 b. at 5.15 p.m. Orders for the attack were issued verbally and the battalion moved off at 5.30 p.m.

The Advance As SERANVILLERS and the ground south of it was definitely reported to be in our hands and the situation to the north of it was uncertain, it was decided to advance south of the village and to attack the objective from the right and not frontally. Two coys (B & D) were to carry out the attack, one was retained in reserve. Battalion H.Q. moved forward with the battalion – a rear report centre being left at the Crucifix in touch with Brigade H.Q. by a wire which was laid by the battalion.

The two leading companies crossed the Red Line at 6.10 p.m. – No definite orders had been received for the attack – it was therefore carried out without orders at 6.30 p.m. These orders eventually reached rear bn H.Q. at 6.35 p.m.

The Attack The attack was carried out by B & D Coys and La Targette was captured without difficulty. The situation on the left was still somewhat obscure as the enemy had a machine gun post north of the buildings, in the Esnes-Cambrai road. This was dealt with about an hour later but touch was not obtained with the King's Own for some considerable time.

The whole advance and the attack was carried out in pitch darkness, which made it very difficult for all ranks to locate themselves.

Seranvillers Shortly after the attack started it became evident that Seranvillers was still occupied by the enemy. Machine gun and rifle fire was still coming from the western end of the village. This fact was reported to Bde H.Q. with a request that orders might be given for it to be mopped up.

The Reserve Coy The Reserve Coy of this battalion which had been ordered forward to H.20 central could not be immediately found in the darkness. Later touch was obtained with it and it was sent forward with exception of one platoon which was retained in battalion reserve. Its orders were to assist the left front company in clearing the road with one platoon, which was then to dig in echeloned in rear of the left flank of the battalion. The second platoon was to dig in, in the same way, in rear of the right flank. These orders were carried out and the line was consolidated as shown in disposition map already forwarded to 9th Inf. Bde.

Seranvillers As soon as the position at La Targette was satisfactory it was intended to mop up Seranvillers with the reserve platoon of the battalion, starting from the eastern end of the village and driving the enemy in a westerly direction; but this operation was rendered impossible by the enemy artillery, which commenced to bombard the village very heavily with H.E. & gas, especially at the Eastern end. It was considered that this bombardment would sufficiently demoralise the enemy in the village, who had given no sign of life for some time, and that they could be collected in the morning. The operation was therefore abandoned.

Remarks The operation was rendered difficult by the hasty nature of the preparations and the absence of definite orders. The difficulties were increased by the darkness of the night and the large amount of gas employed by the enemy round Seranvillers and parts of the valley between it and Crevecoeur.

The Withdrawal Orders were received at 2 a.m. that the bn. would withdraw from the positions gained by 4.30 a.m. in order that the barrage to cover a further advance might be put down on them. This operation was carried out without difficulty.

I called in at the 9th Bde H.Q. on the way back and saw Gen. Potter. He had no thanks to us for taking his brigade objective, which was finally held by the King's Own, the 1st G.H., and the New Zealanders – but censure because the information of success had not got back soon enough. Which certainly was not our fault. I got rather angry and may have been rude, being very tired at the time. I certainly told him his H.Q. were much too far back.

OCT 10TH – NR HAVRINCOURT A bleak bare (except for dirt)

wind-swept slope. However the men soon made themselves little cubby-holes out of old bits of corrugated iron, bivouac sheets, blankets etc. and we had wee houses built for H.Q. and Coy. messes. There was a tent for Orderly Room so Taldo was quite happy. Pearson and the doc. and I shared another tent. And Cabane had salved a stove and a table and some chairs in Masnières, and finally this little bit of desert became quite a comfortable home. We spent the day getting the battalion reorganised, it was all mixed up after three battles owing to casualties etc. In fact 70% of it is completely new since we came out of the line, and of the battalion I took over 6 weeks ago I don't think 10% remains apart from the administrative blokes. No N.C.O.s left at all and none being sent up and one does not know whom to promote because all the men are new. Since I've had the battalion we've had drafts of 479 O.R. and among them six N.C.O.s. It's really wicked.

OCT 11TH – SAME PLACE And doing the same thing, – company commanders still busy getting their companies reorganised. It is a difficult job. We had baths and much needed clean clothes in the afternoon.

OCT. 12TH – SAME PLACE Bathing all the morning, interspersed with a little drill. Just before lunch a very grimy corporal of the R.E. turned up and announced that they proposed to build a railway through H.Q. Mess starting in 2 hours. So we had two hours' notice to have lunch and get our house bodily shifted elsewhere. The sort of thing that might have upset one – once upon a time.

I walked over to Brigade while the house was moved in order to have somewhere to sit out of the rain.

OCT. 13TH – MARCOING Perry has been sent on leave, and about time too, so Pearson has gone temporarily to command the King's Own. Cold damp sort of morning. We left Havrincourt at 10.30 a.m. and marched here, about 4½ miles. Considering the absolute lack of N.C.O.s the march discipline was pretty good. Got in about 12.30 p.m. – the accommodation is not very good because the Boche has systematically destroyed all the houses

[313]

which our shell-fire left. However the men are all under cover more or less rain-proof and it was not very long before most platoons had a good fire going too. H.Q. is located in the remains of a house which the Boche used as a prison, and one of its former inmates has recorded on the wall that he had just been sentenced to a good many years penal servitude for desertion. I think the battalion should be comfortable here if we are not bombed too badly, although most of the best billets are occupied by Portuguese whom we are not allowed to turn out, and Corps. Troops.

Oct. 14th 1918

Dear Father,

At last I have a moment to write you a line. We were withdrawn from the battle a few days ago, after being at it on and off from the first day of the last attack, Sept. 27th. The battalion did well under rather difficult circumstances. We had three definite attacks to do apart from odd jobs, and never got a chance to rest or reorganise at all. When we weren't fighting we were holding bits of the line, and even when you are out you can imagine that a devastated country with no cover and no water does not give one much opportunity to rest and reorganise. When we first came out we were in a bare field, but here we are better off rather, though still in the devastated area. However now we have penetrated the desert and emerged the other side and the further forward one goes the better off one is as far as accommodation is concerned.

What is coming over everyone? Every paper one opens is full of German peace offers, and it's very unsettling for the private soldier. The bonds of discipline are not so very strong in the British Army today and if the soldier gets the idea that there is no real need for him to go on fighting, there may be trouble. I regard the whole thing as the last effort of the Boche to make us slacken our efforts. I would forbid the papers to make any mention of peace until the Boche lays down his arms and retires to his own country. Until he does that the only answer is to give him another knock. It is only a few days since he set Cambrai on fire and sank the Leinster – he is now burning Douai, and Lille is all ready to burn. And I think that proves what his peace offers are worth. There is only one place to make peace with the Hun, with an armed force in Berlin. The Kaiser and Ludendorf and Co are keeping in the background for the moment but they have not changed their spots.

I had my blokes on parade this morning and told them the Hun was not yet beaten and that we had got to go for him again. But as I say all this gup in the papers is very unsettling for them.

Your affectionate son

WILLIE

[DIARY] OCT. 15TH 1918 – CALAIS Started off at 9.30 a.m. by auto for Calais to try and get some N.C.O.s for the battalion. Lambert, M.O. of the King's Own and a fellow from Div. H.Q. came down in the car as far as Boulogne – both going on leave. Very wet raw day and bad roads, so that we did not get to Frevent until 12.30. There we stopped for lunch as the car wanted repair. The clutch was slipping badly. Left again at 1.30 and eventually reached Boulogne about 3.30 p.m. after passing by my old haunts of the days at the Corps School. Which incidentally seem very far away now. The Foret de Hesdin was looking very beautiful in its autumn colours in spite of the grey colourless day. Dropped the other two at Boulogne and after some delay to get some more petrol pushed on to Calais. I didn't know the way and the driver said he did but didn't. After nearly killing a Portugoose who jumped quicker than anyone I've ever seen, we got lost, and then the driver disclosed the fact that he had got a Calais map all the time. So I got that and we got on to the right road. But the car was still going badly and we did not get to Calais until six o'clock by which time it was pitch dark. Went on to the Scottish Base Depot, but Wemyss who commands it was out. So fixed up an appointment for 9 a.m. tomorrow. Back to the Officers' Club but it was full up, so I eventually got rooms for the driver and self at the Hotel Metropole, an indifferent place where hot water for washing purposes was very hard to come by. Went up to the club for dinner and there I saw Wemyss. As soon as I saw him I realised he was the fellow who came out to India with me on the transport in 1910, (a hundred years ago). We had a long buck about old times and he told me a lot about the East African Show, where he had been in the Intelligence branch. He was full of admiration for

[315]

von Letow,[*] the Boche general out there. He seems to be a most marvellous chap, worshipped by the natives almost as a sort of God. And almost as much so by the Germans.

He also told me the truth of why Hoskins got the sack. When Smuts left he was there in supreme command. Presently the Government wired out that they were tired of the business and that it had got to be finished in three months. The climate, the country and the general conditions made that an impossibility, so Hoskins in his blunt way wired back 'Impossible.' Whereupon Smuts who had meanwhile arrived in London, said 'If he can't do it, I can tell you a man who can, Van Daventer.' So Hoskins got the sack and the show is not finished yet, over two years later.

Apparently the conduct of the Dutch out there was at least as ruthless as that of the Boche elsewhere, and with less excuse for they could not plead the 'necessity of war'. It was simply wanton destruction.

At dinner a stout cheery-looking bird came and sat down at my table. He proved to be an inspector of machinery, Hutchinson by name. Had followed the sea for many years as a ships engineer. He had been in the South African War. Then some years later had chucked the sea and had gone in for mining in South Africa. Bought an old mine, made a good thing of it and got married, and had made a beautiful home for himself on the edge of High Veld. His partner was a fellow called Gray, a brother of Sergt. Gray in this battalion who was killed at Flesquières. Which shows how small the world is. Hutchinson was a good fellow, he made one remark which struck me. He said, 'When I see a battalion marching back from a battle, I always look at them and think 'Now probably every man in that crowd has just lost a pal.' And it's very true. He seemed to have learnt sympathy in his journeyings about the world.

OCT. 16TH 1918 – MARCOING[†] Went up to the Base Depot for a start and saw Wemyss. He paraded all the Gordon N.C.O.s he had for me, and I picked out the ones I wanted sent up to the battalion. Found Frame there too, who was commanding a company in the battalion until he was wounded the other day. So

[*] General von Lettow-Vorbeck, a soldier of genius.
[†] South-west of Cambrai.

I arranged to take him back with me. We eventually left Calais about 10.30 laden with fish and other delicacies. Hadn't gone a mile out of Calais when the car broke down completely – big end gone. We managed to crawl back. Spent the next hour and a half trying to find a car to take us back and eventually decided to go by train, a two days' journey. Got to the station just in time to see the train leaving. So back to the club for lunch. Then we saw Preston, who is fit again.

After lunch I spotted a car standing outside, and enquiry disclosed that it was to take a Lieut. Innes to Abbeville. So I got hold of Lt. Innes and he agreed to take us to Crecy where I hoped to get a car out of Monty to go on. However on the way it occurred to me to stop at G.H.Q. and see Dinwiddie on the chance of getting a car there. And we did – Dinwiddie turned up trumps, he gave us tea and took an enormous amount of trouble to get us a car. When it came it was a brand new closed Vauxhall. Before we left G.H.Q. they told me the orders had already been issued for the N.C.O.s I had selected at the base to join the battalion. This also through the good offices of Dinwiddie. We got away about 7 p.m. laden with sandwiches for dinner. Got to Arras about 8.45. From there, not being sure of the way, I called in at a Brigade H.Q. to enquire and found them all at dinner. And who should the Brigadier be but Loch in the Royal Scots, an old friend of the 9th Division days and a splendid fellow. So we had a cup of coffee and a crack and learnt our road.

Continued the journey by the main Arras-Cambrai road, then down through Fontaine–notre-Dame and Cantaing to Marcoing, which we reached at 11 p.m. It was rather interesting to drive through Fontaine-notre-Dame – one's last experience of it in the first Cambrai battle was very different. The whole journey seemed to have been arranged by Providence. At 2 p.m. in Calais without any means of transport, at 11 p.m. back with the battalion 130 miles away and all one's business fixed up en route. Turned in and slept like a log.

OCT. 17TH 1918 – MARCOING Fine warm day. We did a bit of training, the battalion needs a lot. The whole thing is new and the men don't know their N.C.O.s or each other, and they have not got the battalion spirit yet. Got a very stuffy memo from the

[317]

Divisional Commander in the evening complaining of the saluting of the men, or rather the lack of it. Thought it rather unjust as a huge draft had joined the battalion the very day the iniquity occurred.

Dined with the Brigadier in the evening. Saw Gen. Byng, the Army Commander this afternoon walking along the road like an ordinary mortal, and we had a short crack about old times. He is a splendid fellow.

OCT. 19TH 1918 – MARCOING Very cold morning with a damp dense mist which rather interfered with training. However it cleared up about midday. In the afternoon we got a warning order that we move forward tomorrow – operations 'de nouveau'. Saw the Divisional Commander in the afternoon and learnt what is in the wind. Also tackled him about the 'saluting memo'. The news from the north is splendid today. Ostend was occupied by the navy yesterday and today the Cavalry have got Bruges, which must mean the loss of the entire Belgian coast to the Boche. But it sounds like a brilliant withdrawal on his part because one hears no word of any prisoners.

Lots of peace rumours in the papers, but the fact remains that the Boche is fighting very hard and very well where he wants to hold us – as for instance on the American front opposite Mezières, and here. Wonder if we shall have peace this year – personally I am doubtful. I think the Boche will reject the new terms because his people don't yet realise how they are regarded by the rest of the world or what the real situation is. And that we have much very hard fighting before us, because if he thinks our terms too hard, the whole nation will stiffen up. Like the old jackal when you get him into a tight corner.

The German Government, at the beginning of October, had addressed President Wilson to enquire on what terms the Allies would negotiate peace. On 23rd of the month they received a reply which implied, without using the phrase, a demand for unconditional surrender. Meanwhile Ludendorff advised that the Army could continue the struggle if it were absolutely necessary.

[DIARY] OCT. 19TH 1918 CATTENIÈRES We left Marcoing at 2 p.m. and moved to Cattenières,* which we reached about dusk. At last we have got through the destroyed country, and that which we marched through today is cultivated in patches. The country reminds one of Buchan in a way. Most of the civilians were evacuated by the Boche before he went back.

Saw the divisional commander on the way, who expressed himself pleased with the appearance of the battalion. The billets in Cattenières were very good, the houses not at all destroyed, though they were in an awful mess, having been left that way by the Boche and no one having had time yet to clean them up. He (the Boche) appears to have taken away everything of value which was easily portable, but a lot of furniture, pianos, etc. remain.

One of our great difficulties now is transport – in the past one has been helped with lorries, now we have to rely on our own horse transport. Result we have a lot of stuff we can't shift when we move.

OCT. 20TH 1918 – QUIEVY The Corps attacked at 2 a.m. 62nd div. on the right, Guards on the left and it appears to have gone well. We moved at 11.20, I saw the Div. Com. on the way and he told me that we should not attack before the 22nd. It was a wet unpleasant march, sort of thick Scotch mist which turned to rain in the afternoon. The billets in Quievy were much better than I anticipated, the place has not been much knocked about although it was shelled before we came in this morning. Great number of troops in it – result we are very crowded.

Saw Jim Burnett there and dined with him in the evening. He told me the news – his attack was a very good show indeed and took St. Python and Solesmes with v. few casualties. The IV Corps on the right were counter-attacked off their objectives, which held matters up a bit. However it seems pretty successful on the whole. There were 3000 civilians in Solesmes. The first story was that the attack was expected and that the civilians were waiting for our men with hot coffee at 2.15 a.m. but the true story is that the whole show was a complete surprise.

*On the old Le Cateau battlefield of 1914. Willie, as it happens, was within a few miles of the place where 1st Gordons had been largely taken prisoner in 1914 – including the Master of Saltoun.

[319]

We have no orders at all about what we may be expected to do, and of course it depends entirely on the Boche. He may go back, but probably not very far. The fellows who are fighting are the machine gunners and the artillery. On the whole his morale seems pretty low. News from the north very good, we have got the whole of the Belgian coast and are pushing on towards Ghent.

OCT. 21ST 1918 – QUIEVY Nothing much doing in the morning – did some routine work. Reports state that the IV Corps have now got the high ground on our right, so things seem to be going pretty well.

The battalion remained at Quievy, we move tomorrow and attack on the morning of the 23rd. Am sure the battalion will do well. Jim Burnett came to dinner and we had the pipes.

OCT. 22ND 1918 – SOLESMES Late reveille and then got all battle stores etc. issued. The battalion left Quievy at 4 p.m. The march to Solesmes was rather a business because the whole road was blocked with transport and lorries. Luckily the Boche did not shell the road though he pitched one or two near it and there was a lot of gas about near Solesmes. The companies were all in billets there by 7 p.m. Bn. H.Q. in the same house with the King's Own just near Bde H.Q.

We were to attack Romeries at 4.20 a.m. tomorrow morning, the Suffolk & King's Own passing through us at 8.40 a.m. – rather a long wait, but we have to wait for the right flank, which is much further back, to catch up. About 9 o'clock zero hour was changed to 3.20 a.m. which gives us a still longer wait. We shall get all the shelling and the Boche will have time to get his guns away. Am told that he has a lot of machine guns in the orchards in front of Romeries.

We were ordered to assemble two hours before zero, but I have got it cut down to 1¼ hours, which is still too long. These waits when one is not attacking from an organised trench system, where there is cover for the men, are a great mistake. The men get cold and much of the enthusiasm evaporates.

OCT. 23RD 1918 The men had hot tea and sausages before starting and the leading coy. moved off at 1 a.m. followed by the others at intervals of 10 minutes. Battalion H.Q. remained in Solesmes for the moment, but an advanced report centre was sent forward before zero. We had bad luck in the assembly because someone in the front line put up an S.O.S. rocket about 12.30 a.m. and our guns opened very heavy fire. The reason the S.O.S. was put up was apparently a Boche patrol which approached the line, and instead of shooting them the N.C.O. in charge of one of our posts lost his head and put up the S.O.S. The Boche retaliation was very heavy on the exits from Solesmes and we had several men wounded and gassed. All high explosive shells contain gas now – it's very unpleasant but not very serious. However it's quite enough to take the enthusiasm out of the faint-hearted. Of whom there is a fair proportion these days. And it's very hard not to lose men in a big town if they want to be lost. We collected ½ dozen out of a cellar later on. A good deal of disorganisation resulted, but eventually the companies were reorganised and went on.

Eventually the situation got more normal and at 2 a.m. I went round companies in the assembly positions. There was a little shelling there but not too much. Got back to HQ just before zero. The companies went forward under the barrage and the story of the attack is more or less as written in the official account which follows. Beveridge was killed, doing most gallantly, – he is a great loss. Of course the story of a battle is never really as one writes it – one couldn't write it as it is!

OPERATIONS BY

1ST BN. THE GORDON HIGHLANDERS

OCT. 23RD AND 24TH 1918

Assembly (1) At 4 p.m. Oct. 22nd the battalion marched from Quievy* to Solesmes. The march was rendered somewhat trying by the enormous amount of traffic on the road, which made progress very slow.

In SOLESMES the battalion was billetted in houses. In view of the size of the town and the large number of civilians in it, special

---

*Quievy is a village five miles west of the town of Solesmes and Romeries two miles north-east of that place. This was country which had not been fought over since 1914.

orders were issued to prevent men straying. At 12.30 a.m. hot tea and sausages were issued to the men, and at 1 a.m. the companies moved off at intervals of 10 minutes. About 12.30 a.m. a S.O.S. signal was put up from the front line in response to which our artillery put down a very heavy barrage in front of ROMERIES. The enemy reply was very heavy, especially on the exits from SOLESMES and a considerable number of casualties were caused (the O.C. 'A' Coy was wounded) and a great deal of disorganisation. Companies were reformed outside the town and the advance to assembly positions continued. Reorganisation was facilitated by the bright moon-light. A few further casualties were suffered in the assembly positions from enemy shell-fire. The positions had been carefully reconnoitred by companies earlier in the evening and no difficulty was experienced in finding them.

Plan of Attack (2) The task of the battalion was to capture and mop up the village of ROMERIES and to consolidate the line of the light railway beyond it. In view of the difficulties recently experienced owing to inefficient mopping up, it was decided to detail certain platoons to go to definite points in the village where they were to make posts and from these posts to carry out the mopping up in their vicinity.

The general plan was as follows:

The B & D Coys were to make good the N.E. bank of the river HASPRES, on which line A & C Coys were to pass through them and advance to the final objective. In addition 'B' Coy was to detail one platoon to deal with the wood in W.27.d. and one platoon to deal with the main railway. These platoons were then to make posts in W.28.a. as shown on the attached map.

Details of objectives of companies and platoons were as shown on the attached map.

The Attack (3) At 3.20 a.m. B & D Coys. (B on the right) advanced under the barrage. A considerable number of machine guns were encountered in the cemetery, the orchards and the railway in front of the village. In particular the former was very strongly held. The opposition on the right was not so determined as on the left and 'B' Coy. captured several machine guns and reached its objectives under the barrage.

[322]

A. Coy. then passed through and captured and consolidated the final objective.

On the left D. Coy was held up almost immediately by intense machine gun fire from the cemetery and the orchards behind it, and lost the barrage. The advance was continued by rushes but at considerable cost. The HASPRES was found to be a considerable obstacle and the bridges had been blown up. Eventually the objective on the N.E. bank was gained and 3 platoons of C Coy passed through and continued the advance. One platoon of 'C' Coy, finding the advance on the left to be held up by machine gun fire, advanced round the right of the village and reached its objective. Heavy machine gun fire was still coming from a house 100^x south of the church, and Capt. BEVERIDGE comdg. 'D' Coy, was killed in a most gallant attack on these guns. Sgt. Lawson who was in command of the platoon concerned, then formed up some prisoners already captured[*] and screened by them, advanced against the house, and succeeded in silencing the opposition by shooting the gunners.

(4) Resistance was very determined at certain points both in the village itself and in the orchards in front of it, but on the whole the enemy surrendered easily. A large number of prisoners were captured, including a battalion commander.

Remarks (5) (a) A field gun barrage has little effect on machine guns in houses, and such guns do great damage when manned with determination.

(b) The system of establishing posts at certain selected points in villages and mopping up from these posts is a good one, as it prevents the enemy reappearing after our troops have passed through. In this case the whole village was mopped up very quickly after the leading troops had reached their objective.

(c) A S.O.S. signal sent up without due cause during assembly may do great harm.

(d) In cases where there is no cover in assembly positions, a long wait in these positions should be avoided. The men get cold and much of the enthusiasm evaporates. Where the assembly presents no great difficulties a margin of ¼ to ½ hour should be ample.

[*] Illegal of course, but recorded without observation.

(e) It is strongly recommended that boys of 18½ years should not be sent to fighting battalions. Although perhaps 10% of these boys may do quite well, the remainder are quite useless. They do not possess the necessary stamina and a battalion however weak is better off without them.

To continue the story from one's own point of view. The companies got a good bit mixed up at the entry to the village, but they got to their objectives pretty well. I went up about 6 a.m. and H.Q. followed shortly after.

A few prisoners had come down before I left but not many. However I met a lot on the road. Always too many men are sent down as escorts, and by the time I got to Romeries I had about 20 men with me from thinning them out. Went round D & C Coys first – they were both disorganised with a good many men missing, and D Coy had only one officer left – Robertson. A very quiet and rather awkward fellow, but his father won a Victoria Cross in S. Africa, and I think he might easily follow in his footsteps.

The village itself was being very heavily shelled all the time by the Boche. Have not seen his artillery fire so heavy in a battle for a long time now. Afterwards went round to the other flank but had to wait for a bit owing to the shelling. Had Henderson with me and a few men still. We took shelter behind a ruined cottage. By this time the Suffolk and the King's Own were passing through. I saw an officer of the Suffolk who was wounded and asked him how they were getting on. He said they were going on, but had had many men wounded and that all the officers in his coy. had been knocked out. It afterwards transpired that the casualties in the whole battalion at that time were one officer (the one I saw) and 9 men wounded. One expects better information than that from an officer.

Eventually saw all the companies and found bn. H.Q. which had been established in Romeries. Some time later the shelling on the village died down, and we got the battalion re-organised and ready to move forward. About 2 p.m. we were ordered up to take up a line south of Escarmain on the far side of the St Georges River. The King's Own and the Suffolk had pushed on to a sunken road about 1000 yards in front of this line without much opposition. Moved off at 3 p.m. Halted the battalion on the way as the position we were to occupy was being shelled. An unlucky shell arrived just as we were moving off again, which wounded three men and Sergt. Lawson – him for the third time today. This time he had to retire.

Battalion H.Q. moved to a small house in Escarmain close to our line. We dug in on the position as ordered. About 11 p.m. we were ordered to withdraw again.

OCT 24TH 1918 – ROMERIES At 12.30 a.m. we withdrew, the 9th Bde taking over the line preparatory to continuing the advance under a barrage at 4 a.m. We moved back to a sunken road about 1000 yards east of Romeries. We were shelled when we got there and had to move a bit. It was very cold and no one got much sleep.

Also at 4 a.m. two field batteries opened fire just behind us. Anyone who can sleep with a battery of field guns firing over his head from 100 yards away is a marvel. However by 5 a.m. it was quieter and I got to sleep for two hours or so. The cookers arrived about 8 a.m. and the men had hot tea and bacon. Kelly our H.Q. cook also made a fire, and soon we had a most scrumptious breakfast too. Got a letter from Pam just before breakfast which I answered on the spot. About 10 a.m. we got orders to move back to billets in Romeries. At first we were told to be ready to go forward again at 4 p.m. but this was cancelled later and we stopped the night. Surplus N.C.O.s etc. came up from details and we got down to reorganising the battalion properly. There were 1150 civilians in this village yesterday when we captured it, and really it's almost like the beginning of the war, they are so pleased to see one. And their houses, or rather what remains of them, they put entirely at our disposal. But the Hun has left his mark on them – they are pale and very subdued, they haven't really got much power of enthusiasm left. They all say that the men in the Boche ranks are much demoralised and that the food is bad. The old lady in our H.Q. told me that sometimes all the rations the officers would get for days at a time were some black bread and honey and coffee. Think of the spirit that keeps them fighting on that. She remarked how patriotic they were, she told me of one boy – a budding officer, whose father was a general. He was good, she said, he was all on fire to die for his country. Of another two she spoke, who drank 13000 francs worth of wine in three weeks to celebrate the Boche victories in March.

To bed at 9.15 p.m. very tired.

Oct. 24 1918

Dear Mother,

A very hurried line, as time is short. Battalion had a very good show yesterday, about 800 prisoners. But there is no time for sleep, we are trekking on. Think we have given the Boche a biff but he has run and not left much behind at present.

Love to father.

Your loving son
WILLIE

[DIARY] OCT. 25TH 1918 – ROMERIES More reorganisation, but no other work. The A.B. turned up in the morning and was full of congratulations for the show. A most enthusiastic (for him) letter of congratulations too from the Divisional Commander. We were expecting orders to move all day, but none came until late at night, when we got orders to move early next day to Escarmain.

OCT. 27TH 1918 – RUESNES Various inspections and a little physical training in the morning, followed by a voluntary service which I did not attend, as I wanted to ride out and reconnoitre the country forward. But about 75% of the men did and sang lustily. I think a voluntary service is much better than a church parade.

Had quite a good ride round and had a look at Le Quesnoy and the Foret de Mormal, both of which are rather hard nuts to crack. Wilson's reply to the last Boche Note was in the paper today and seems to meet the case pretty adequately.

At 2.45 p.m. I was summoned to Bde. H.Q. and was ordered to relieve the main line of resistance on our front. Relief to be complete by 8 p.m. Issued the orders and then rode up to the H.Q. of the battalions we were to relieve and made the necessary arrangements about guides. The companies were delayed by traffic on the way up and one of the guides went wrong, so the relief was not over till 9 p.m. Very dark night.

It seems that brother Boche shells a bit round about and he certainly put one or two rather close to H.Q. during the night, but no damage done.

OCT. 28TH 1918 – RUESNES Went round the company posts early – a lot of them need altering considerably. Then the general came up and we went round again. Inundated with gunners today who all apparently want to put their guns just beside battalion H.Q. so we shall probably be shelled some more. However we have had our cellar strutted, which makes it a bit stronger, though it doesn't protect our men.

OCT. 29TH – ST PYTHON Lots of gas shelling about 2.30 a.m. but no harm done. I sent for Cpl. Houston, the gas N.C.O. to H.Q., when it started and sent him off to investigate it. He ambled off hugely delighted at having a chance to ply his trade, sniffing the air like an old dog after a rabbit, and the next day produced an A.1 report on the affair.

There is a great deal of gas of all sorts about just now, the Boche is using it very extensively. Walked round the posts about 9.30 a.m. – a lot of good work has been done. We were to be relieved in the evening and I expected someone from the in-coming battalion to come up and see the line and make arrangements about guides etc. However no one turned up. However it went off all right in the end and the relief was complete about 7.30, and we got back here (St Python) about 9.30.

Great rumours of peace in the air tonight and one seriously wondered as we left Ruesnes, whether one was in the line for the last time or not. Two companies had arrived before us and two came in just after.

A meal and then to bed at 11 p.m. And tomorrow a day of rest I hope.

OCT. 30TH – ST PYTHON And a day of rest it was – we did nothing except clean up. I rode up to Brigade H.Q. in Vertain in the morning and got early information about our move tomorrow. In the afternoon Taldo and I paid a visit to Solesmes to have a look at it by daylight. We had not seen it since the night before the Romeries attack. It's not a bad town. Reminds me of an incident on our way back from the line last night. We took a wrong turn and found ourselves at Solesmes.

'What place is this?' says Taldo to a military policeman who was standing in the road.

'Sollum, sir,' was the answer, 'or Sollumy as some people prefer to call it.'

Our soldiers don't take very readily to the French language. Have arranged for two companies to get baths before we move off tomorrow, through the kindness of the 2nd Division.

OCT. 31ST 1918 – CARNIÈRES We moved off soon after 11 a.m. marching as a battalion. Traffic was not too bad on the road and we got to Carnières by 2 p.m. This is a good village – it has not been knocked about and there are no civilians in it at all. So the men are all in houses, and very comfortable. A fortnight here would do us a lot of good.

We got a draft of 200 this afternoon, mostly 7th battalion men, but the physique by no means as good as the last one we had. The battalion is now very considerably over strength.

NOVEMBER 1ST 1918 – CARNIÈRES Started training and two companies had baths. In the afternoon I rode over to Corps H.Q. to see the A.B. and find out how long we were to be out of the line. The A.B. was out but I found out the other thing and I find our promised fortnight is not likely to materialise and that we move forward again the day after tomorrow. Which is sad.

The news is good though – Austria really appears to be right out of it, and the Armistice terms with Turkey seem to be satisfactory enough. Our terms to Germany are nothing short of unconditional surrender – so rumour has it – and it's not likely that she will accept that at present, so I suppose we may look forward to another winter's campaign.

Within Germany matters were approaching crisis. Ludendorff, 'First Quartermaster General' and the implacable spirit behind

the High Command, had resigned on 26 October, rightly appreci-
ating that unless he did so the German Chancellor, Prince Max
of Baden, would; and the Kaiser, at that stage, would prefer to
keep the Chancellor and dispense with Ludendorff. But already
the cries in Germany for the Kaiser's abdication were deafening;
and equally strident were the demands that, somehow, the war
be ended. Yet in the recent battles the Germans had fought with
vigour, and the situation behind the enemy's front did not show
itself to the Allied soldiers.

Nov. 6th 1918

Dear Father,

Many thanks for your letter. I should have answered it earlier, but sudden moves have been the order of the day lately, and one never knows where one will be in 24 hours.

We are in reserve at the moment, but not for very much longer I should think. The battle seems to be going not too badly, but we think the Boche has got a strong position on the Mons-Maubeuge line and that we shall have a stiff battle there. The general impression seems to be that we shall go on fighting until the Boche sends over a white flag and asks for an armistice. So it may go on for some months yet. But I really think the time can be measured in months, and not in years now. He has got quite a lot to pay for, the old Boche, hasn't he. The people in the occupied territories of France wouldn't have much mercy on him if they had their way. It would be a good scheme to collect a few of them to go over and speak at some of these labour meetings where they sing the Red Flag and advocate letting the Boche down lightly. In this village they have got hold of an old story which they think is new and delight hugely in: 'In the beginning God made man. The devil being jealous decided to make one too, and he made a German. He saw there was something wrong. "Lor," says he, after scratching his head for a minute, "I've gone and made him with two stomachs and no heart."'

The weather is perfectly awful, and of course rain is the last thing we want just now. However it will take more than rain to stop us hammering at the Boche just now. Only it makes things slower. I don't think anyone is for a return to trench warfare if it can be avoided. And the only way to avoid it is to beat him now.

Au revoir and love to Mother.

Your affectionate son
WILLIE

[DIARY] NOV 8TH 1918 – GOMMEGNIES Orders had come yesterday to move forward and we marched off at 10 a.m. A wet morning and much mud on the roads, also a vast number of motor lorries and cars. So the march was not altogether a pleasant one. Our destination was to be Fasnoy but there was no room when we got there so we came on to Gommegnies. We are in quite good billets here but as things stand at present we have got to move out at 9 a.m. tomorrow to make room for Corps H.Q. which is coming in here. I saw Uncle Harper on the way – he was in very good form and looking very well.

The news today – the Americans are at Sedan and the French at Mezières, and the Boche plenipotentiaries are being interviewed today by Foch at Paris with a view to an armistice. A mutiny in the Boche fleet is also reported. It looks as if the end were very near. Pray God it is.

NOV 9TH 1918 – LE GRAND SART Marched here early in the morning, as we had to turn out of the other place to make room for Corps H.Q. Got in about 10.30 a.m. The billets are much better than the other place; bn H.Q. the best I've ever had. Did a little training and got billets cleaned up, also found a party for work on road-mending.

The population were enthusiastic in their reception – it was like the early days of the war back again. After the pipes had played 'Retreat' in the evening there was great clapping of hands and cries of 'Vive l'Angleterre'. When will these people learn to distinguish between England and Scotland! Went for a ride in the Forêt de Mormal in the afternoon, only the Boche has cut down most of it. But some still stands and I found one beautiful bit, all green and gold. It was a glorious autumn day.

Dined with Uncle Harper at Le Quesnoy – he sent a car for me.

News came while we were at dinner that the Kaiser had abdicated and the Crown Prince had renounced his claim to the throne, but it's hardly official yet. The armistice is to be signed by 11.00 a.m. on Monday if at all and everyone said that the Boche was certain to sign it. We played bridge after dinner.

Had expected to be here two or three days but orders came in this evening to move early tomorrow to Longueville. Thought these billets were too good to be true.

The Boche has apparently gone off and the 3rd Div. is to be the advanced guard for the 3rd Army, and the 76th Bde for the 3rd Division. So we may have some long treks ahead of us – if the Boche does not sign the Armistice.

NOV. 10TH 1918 – LA LONGUEVILLE[*] Left soon after 9 a.m. The mud on the roads was simply awful, and a lot of lorries into the bargain made the march rather an unpleasant one. We got in about 2 p.m. Lots of rumours to effect that revolution has broken out in Germany, especially in Berlin, and that Bavaria has declared itself a republic.

A hitch occurred about the armistice, because when the Boche plenipotentiaries came over under the white flag, the French thought it would be a good opportunity to do a raid, and they did and scuppered 350 Huns. Result – when the emissaries tried to return they were fired on from the Boche lines and could not go. Eventually they had to be sent over by aeroplane.

We leave here tomorrow very early and march up to the front. If it's peace we shan't have much to do, if it's war we do the advance guard stunt. It's odd sitting here and wondering, 'Is this the last day of the war, or not?' One can still hear guns going. I don't know that one is very excited about it, it's in the day's work either way – but it will be a disappointment if we find the war has got to go on. One expects it to end. Early rise tomorrow and I'm tired.

NOV. 11TH 1918 – LA LONGUEVILLE I suppose this has been a memorable day in the history of the world – though we took it

[*] About ten miles south of Mons, where the British first met the Germans in 1914; and here Willie's war ended.

very quietly on the whole. Just as we were about to move off to go and fight the Boche, I got a message from Furnell through Cabane that our move was cancelled, as the armistice would be signed at 11 a.m. So we stood by and I send down to get official confirmation of the order – which arrived about 8.30 a.m. So the war is ended – rumour has it that the Boche has accepted all our conditions, and ends by begging us to do what we can to feed his starving people.

How does one feel about it all – not very excited certainly; I don't think we realise it at present. It makes no immediate change for us, demobilisation will take months, and we shall probably stand around making roads, etc. Only the danger of life is missing and the excitement, and the 'great end' for which one has been keyed up all these years.

Because the end has come. It's all very strange, but I don't think one could begin again, or go back to yesterday. It's a very difficult time coming in many ways; – the men, or many of them, will be difficult to hold now, – the purpose which has held them together is gone, discipline as a power in itself is not a very strong one in our army. But they are good fellows with plenty of common-sense; in that fact and in keeping them occupied the solution lies.

To get back to the events of this day of days – as soon as the news was confirmed the pipes and drums paraded and played national and regimental tunes all round the town, followed by a great concourse of good east country faces in balmorals.

I went down to Brigade H.Q. but they had no more news there. They had got theirs from a fellow on the Corps Staff, who was touring the country as fast as his car would go in pyjamas and an overcoat. We waited about until 11.15 when an official wire came to the effect that hostilities had ceased at 11 a.m. So at 12 noon we had a battalion parade and told the men, adding a few sage words about patience as regards demobilisation. After which the battalion stood at the 'slope' while the Pipes and Drums played the regimental march. Then the companies marched off to the pipes.

After lunch we had a church parade, or rather a voluntary service – but nearly all the men were there. The band played in the square during the afternoon.

No news came in beyond what we had already had, and no information about our immediate movements – we shall be here for a day or two I should think. All the officers of the battalion dined together in the evening, thirty-four in all, and danced reels after dinner. But they are bad at that. And the doctor recited 'Tam-o'-Shanter', which is almost a 'rite' in the battalion now, and a right good job he made of it. Then Pearson played the Marseillaise on the piano and Cabane sang it, accompanied by the people of the house – and then to bed at midnight.

And so ended the last day of the great war. One has been feeling one's way through the dark for 4½ years, and now one has come out into the sunlight – and behold!! one is blind, one cannot see the sun. But the blindness will pass in time. But we shall be exiles for a few months yet, I'm afraid.

NOV 12TH 1918 LA LONGUEVILLE Most glorious weather – bright days and hard frost. No news of our future moves, no newspapers, as the mail has ceased to arrive with any regularity whatever, and practically the whole battalion on work cleaning up roads. Peace, perfect peace.

Willie's diary continued into 1919, giving a daily account of the great march into Germany of the Allies, including a British army of eleven divisions. The diary records speculations about the phenomenon of Bolshevism, which seemed to threaten not only Germany but all Europe; about how rapidly demobilisation would start: about his own personal future. But it records no doubt about the nature of the triumph he felt.

[DIARY] NOV 24TH 1918 – LOBBES Well today I suppose the march to Germany may be said to have begun. Eleven British divisions are going – and surely it is the greatest march in history. The tramp of our marching feet will sound down the ages as the symbol of the progress of the Liberty of the World. Was ever a time like this? And we don't realise it, and we must. We have let those materialists pollute us who are so fond of telling us that our country came into the war to save it's own skin – but it's a lie. Politicians may have come into it for that reason, the country came into it to fight for the liberty of the World and *no other reason*. And this march marks the ultimate triumph of our cause after 4½ weary years, which have cost us most of our friends into the bargain.

And everywhere the welcome was affecting.

[DIARY] NOV 28TH 1918 – ANHEE A fairly long and very wet march. It's a pity the weather has broken. The billets in Anhee are fairly good, but much better for officers than for men. H.Q. is a very nice chateau on the banks of the Meuse. Our host, M. Henry, a banker of Dinant with three pretty daughters, asked us all to take coffee with him after dinner, and we heard many a tale of the Boche.

It was in 1914 that he committed most of the crimes in this part of the world – in Dinant he shot some 700 civilians, among them the brother and two nephews of our host. He told me much of the Boche administration of Belgium, including many ridiculous orders, many of which were obviously issued in order to make money by fining those who disobeyed. And the retreat in 1918 – much disorder and thieving. His eldest daughter shook hands with the last Boche officer to leave the house,

'Why do you take my hand?' he asked.

'Because you are the last – for the last time.'

It is certainly a very comfortable billet, and the daughters have the frank unaffected manners which seem a characteristic of French and Belgian girls.

There were occasional opportunities for sightseeing: as in the Ardennes:

[DIARY] DEC. 1ST 1918 – CINEY Sunday – we had a joint Corps H.Q. and battalion service which combined the celebration of St Andrew's day, which was yesterday. The A.B. was present. Lunched with him at one a.m. after getting a lecture on the general situation and education etc. for the benefit (we hope) of A. Coy off my chest.

After lunch we set out to Han, I in an open car, and bitterly cold it was. It was a long drive through lovely country, and passing through Rochford on our way. At last we reached our goal, and proceeded to investigate an underground river in a boat. And presently we came out in great halls, one 400 feet high, under the rock and filled with stalactites most marvellous to see, and some of them wondrous beautiful. It would take a long time and the pen of a readier writer than I to describe the place – some of the most beautiful stalactites had been broken by the Boche out of sheer lust for destruction. The guide who was with them turned and said, 'In a thousand years we shall point to that and say, the Boche destroyed that.' – But they paid no heed. We did not see all the grotto, one can walk for 4½ kilometres through similar marvels. Some of the forms taken by the stalactites were very interesting – one a huge beehive – one like the head of Socrates, and so on. As we approached the exit to the grotto, the view was most beautiful, a little patch of country all mysterious in the twilight, framed in the opening of the rock.

We drove home by a shorter route, but again the cold was awful. But it was well worth it.

And on 11 December the 1st Battalion Gordon Highlanders crossed the frontier and entered Germany. The battalion's colours had been collected from the Depot in Aberdeen.

[DIARY] DEC. 11TH 1918 NEIDINGEN & BREITFELD Moved off at 10 a.m. – the battalion leading the Corps except for a section of R.E. Bayonets fixed and colours uncased for the first hour's march. The Corps Commander was present on the frontier, also a large number of gilded staff officers with cameras. We had quite a long march and a very wet one as it started to rain hard after the first hour, and by the time we got into billets everyone was soaked.

We are rather scattered in two very poor villages, but most of the men are in houses and have got fires to dry their clothes. We were to have gone to St Vith which is quite a large town, but there they have had an outbreak of small-pox, which has put it out of bounds. The people here are more or less friendly – not demonstrative, but not hostile; they are supplying milk and eggs and butter which does not look as if they were short of food. There are several men back from the war in the village. We move on again tomorrow.

And the march continued, day by day, towards the Rhineland where the Army of Occupation was to be quartered.

[DIARY] DEC. 16TH 1918 MÜNSTEREIFFEL Quite a pleasant march in spite of a sort of driving rain at first. It cleared up later and blue sky appeared – it's fairly cold.

This is quite a pleasant old walled town, nestling under the steep cliff on one side of the valley. The battalion is all billetted in one enormous building, a sort of college for budding priests, I think.

Battalion H.Q. is in a quaint old house, now an hotel. I find that my bedroom was inhabited in 1847 by Friedrich, father of the late Kaiser Wilhelm. However he was a better fellow than his son. The pipes played in the square in the afternoon.

It's hard to know what is happening inside Germany, but from what the people here say, things are really quite quiet except perhaps in Berlin: the fellow who owns this house appears to think that Germany will divide up into four republics – 1 Prussia: 2 Bavaria: 3 The Rhine Provices and Westphalia; 4 Saxony, Wurtemberg etc. Perhaps!

We move tomorrow to Euskirchen, which is quite a big place – our final destination appears to be somewhere east of Duren on the Cologne road.

For the first weeks of 1919 Willie was on leave in England. The coming of peace brought anti-climax and uncertainty as well as relief. The family, however, were united for the first time since 1914 – the Master of Saltoun was at last home.

[DIARY] JAN 25TH 1919 My last day at home. Spent the morning doing a few last jobs and then went to the War Office. My idea was to see Gen. Furse and ask him whether he thought one ought to go to Russia and fight the Bolshevists. He was away unfortunately. I saw the fellow who is in charge of the Russian Section at the War Office, and he told me that they had plenty of fellows of my rank wanting to go. They had asked for six commanding officers a short time ago, and twenty-four names had been immediately forthcoming. I could register my name – Russia was probably a good place for an ambitious soldier, especially just at present, and so on. That was his point of view, but mine was a bit different, because I don't *want* to go to Russia a bit. And at present no one knows what our policy in Russia is to be.

JAN 28TH 1919 EUSKIRCHEN The train made up time during the night with the result that we were thrust out on a cold and inhospitable platform at Duren at 5 a.m. Tweedie and I tried a hotel but were unable to get in, so he went back to the station to await his train on, and I dived into the room I had occupied before at Corps H.Q. and went to bed. Got up at 9.30 and had a bath, then to see Kearsley and cadge some breakfast. I also cadged lunch, and a car afterwards which took me to Euskirchen, where I heard Gen. Maxse was, in temporary command of the IXth Corps. He made me stop the night and promised to recommend my application to go to Sandhurst as an instructor. But even now I'm not sure it won't be Russia.

JAN 29TH 1919 KIERDORF Left Euskirchen at 10 a.m. and drove down here – about ten miles. The roads very icy, the country covered with snow. So here one is back with the battalion – the best place to be after all, if one is not in England.

Things have been going on very well I think – the education is getting more into it's stride – we are doing well in football and boxing – cookhouses have got on pretty well. But when all is said and done it's a dull life for the men. And for us too, but of course one has always got books, and so forth.

JAN 31ST 1919 Started the day with a battalion parade at 9 a.m. It was bitterly cold, which made the parade rather a scratch affair. The rest of the morning I spent with the education classes and in mastering the conditions of re-enlistment for the soldier. Went round the dinners of A & B Coys. The general came to lunch, and afterwards we walked round the cookhouses, recreation rooms, etc. – and then on to Brigade H.Q. where I started to learn to skate. Having been on roller skates a few times was some help, but it's a dangerous business for a beginner I must say! However I only took one toss. Found Pearson over there, he is rather an expert, and we drove back together in a four-wheeled buggy we borrowed from our Burgomaster here. I'm not sure 'borrow' is quite the right word.

After tea I pelmanised until dinner time. All the available information points to the battalion going home before very long – as a cadre that is, and after handing over everybody and everything not connected with the 'post-bellum' (horrible word) army to the relieving unit, which I should think will be another battalion of the regiment.

The weather is dull and cloudy and the whole country is a dirty grey colour, because all the snow is darkened by the dust of the briquet factories, for miles around.

FEB. 23RD 1919 Sunday – we had a church service in the morning. The Doctor and Pirie and I all went over to lunch with Crawfurd at his H.Q. and took the pipe-major with us. After lunch he piped for us, he is a wonderful piper. Percy Brown turned up about 4 o'clock, having motored over from his place at Rheibach. No further information about when we go home.

I hear that the final armistice conditions are to be presented to the Germans on the 25th, and that they will be given 48 hours to consider them. If they do not sign them, we give them 24 hours notice, and then the war starts again. That is to say we advance 50 miles and then give them another chance to sign. So that's that.

MARCH 2ND 1919 Sunday. Today we put all the retainable men into separate companies, and formed demobilisation companies. And we hear too that we move to Cologne on Tuesday although no orders are in about it. Here no one troubles about us any more and we have had no mail for two days which is the limit.

Master left about 11.30 this morning, after prophesying a future of anarchy and barbarism, to look for a really luxurious house for the Corps Commander in Cologne.[*]

In the afternoon Taldo and I went for a ride in the woods, and up on to the ridge beyond, from where we could see down to the Rhine. I got back to find Doc. Stewart had been ordered off to another battalion and an American sent in his place. It's the limit, the A. may be a very good fellow, but the doc. has been with us since September 1914.

MARCH 6TH 1919 The last day of the existence of the present battalion. The replay of the final of divisional football cup was to take place in the afternoon, and we arranged a hurried concert for the evening. At 12 noon I said goodbye to the battalion.

After lunch we made our way to Blucher Park, where the match took place, and we managed to win, 5 goals to 3. The game was played in the pouring rain, and Blucher Park is miles away. However there was plenty of enthusiasm. I went back to tea at Brigade H.Q. and then back home to have a German lesson – the last for the moment as things are so uncertain.

Then to concert which got started about 7.30. Nearly the whole battalion turned up, and it was a great success, and quite a fitting ending in a way. For a last event I took the cup we had won on to the stage filled with champagne, and made the football team come up and empty it, while the pipes played the regimental march.

Then we all sang Auld Lang Syne, and the din was tremendous. Finis.

[*]The Master of Saltoun had been sent out as ADC to Sir Aylmer Haldane.

Biographical Index

Baird, A. W. F., took command of 1st Gordons at First Ypres, whither the battalion was moved (less the considerable part of it captured at Le Cateau) in November 1914. Later promoted brigadier-general.

Bonham-Carter, General Sir Charles, was a staff officer on divisional, corps and GHQ staffs in France, rising from major to brigadier-general. He was Governor of Malta in the early stages of the Second World War.

Brand, Lieutenant-Colonel J. C. ('Jack'), Coldstream Guards.

Bridges, Lieutenant-General Sir Tom, commander of 19th Division, and in 1914 commander of the cavalry squadron which first exchanged fire with the German army. A much decorated officer who had served extensively in Intelligence and as military attaché, beside distinguished active service in South Africa. A nephew of the Poet Laureate, Robert Bridges.

Brooke, Captain Otho, VC, son of Sir Harry Brooke, a distinguished Gordon Highlander, was awarded the Victoria Cross for his actions at First Ypres – in the same 2nd Gordons as Willie Fraser. The Germans had broken through on the Menin road and were attacking from both front and rear. Brooke's gallantry helped save something of the situation. Simon Fraser was killed that day (29 October 1914).

Brown, Alexander, the factor at Philorth for many years, lived at Witch Hill – giving shelter to the Saltouns when their house was destroyed by fire in 1915. He was a man of utter integrity, considerable learning, unshakeable loyalty to the family of Philorth, and irresistible quiet charm. He was also for a time a (very distinguished) Provost of Fraserburgh.

Brown, Lieutenant-Colonel Percy, commanded 2nd Gordons during the Battle of Arras, and later commanded a brigade.

Burnett, Major-General Sir James ('Jim'), 13th Baronet of Leys, a Gordon Highlander of immense renown was wounded eleven times and Mentioned in Despatches eighteen. Known as 'Maxim' because of his staccato and formidable bark he was a man of legendary charm as well as a superb fighting soldier. Colonel of the Gordon Highlanders later in life.

Byng, General Hon. Sir Julian, later Field-Marshal Viscount Byng of Vimy. Known as 'Bungo' Byng, he was a cavalryman with a reputation for commonsense and the common touch. He commanded 3rd Army after commanding the Canadian Expeditionary Force – both with distinction.

Carr, Laurence, took temporary command of 2nd Gordons as a young captain after the Battle of Loos in October 1915 – fighting in which the battalion lost seventeen officers. Thereafter Laurence Carr filled a number of staff appointments. He and Burnett (*q.v.*) married sisters, and he finished his career in the Second World War as a lieutenant-general.

Cator, Albemarle, known as 'Alby', commanded 2nd Scots Guards and then 37th Infantry Brigade. Willie was a frequent visitor to the Cator family home at Woodbastwick in Norfolk.

Churchill, Winston Spencer, resigned office as First Lord of the Admiralty in the wake of the Gallipoli disaster, then (to his great credit) managed to insert himself into the British Army in France – first 'learning' with 2nd Grenadiers, then commanding a battalion of Royal Scots Fusiliers.

Clarke, Donald, 6th Gordons, was a company commander of great reputation, popular, gallant and efficient. He won DSO and MC and was killed during the Germans 1918 offensive on the Lys.

Codrington, Commander Jack, RN, married Mary Fraser, Willie's only sister, and was killed before the war's end.

Congreve, Lieutenant-General Sir Walter, Billy Congreve's father and commander of XIII Corps and later VII Corps. A Rifleman like his son, he had been awarded the Victoria Cross at Colenso in the South African War, and together the Congreves represented one of only two father-and-son VC combinations in the British Army (the others were the Roberts family). Walter Congreve suffered severely from bronchial trouble and drove himself ruthlessly in the performance of duty despite ill-health.

Congreve, William ('Billy'), whose best man Willie was in June 1916, was killed early in the Somme fighting on 20 July at the age of twenty-five – already a brigade major with DSO, MC and Croix de Guerre. He was awarded the VC posthumously.

Craufurd, Lieutenant-Colonel S. G., commanded 1st Gordons on the Somme.

Daly, Major-General Arthur, commanded 24th Division for the last year of the war. He later held the post of Military Adviser in Iraq.

Duff, Arthur, Willie's second-in-command in 6th Gordons and later their commander. Younger brother to the laird of Fetteresso.

Dugan, Winston, Worcestershire Regiment, later in life Lord Dugan of Victoria and Lurgan, he commanded first 184th and then 73rd Brigade in France. A trainer of skill whom WF admired.

Duncan, Major-General Francis, commander of 165th and later 60th Brigade, was afterwards to command 61st Division.

Falkenhayn, General von, succeeded von Moltke (the younger) as Chief of the German General Staff. Alleged by his enemies to be a vain and obstinate man, he was the architect of the German offensive at Verdun and was replaced thereafter.

Fergusson, Sir Charles, Bt., of Kilkerran, commanded II and later XVII Corps. A Grenadier, he was a friend of Willie's father. He, like Gough, had held a command in Ireland in 1914 – and had taken an entirely opposed view of where duty lay.

Fleming, Captain Ian, a company commander in 6th Gordons, commanded the bombing raid which had spectacular success in 1916, occupying a section of German trench and bombing every dug-out, withdrawing thereafter. He was one of the original officers of the battalion who went to France with it in November 1914, and was killed in 1917.

Fraser, Alistair, Master of Saltoun, eldest of the Fraser brothers and always known in the family as 'Master'. He joined 1st Gordons as a Reserve officer in 1914, went to France with them and was taken prisoner with that part of the battalion captured at Le Cateau – of which incident he later wrote a vivid and private factual account. Thereafter he was imprisoned in Germany (escaping and being recaptured several times) until exchanged through Holland. In 1933 he became 19th Lord Saltoun.

Fraser, George, the second Fraser brother, joined the Royal Navy from Britannia Royal Naval College and served until the end of the Second World War, retiring as a rear-admiral.

Fraser, Mary, Willie's sister, married Commander Codrington (*q.v.*) and, later, Balcarres Wardlaw-Ramsay of Whitehill.

Fraser, Simon, the third Fraser brother, was two years Willie's senior, and joined 2nd Gordons as a Reserve officer. Killed at First Ypres.

French, General Sir John, later Earl of Ypres and Field-Marshal. The first commander of the British Expeditionary Force, he had won a great reputation as a dashing cavalry commander in the South African War. His temperament in 1914 failed to show the robustness necessary and his senior commanders, notably Haig (*q.v.*) had little confidence in him. Haig replaced him after the disastrous fighting at Loos.

Gough, General Sir Hubert, commander of 5th Army. Adored by some, execrated by others, 'Goughie' took the blame for the German breakthrough in March 1918 – in Willie's view most unjustly. Gough had gained a certain fame (or notoriety) at the time of the Curragh Incident in 1914.

Gray, Private, was Willie's soldier servant in 6th Gordons.

Haig, General Sir Douglas, later Earl Haig and Field-Marshal, initially commander of I Corps, succeeded French and undoubtedly impressed the whole Army with the force of his determination, the strength of his will. His strategy – or, perhaps, his detachment from the appalling tactical realities of the battlefield – have often been criticised, but Willie never wavered in his view that the overall strategy was as sound as it was inevitable.

Haldane, Lieutenant-General Sir Aylmer, 'The AB', a Gordon Highlander, commanded VI Corps. In 1918 the Master of Saltoun, after repatriation, went to Germany as Haldane's ADC.

Harper, Sir George, later lieutenant-general and a corps commander, was the profoundly respected commander of 51st Highland Division. A Royal Engineer in origin, he was thoughtful, thorough and effective. Universally known as 'Uncle'.

d'Hespel, Comte, was the proprietor of Willie's billet at the Château d'Eperlecques, and, with his family, was a hospitable friend.

Hill, Major-General John, Indian Army, commanded 52nd Division.

Hunter-Weston, Lieutenant-General Sir Aylmer, successor to Maxse (*q.v.*) in command of XVIII Corps. Invariably known as 'Hunter-Bunter', he had a reputation, perhaps undeserved, for a certain rather bombastic pomposity. He had commanded, earlier, a corps at Gallipoli and VIII Corps – which suffered severely – at Beaumont Hamel on the Somme.

Hutcheson, Major, awarded DSO and MC, was a company commander in 6th Gordons.

Joffre, Marshal, French Commander-in-Chief in 1914, was architect of the Battle of the Marne – the 'Miracle of the Marne' – which turned the German tide in front of Paris.

Johnson, Sir Harry, explorer and governor, a great naturalist, a knowledgeable lover of Africa, a gifted artist and a renowned conversationalist.

Lansdowne, 5th Marquess of, had been Governor-General of Canada, Viceroy of India, Secretary of State for War and then Foreign Secretary (1900–05), beside holding other Cabinet port-folios – a spectacular proconsular and ministerial career. The 'Lansdowne Letter' discussing the possibililty of a negotiated peace created a furore in the (inevitably obsessive) atmosphere of 1917.

Lee, Captain C. H., a very gallant company commander of 1st Gordons who won an immediate DSO at Flesquières.

Little, W. B., staff captain 151st Brigade at the time of Willie's accident as brigade major.

Lochbuie, see Maclaine.

Long, Lieutenant-Colonel A. de L., commanded 7th Gordons at Cambrai and was wounded in March 1918.

Ludendorff, General, officially styled 'First Quartermaster General' was effectively Chief of Staff of the German Imperial Army and its driving force – in conjunction with von Hindenburg who held the official position of 'Chief of Staff' – after von Falkenhayn's removal. Ludendorff – ruthless and brilliant – held a particular place in Allied demonology.

Mackay, Captain, a company commander in 6th Gordons, won the MC.

Mackechnie, Samuel, head keeper at Philorth, and perhaps the man whom Willie loved and revered most in his young days. A genius at his job, a man of dedication and loyalty, he possessed great physical strength and a head that cried out to be painted by Raeburn.

Mackenzie, Major-General Sir Colin, later Colonel of the Seaforth Highlanders, commanded 61st Division.

Maclaine of Lochbuie, Kenneth, was an officer in the 15th Hussars.

Macnaughten, General Andrew ('Andy'), was a Canadian Artillery officer – later a Canadian statesman, of great brilliance and distinction who commanded Canada's forces overseas, at one stage, in the Second World War.

Makgill-Crichton-Maitland, Mark, a Grenadier with a great fighting reputation, commanded 1st Grenadiers in France – and returned to command the regiment in 1939. His brother, Freddie, was a Gordon Highlander, as had been his father.

Malcolm, Major-General Sir Neil, was Gough's (*q.v.*) chief of staff at 5th Army and later commander of 66th Division.

Maxse, Lieutenant-General Sir Ivor, Commander XVIII Corps and a Coldstreamer, was a trainer of great skill and renown.

Maude, Pamela, younger daughter of Cyril Maude, married Billy Congreve (*q.v.*) and, in 1919, WF.

Montgomery, Sir Archibald (later Montgomery-Massingberd), was to become Chief of the Imperial General Staff. He was Chief of Staff – officially MGGS, 'Major-General, General Staff' – to 4th Army (Rawlinson *q.v.*).

Nugent, Major-General Sir Oliver, a Rifleman, commanded 41st Brigade in France and then the famous 36th (Ulster) Division from 1915 until 1918.

Ogilvie, Lieutenant-Colonel T., a very experienced Territorial officer commanded 4th (Territorial) Battalion, Gordons, in 1914–15.

Oldfield, Major-General Sir Louis, was ultimately General Officer Commanding in Malaya in the 1930s. He commanded the Artillery in 51st Division and then an infantry brigade – first 117 then 15 – for the last year of the war.

Paget, (later General Sir) Bernard, one of WF's lifelong friends, was to become Commander-in-Chief. An officer in the Oxford and Buckinghamshire Light Infantry, he had gone out to India with WF on the latter's first joining.

Pelham-Burn, 'Harry', ('Pelham' or 'HPB') was Willie's first company commander in the 92nd and was to be his brigade commander (152 Brigade) in the 51st Division after commanding 8th/10th Gordons.

Plumer, General Sir Herbert, later Field-Marshal Lord Plumer of Messines, had the – probably deserved – reputation of being the most thorough army commander on the Western Front and the one most careful of his soldiers' lives.

Potter, Brigadier-General M. C., commanded 9th Brigade (in 3rd Division) for three years from March 1916 until March 1919.

Rawlinson, General Sir Henry, later Field-Marshal Lord Rawlinson, 'Rawly', was Commander 4th Army – the army chiefly concerned in the Somme fighting.

Rollo, Company Sergeant Major, described by WF as the 'quintessential Gordon Highlander', was killed (1st Gordons) in 1918 at Flesquières.

Ruggles-Brise, Brigadier-General H. G., commanded 20th Brigade in 7th Division, the brigade in which WF first went to war.

Saltoun, Alexander, 18th Lord Saltoun, Willie's father, previously a Grenadier, recalled to command a reserve brigade at home in the early part of the war. He had an explosive temper and was known to his contemporaries as 'The Dove'.

Saltoun, May, née Grattan-Bellew and a descendant of the Irish statesman Henry Grattan, was Willie's mother. A highly intelligent and original woman, she was interested in photography and many kinds of scientific experiment, setting aside a room at Philorth (and in her London house) as a laboratory.

Seely, Colonel 'Jack', later brigadier-general, later 1st Lord Mottistone, had been Secretary of State for War in Asquith's Government, 1912–14. He took responsibility at the time of the Curragh Incident (see Fergusson, Gough), resigning thereafter and commanding a brigade on the Western Front.

Smith-Dorrien, General Sir Horace, commanded II Corps during the retreat from Mons and at the Battle of Le Cateau; and commanded 2nd Army when it was formed in 1915. He was regarded by many as the best senior officer in the war's early years, and was regarded with disfavour by French (*q.v.*).

Stewart, Dr, was medical officer, 1st Gordons, throughout the war – a remarkable record of a remarkable and greatly esteemed man.

[347]

Stewart-Menzies of Culdares, Ronald ('Rony'), Chief of the Menzies, was a cousin of the Frasers, his father, 'Willie Menzies', being a particular crony of Lord Saltoun. An officer in the Scots Guards, he was taken prisoner in 1914.

Thom, Lieutenant-Colonel J. G., commanded 6th Gordons, then 8th/10th at Third Ypres and 6th (again) after WF; and, later, 6th/7th. A commanding officer with a magnificent reputation.

Townshend, Major-General Sir Charles, conducted a dashing offensive in Mesopotamia, capturing Kut-el-Amara in the valley of the Tigris. A further advance to Baghdad was checked and Townshend's force finally besieged by the Turks in Kut, where he ultimately surrendered. He was well treated by the Turks, whose firm advocate he became later in life.

Trotter, George, a Grenadier, commanded 1st Grenadiers in 1915, and in 1916 27th Brigade; and, subsequently, 51st Brigade.

Uniacke, Lieutenant-Colonel H. P., was WF's commanding officer in the 92nd at First Ypres. Very much the 'father of his battalion', Colonel Uniacke was wounded at Ypres, rejoined in January 1915 and was killed in March at Neuve Chapelle.

Westmorland, Brigadier-General T. T., commanding 151st Brigade in 50th Division, was WF's commander when he, as brigade major, had his accident in June 1916.